SABOTAGE AT BLACK TOM

ALSO BY JULES WITCOVER

85 Days: The Last Campaign of Robert Kennedy (1969)

The Resurrection of Richard Nixon (1970)

White Knight: The Rise of Spiro Agnew (1972)

A Heartbeat Away: The Investigation and Resignation of Vice President Spiro T. Agnew (1974) (with Richard M. Cohen)

Marathon: The Pursuit of the Presidency, 1972–1976 (1977)

The Main Chance (A Novel) (1979)

Blue Smoke and Mirrors: How Reagan Won and Why Carter Lost the Election of 1980 (1981) (with Jack W. Germond)

Wake Us When It's Over: Presidential Politics of 1984 (1985) (with Jack W. Germond)

SABOTAGE AT BLACK TOM

IMPERIAL GERMANY'S SECRET WAR IN AMERICA · 1914-1917

JULES WITCOVER

DOING *HIS* BIT

MYSTERIOUS BLAZE

LOYAL KAISERITE

ALGONQUIN BOOKS OF CHAPEL HILL 1989

Published by
Algonquin Books of Chapel Hill
Post Office Box 2225
Chapel Hill, North Carolina 27515-2225

a division of
Workman Publishing Company, Inc.
708 Broadway
New York, New York 10003

Library of Congress Cataloging-in-Publication Data

Witcover, Jules.
Sabotage at Black Tom: Imperial Germany's Secret War in America /
Jules Witcover

Includes index.
ISBN 0-912697-98-9

1. World War, 1914–1918—Secret service—Germany
2. Sabotage—United States—History—20th century.   I. Title
D639.S7W56   1989
940.4′87′43—dc19

88-24267
CIP

First Printing
10   9   8   7   6   5   4   3   2   1

To Bob and Mary

"The day will come when people in Germany will
see how much you have done for your country in America."

*—Letter of farewell to Count Johann von Bernstorff, German ambassador to
the United States, from Colonel Edward House, personal confidant of President
Woodrow Wilson, upon the breaking of diplomatic relations between the two countries, February, 1917*

CONTENTS

IV: GERMANY ON TRIAL, 1919–1939

Introduction

What follows in these pages is history—and detective story.

It is the history of Imperial Germany's extensive acts of sabotage against the United States, on American soil and on the high seas, in the nearly three years leading up to the American entry into World War I. And it is the history of how the American president, Woodrow Wilson, sought to preserve American neutrality in the face of this Imperial German deception, overseen by the very German ambassador to Washington, Count Johann von Bernstorff, whose prime mission was to keep America neutral.

It is also the detective story of how, after the objectives of both Wilson and von Bernstorff were dashed and Imperial Germany defeated, the perpetrators of the sabotage were hunted down and the governments of postwar Germany were brought to trial in an unprecedentedly bizarre international lawsuit. And it is the detective story of how American sleuths and lawyers for two decades thereafter sought to establish Imperial Germany's guilt and to exact reparations for the two most heinous of these acts of sabotage, first from the successor Weimar Republic and then from the National Socialist regime of Adolf Hitler.

The suit was popularly known as "The Black Tom Case," after a huge munitions supply terminal on the New Jersey side of New York Harbor, directly across from the Statue of Liberty. The depot was blown up in the early hours of July 30, 1916, when the United States was officially neutral in the Great War but had already become "the arsenal of democracy"—the chief armaments supplier for the Allied powers. The suit also embraced the destruction of a very large shell manufacturing plant at Kingsland, New Jersey, near what is now Lyndhurst, only eight miles northwest of Black Tom, about five months later.

Together, these two acts of sabotage against a neutral power caused millions of dollars of damage and were the catalyst for a worldwide search for the perpetrators after the war. They were singled out from nearly two hundred suspected acts of German sabotage because of their scope and because the private American claimants in the two cases were willing to go to incredible lengths to seek justice in them. On tying the Black Tom and Kingsland disasters to Germany rested the chances of the claimants to recover their losses in accordance with the Treaty of Berlin between the United States and Germany —signed in 1922 after the United States Senate had refused to ratify the multinational Treaty of Versailles.

Every character in this narrative was an actual participant in the events described. Every word attributed to the individuals herein comes from signed affidavits, contemporary interviews, memoirs, and transcripts of official hearings. All but a few of the principals are deceased, but the details of the whole episode have been stored for half a century now in the stacks and dusty files of the National Archives of the United States in Washington, D.C., and nearby Suitland, Maryland.

This book is the result of four years of research among these stacks and files, and of inquiries at the Foreign Office of the Federal Republic of Germany in Bonn and the Bundesarchiv in Koblenz, and in Sarajevo, Yugoslavia, where the whole story really began in June, 1914 in what was then Serbia. Special thanks are due first to the staff of the National Archives, especially the diligent and helpful employees of the Central Research Room in downtown Washington, and to the former administrator of the General Services Administration, Gerald Carmen, who helped me gain access to the files. Amateur librarians Kathy Bushkin and Melody Miller, for their intercessions with the Library of Congress, also were indispensable, as were Julie Witcover, for constructive suggestions on the manuscript, and my most industrious agent, David Black.

Finally, I am indebted to the only surviving major player on the American side of the drama, John J. McCloy, and his associate in the case, Benjamin Shute. Mr. McCloy was a counsel and principal investigator to the American claimants, later assistant secretary of war in World War II and military governor and high commissioner of Germany thereafter. Past age ninety, possessing a bell-clear memory, Mr. McCloy helped put the complex pieces together in two long interviews in his office high in Manhattan's World Trade Center.

As we talked, we could look out across the Hudson River and Upper New York Bay to the promontory on the New Jersey side once called "Black Tom." Now it is known as Liberty Park, where tourists board small boats to the Statue of Liberty, recently refurbished to remove the scars of time—and of the shrapnel that tore into it on that summer night in 1916 from the explosions that came to be the centerpiece of "The Black Tom Case."

This history/detective story is a complicated one, with a large cast of characters bearing unfamiliar names and frequent aliases. Therefore, the reader from time to time may want to refer to the list of the most important individuals and the chronology assembled at the back of the book in the course of addressing one of the least-remembered true stories of American vulnerability, gullibility—and tenacity—of the twentieth century.

Washington, D.C.   JULES WITCOVER

I: THE GREAT WAR COMES TO AMERICA, 1916

7

I. A Pleasant Saturday in New York

Saturday, July 29, 1916, dawned clear and cool in New York City. It was one of those pleasant summer days when normally it would have been ideal to pack a lunch and take the children off to Coney Island or Rockaway Beach, and many New Yorkers did just that. But many others, unnerved by reports of shark sightings off the Brooklyn and Long Island beaches and by an epidemic of infantile paralysis, spent a lazy Saturday morning at home, sleeping late, scanning the morning newspapers or just gossiping with a neighbor.

On West Fifteenth Street in Manhattan, a street of sedate brownstones with an occasional motorcar parked in front, the talk was of the usual things—work, children, happenings in the neighborhood and, to a lesser extent, in the city, in the country and the world.

Happenings in the neighborhood, or at least suspected happenings, were a matter of particular concern on West Fifteenth Street, as they had been ever since the outbreak of the Great War. Down at No. 123, in a shuttered row house, the nocturnal comings and goings of mysterious men, many of them Germans, through a basement door under the steep front steps disturbed and distressed many neighbors.

They were suspicious not because the callers were Germans of rank—diplomats and sea captains; the neighbors did not know that fact. Rather, it was because the address was thought to be a house of ill repute. Its proprietress was a hefty former German opera singer named Martha Held, whose duties included wining and dining the visiting Germans and providing them with attractive young women companions.

On the previous night, the neighbors of the house at 123 West Fifteenth Street once again had seen, and some had been affronted by, a parade of visitors to the suspect address. Those neighbors who sauntered by in the late hours could hear, as they often did on similar weekend nights, the sound of powerful operatic arias from the booming voice of the hostess of the house, or the boisterous singing of patriotic German songs from the male guests. That merrymaking did not in itself particularly disturb the neighborhood; Germany as the leader of the Central Powers was at war with the Allies, chiefly England and France, but the United States was neutral—in official government policy, at least.

Unknown to the neighbors, however, the visitors to the suspected brothel on that Friday night had more serious business on their minds. Behind the shuttered windows they had spread large maps, blueprints and photographs on the dining table and engaged in lengthy, animated discussion over them. Even the uneducated eye of one of the young women present, a self-styled model named Mena Edwards who spoke little German but understood a bit more, could see that the maps, blueprints and photos depicted areas of the New York waterfront and facilities along its shores.

What Mena Edwards saw and heard, in fact, persuaded her to leave the city hurriedly for the weekend. On Saturday morning, she boarded a train for Atlantic Highlands, on the New Jersey coast, to visit a friend—a decision she would not regret, for reasons we shall learn.

To others on West Fifteenth Street not privy to what had been discussed and planned at No. 123 the night before, however, Saturday, July 29, was like any other summer day in the city. The Great War in Europe was a remote, impersonal thing that New Yorkers willing to part with a penny read about in the sixteen pages of the *New York Times* with less than consuming interest. These Saturday morning readers learned that the war, just entering its third year, seemed at last to be moving in the Allies' favor. In the province of Galicia in what one time had been Poland, the armies of the Russian czar were pushing back the combined German and Austrian forces at Brody, a town only fifty-eight miles from the Galician capital of Lwow. And in eastern France, the British had driven the Germans' Fifth Brandenburg Division from Delville Wood.

In the air, German zeppelins dropped bombs on the English northeast coast, while a gallant French "aeroplane" pilot, his machine gun jammed, was seen to "swoop upon his adversary at full speed, crash into him and fall with him to the ground," taking two German airmen to their deaths with him at Chalons on the Marne, eighty-five miles east of Paris. At sea, a German U-boat sank the British patrol boat *Nellie Nutten*, with three British crewmen perishing and eleven others rescued by a Dutch fishing boat.

By this time, most Americans were likely to share the view that

Germany was the guilty party in the Great War. Yet there were considerable pockets of sympathy for her cause, in New York and elsewhere around the country. On Manhattan, the Yorkville section in the East Eighties hosted a large and lively German population and some of the better German restaurants.

Along the Hudson River waterfront eighty German ships were interned for the duration of the war under American neutrality laws; their seamen frequented the rough-and-tumble bars. With time on their hands, they were forever looking for entertainment and, sometimes, information from other sailors about shipments of munitions and other supplies to the Allied powers.

This information often made its way to the house at 123 West Fifteenth Street, where it was put to use in predictable but secretive ways by the mysterious gentleman callers, under the very noses of those neighbors whose thoughts and interests were far from the Great War in Europe.

At home, the war in Europe was not a matter of first priority on this Saturday in late July even in the realm of foreign affairs; American relations with Mexico commanded the spotlight. There was encouraging news that President Woodrow Wilson had agreed to the appointment of an international joint commission to work out the evacuation of American forces in Mexico. Wilson had dispatched them to pressure the despotic General Victoriano Huerta to relinquish the government control he seized after the murder of revolutionary leader Francisco Madero.

In New York City, Saturday, July 29, was a good day to stay home. A strike was under way by employees of the Third Avenue Railway Company, which ran many of the city's streetcars. The strike was spreading from the Bronx into Manhattan and Brooklyn, tying up the city's "Red Line." Streetcars on the city's "Green Line" and elevated trains continued to run, but the labor unrest kept many New Yorkers off all public transportation.

Many therefore did stay home, just reading the newspapers and puttering around. The baseball fans among them learned in the *Times* that on the previous day, a pinch-hitter for the Brooklyn Robins named Casey Stengel had belted a triple that broke an eighth-inning tie and gave the league-leading Robins a narrow victory over the St. Louis Cardinals. In other words, Saturday, July 29, 1916, was a pretty average day for a country that watched with interest but without undue alarm, and at a safe distance an ocean away, the greatest war the world had ever seen. And it was a pretty average day for a city accustomed to the ups and downs of labor unrest, summer health scares and the national pastime.

As this Saturday unfolded, the streetcar motormen's strike broadened and tightened its grip on transportation in the Bronx, Manhattan and Brooklyn, affecting more than a quarter of a million daily passengers. In certain parts of the city, rioters fought the police, and in downtown Manhattan, a mob of International Workers of the World—the infamous "Wobblies"—wrecked the office of the Italian-American newspaper *Il Progresso*, with the notorious Irish labor agitator James Larkin in the forefront of the attack.

For all that, however, the first signs of pennant fever were infecting New York, and on this warm afternoon some 21,000 baseball-loving souls managed to make their way to Ebbets Field—by private car, on streetcars that were still running, or on foot. There they watched the Robins maintain their National League lead by splitting a double-header with the Cincinnati Reds and their new manager, former New York Giants pitching great Christy Mathewson. An even larger crowd of 30,000 poured into the Polo Grounds in upper Manhattan, where they watched John McGraw's Giants sweep a pair from Honus Wagner and the Pittsburgh Pirates and pick up a game on the hated, front-running Brooklyns.

Other New Yorkers not smitten by the baseball bug nor intimidated by the strike ventured to midtown Manhattan for a Saturday matinee or a show at one of the many moving-picture houses that had blossomed amid the theater district. Children under sixteen, however, were barred because of the infantile paralysis threat. The upper crust filled the orchestra and boxes of the New Amsterdam, "The House Beautiful," on West Forty-second Street off Times Square for the fabulous *Ziegfeld Follies*, featuring Fanny Brice and her hilarious impersonation of screen vamp Theda Bara, and the songs of Irving Berlin. Good second-balcony seats could be had for fifty cents.

Not all New Yorkers, however, could enjoy this Saturday in such leisurely pursuits. Governor Charles Evans Hughes, at his summer residence at Bridgehampton, Long Island, spent the day toiling over the manuscript of his speech accepting the presidential nomination of his Republican party, to be delivered the approaching Monday night at Carnegie Hall. Conferring closely with him on the speech was Republican National Chairman William Willcox. Word had already leaked out that the nominee would address himself to the thorny Mexican situation and to the role he envisioned for the United States in the reconstruction of Europe upon the conclusion of the Great War.

As Hughes thus labored, the man he hoped to replace in the White House, President Woodrow Wilson, spent the day cruising with relatives aboard the naval yacht *Mayflower* off the coast of Cape Charles, Virginia, at the mouth of the Chesapeake Bay. As he worked on his own speech accepting renomination as the candidate of the Democratic Party, he watched naval ships, including the armored cruiser *North Carolina*, steam in from neutrality patrol duty within the three-mile limit in the Atlantic.

At the outbreak of the Great War, Wilson had firmly proclaimed neutral status for the United States, and an integral part of that posture required the preservation of American waters as a neutral zone. Most ships of the Central Powers that at the start of hostilities had sought refuge in American ports from British sea superiority had been immediately interned with their crews for the duration of the war.

Wilson, who would campaign for reelection on the slogan "He Kept Us Out of War," was fiercely determined to do so, in spite of growing sympathies in the country for the Allies' cause—and mounting manufacture and sale of American munitions to them. The Allied powers alone had the shipping and surface control of the sea-lanes to deal in that deadly commerce.

The complications for Wilson in maintaining neutrality under these circumstances were underscored on this very Saturday in two separate developments.

In nearby Norfolk, Judge Edmund Waddill, Jr., of the United States District Court ruled that belligerent nations could not use American ports as asylums for their prizes of war. Specifically, he found that the British steamer *Appam*, seized by the German raider *Mowe* in international waters of the Atlantic the previous January and brought into Norfolk Harbor, remained British property. He ruled that the ship be turned over to the British, and that the German crew that manned her be interned in the United States.

The German government immediately appealed the case to the Supreme Court. Meanwhile, American and British authorities kept a close watch on the ship, lest the Germans make good on their threat that if faced with having to give up the prize they would take it out into international waters and scuttle it.

The second development was unfolding up the Chesapeake Bay at the port of Baltimore. There, three weeks earlier, the German merchant submarine *Deutschland* had completed its maiden Atlantic crossing and was docked just northwest of historic Fort McHenry. As the unique vessel took on commercial cargo and underwent emergency repairs to her engines, plates and batteries as permitted under the neutrality laws, curious Baltimoreans flocked to the pier. "She is grounded there," the *Baltimore Sun* reported, "with a completeness that is in proportion to the acute and worldwide interest in her. Scows, high board fences, barbed wire fences and chains of floating logs protect her from the numerous inquisitive and possibly dangerous [visitors]. Moreover, a cordon of determined-looking officers constantly is about her."

The U-boat's skipper, Captain Paul Koenig, was readying his vessel for a dramatic dash down the Chesapeake Bay and out beyond the Atlantic's three-mile limit toward home, in the face of waiting and watching British and French cruisers bent on capturing or sinking her.*

The German government, President Wilson had just learned, was formally requesting that United States naval vessels provide escort protection for the *Deutschland*. But the United States was not inclined to provide such escort because it went beyond the usual measures of preserving American neutrality.

The *North Carolina* and three American destroyers were already guarding the entrance of Chesapeake Bay at the Virginia Capes, Charles and Henry, to bar the entry of the British and French warships inside the three-mile limit. American naval authorities judged that Captain Koenig intended to sail the *Deutschland* parallel to the American coast within the three-mile limit until he could find the opportunity to elude the Allied ships and make his escape. It was not a proper function of the American navy, they held, to facilitate that maneuver.

Complicating Captain Koenig's task of slipping out was the probability that enterprising American newspaper correspondents, some

*This Paul Koenig is not to be confused with another German of the same name, to be introduced later in this narrative, whose activities were of a distinctly less commercial nature.

from the major New York dailies, would hire small boats to follow the *Deutschland* in order to provide their readers with eyewitness accounts of the dramatic escape attempt. The correspondents already knew that a certain Captain Frederick Hinsch, in charge of all activities concerning the merchant U-boat in the United States, had been negotiating for the services of an American tug to assist in the submarine's departure, presumably under cover of night, and that shore leave for the German crew had been cancelled.

What the correspondents did not know was that Captain Hinsch's duties far transcended those of overseer of the *Deutcshland*'s safe passage; that as he pursued this harmless commercial venture he was inextricably linked to those other Germans who, on the previous night, had hunched over the maps and blueprints of the New York Harbor and waterfront at the dining table in Frau Held's Manhattan hideaway.

For the reporters in Baltimore, however, the drama of the *Deutschland* was quite enough to hold their attention. In order not to miss the dash for freedom, they kept a close eye on Captain Koenig from early morning, when he met with Captain Hinsch and a certain Paul Hilken of Baltimore. Hilken was an American official of the North German Lloyd Line who, like Hinsch, had ties to those Germans in Manhattan who secretly displayed such special interest in the geography and facilities of the port of New York. Koenig, Hinsch and Hilken conferred at the submarine secured at the Andre Street pier and then up Charles Street at the Hansa Haus, Baltimore headquarters of the shipping line.*

The Hansa Haus was a favorite gathering place in Baltimore for the many German sailors and shipping officials who visited or worked in the large port city, as well as for diplomats who often came up from the German embassy in nearby Washington on various matters of business. Some of that business, unknown to American authorities at the time, would in due course far overshadow the matter of extricating one merchant submarine from the jaws of the British fleet.

The surveillance of these three men by the reporters was the extent of scrutiny focused on them at the time. But likewise, before too long, all three, and Hinsch and Hilken especially, would become much

---

*The Hansa Haus, built in 1912, remains a distinctive landmark of German architecture in the heart of revitalized downtown Baltimore. Modeled after an early seventeenth-century courthouse in the Hanseatic League town of Halberstadt, it now houses offices of the Savings Bank of Baltimore and a discount catalog store.

sought-after by American security officials and other sleuths.

When the reporters finally cornered Captain Koenig, he was cordial and outgoing as he joked with them in an interview at the pier. He made no effort to hide the fact that he and his vessel would soon be departing.

Asked when he would leave, Koenig replied lightly: "Well, if any of you men from New York want to go to Germany tomorrow to attend church, we'll go today just to oblige you." As for his stay in Baltimore, Koenig said, "Everything has been done to make our stay pleasant. . . . It will mean much when we get back and tell our friends, and of course the whole German nation, what American feeling is toward Germany."

A reporter asked: "Then, Captain, you feel America is trying to be neutral and fair, no matter how sympathies may go in the war?"

"Why, yes, without doubt," Koenig replied. "What differences of opinion the nations may have is due to this"—and with that he placed his palms together and then spread them out. "There is the ocean between," he went on, "and with the war going on there is not good communication. The nations cannot understand each other. When Germans come over here as we do and talk with the people and read your newspapers, then we can understand a great deal better."

Another reporter asked: "Do you Germans feel angry against us, Captain, for selling munitions of war to the Allies?"

Koenig threw his head back, laughed and, according to the *New York Times*, said: "No, no. There is no reason for them to be angry. If Germany could come here after arms and munitions, you would sell them to her, wouldn't you?" And he concluded: "Goodbye, but remember everything in America has been fine. We like Baltimore, and we're coming again."

It was a promise some of those most closely associated with the *Deutschland* would later keep, in the performance of duties Koenig's listeners on that pier this Saturday could not have imagined.

While the imminent departure of the merchant submarine and talk of German-American relations thus captured the attention of the American press, still other American working men, and some alien workers as well, spent this Saturday in labors that belied the official Wilson posture of neutrality.

At the plant and piers of the National Dock and Storage Company in Jersey City on the New Jersey side of New York Harbor, the work force was completing its normal six-day week, loading and storing commodities brought by barges and freight cars of the Lehigh Valley Railroad Company, which owned the massive facility.

The men worked with customary care, because the goods they were handling would not suffer carelessness: explosive powders and munitions manufactured in American factories throughout the Northeast and Midwest and brought to this terminal for shipment by sea to their British and French purchasers. The men worked until the regular five-o'clock quitting time. Then the place shut down for a short weekend of Saturday night and Sunday, leaving the private detective and night-watchman force hired by the railroad and the British on guard in the "dead yard" through the balmy night.

Black Tom Island they called the site, though it was no longer an island but a promontory jutting out into Upper New York Bay; long since, land had been filled in to provide easier access. It was almost directly across from the Statue of Liberty on what was then called Bedloe's Island and not far from Ellis Island, where the "huddled masses yearning to breathe free" welcomed by Miss Liberty were brought and processed for immigration, or detained.

Some who had passed through Ellis Island now worked at Black Tom, and along with the native-born Americans employed there, they were glad to see the work week end. Now they could have a free day at home, or perhaps an outing to Coney Island, sharks or no sharks, or to the Polo Grounds or Ebbets Field.

For these hard-working dock and warehouse railroad men, and for all the other New Yorkers and Jerseyites, Saturday, July 29, 1916, ended as it had begun—cool and clear. The sixty-five degrees Fahrenheit that had been recorded in New York well before daybreak, offering the populace a welcome respite from summer's heat, had climbed to only seventy-four degrees by 4:00 P.M., and by bedtime had slipped down again to that same comfortable sixty-five degrees. It was a good night for sleeping.

Most of the city, and the residents of Jersey City, Hoboken and the other ethnic communities across the Hudson River in New Jersey, were bedded down for the night by 2:00 A.M.—or, more precisely, 2:08 A.M.—when with terrifying, ear-splitting explosiveness the Great War of Europe suddenly came to America.

2. Fire on Black Tom!

In the blackness of the summer night, only the faintest silhouette of
the Statue of Liberty, its torch lamp lit, could be discerned there at
the entrance to New York Harbor. The stillness was disturbed only by
the spasmodic, muffled sounds of what seemed to be firecrackers
being set off, perhaps by a gang of young hoodlums, across the Upper
New York Bay along the New Jersey waterfront.

And then, suddenly, a thunderous blast—"like the discharge of a
great cannon," the *New York Times* reported the next morning
—shattered the calm, and night turned into day. Flaming rockets and
screeching shells pierced the sky, like a great fireworks display, illu-
minating Miss Liberty from torch to base. Beyond her, the tip of
Manhattan and much of the world's most spectacular skyline instantly
were awash in light.

With the huge explosion, the whole harbor seemed to shudder,
sending shock waves pounding against skyscraper windows, shattering them by the thousands and sending deadly splinters of glass plunging into the streets and sidewalks below. Shrapnel pellets tore into
the giant statue and ripped gaping holes in the walls of buildings on
nearby Ellis Island, terrifying newly arrived immigrants who thought
they had escaped the Great War in Europe.

Late-night revelers in Brooklyn were knocked down and sleepers
were thrown from their beds. A ten-week-old boy, Arthur Tosson, was
hurled from his crib in Jersey City to his death. And incredibly, as far
south as Philadelphia, others were awakened by what they feared was
an earthquake—or worse. Police in towns even farther south, in Maryland, received telephone inquiries about the mysterious disturbance.

After the first jolt, an eerie quiet settled for a moment on New York
Harbor and the city. Then, panic-stricken residents of Manhattan's
teeming tenements, and those in Jersey City, Bayonne and Hoboken
on the New Jersey side, threw open their windows and craned for a
view of the orange-red heavens over the Hudson. As they gawked,
the bombardment resumed as if the harbor itself were under attack
from some mighty, invisible armada. It continued undiminished for

about twenty minutes, when a second stupendous explosion rocked the buildings on both sides of the river, unleashing yet another tremendous fusillade into the sky.

All at once, greater New York was alive as thousands upon thousands of people poured into the streets, bewildered. In midtown Manhattan, the *New York Times* reported the next morning, "from the large hotels women rushed out scantily clad, and men who wore pajamas covered with overcoats. . . . Many women became hysterical. . . . Police whistles were blown frantically, but the police themselves did not know what it was all about."

Burglar alarms went off by the hundreds; proprietors of all-night joints dashed into the streets blowing police whistles of their own. In the Times Square area, where plate-glass storefront windows came crashing down, police rushed into the open stores expecting to find safes blown and robbers at work, but they found only rubble. Panicky onlookers stumbled wildly over the shattered glass, seemingly oblivious of the danger.

The explosions also activated fire alarms all over the area, sending fire trucks roaring into the streets on journeys of confusion and frustration. Ten of them converged at the intersection of Fifth Avenue and Forty-second Street, jamming traffic as cab drivers frantically honked their horns. Police commandeered taxis as calls for help clogged police telephone lines throughout the city. Fleets of cabs raced downtown toward the hypnotizing glow, making raceways of Manhattan's great avenues. Ambulances from every hospital in the area set out for the origin of the explosions, thought at first to be in the Lower Manhattan financial district.

Terror struck motorists crossing the Brooklyn Bridge as the giant edifice swayed at the impact of the shock waves, and windshields in their autos shattered. Beneath the surface chaos, a water main burst on Sixth Avenue near Forty-second Street, flooding a four-block area.

The blast jolted the Hudson Tubes under the river connecting Lower Manhattan with Hoboken and Jersey City, panicking the underground passengers who were still making a Saturday night of it. Men on the night shift in a midtown subway excavation climbed out and fled. Even the dead were disturbed; in the Bay View and New York Bay cemeteries, monuments and tombstones toppled and some vaults were jolted askew.

Inevitably, reports circulated of looting of Fifth Avenue's finest shops.

Police reserves—except those guarding the homes of infantile paralysis victims—were called out. But they were needed for the more immediate task of warning people away from dangerous areas. Later, the *New York Times* reported that "although the police feared that thieves and gangsters would flock to the lower part of the city to prey on the banks and jewelry stores as soon as word reached their haunts that there might be easy picking, this source of trouble did not develop. Only one case of theft was reported, and that was a few dollars' worth of clothing from a Broadway store." And in the ethnic consciousness of the day, the reporter added: "An Italian was arrested in the act of taking the goods."

All telephone lines between New York and Jersey City went dead, and into the vacuum of information swept the most fearful rumors. Hospital patients particularly panicked, as did prison inmates. Those incarcerated in a new jail in Hackensack, northwest of Jersey City, aware of earlier underworld threats against its construction, feared for a time the jail was being dynamited.

Similar conclusions raced through the minds of night watchmen everywhere. "Watchmen employed in the financial district," the *Times* subsequently reported, "rushed frantically to telephones, each convinced that the building of which he was in charge had been dynamited." At police headquarters at City Hall, itself badly shaken by the explosions, the immediate impression was that "the Wobblies" who had wrecked the *Il Progresso* office earlier in the day had now committed a massive act of vengeance for the arrest of some of their cohorts.

The site of the greatest explosions ever to wrack a major American metropolitan area was, in fact, the principal terminal for the nation's vast commercial traffic in death—Black Tom Island, the storage and shipping depot for explosive powders and munitions manufactured for the warring nations of Europe. Yet only a very few individuals who heard the thunderclap, felt the shock waves and saw the sky light up in the depths of night knew, or strongly suspected, the cause.

Among them was the young model from the house on West Fifteenth Street, Mena Edwards, who had gone to a friend's cottage about twenty-five miles down the New Jersey coast for the weekend. When the first blast occurred, she lay awake in the cottage's one bedroom with her sleeping hostess, Marie McDermott.

"I remember particularly how nervous I was that night," Mena Edwards testified later, because I could not tell Mrs. McDermott what I knew was probably going to happen. Our bedroom was on the first floor and you could step right out on the veranda. We had been in bathing that afternoon and had left our bathing suits on the line to dry. Mrs. McDermott was asleep when the first explosion occurred, but I was not.

The vibration of the house was terrible. Mrs. McDermott awakened with a great start and we both ran out in the yard. She thought at first it was a terrible thunderstorm and said, "Let's get our bathing suits. They will get wet." We ran out on the lawn in our kimonos. I remember that it was a clear night and we saw the light, and later watched the fire as it developed at Black Tom.

The reason Mena Edwards was on the Jersey shore on this particular night, and unable to sleep before the blast that rocked Black Tom Island, was simple. The serious business discussed by the German men in her presence in Martha Held's house on West Fifteenth Street was the blowing up of this very site, as the crowning undertaking in a continuing program of sabotage against the American munitions industry supplying the British and French.

In the days, months, and years after this memorable night, investigations went forward to establish the cause of the disaster at Black Tom and to find and bring to justice its perpetrators. Eyewitness accounts graphically painting the picture of the chaos and destruction, many of them conflicting, were pored over for clues. At the beginning, however, and for a considerable time after the event, there was little suspicion that the blowing up of Black Tom had been anything but an accident.

The accounts of those eyewitnesses provide, however, a sense of the drama of the early morning hours of July 30, 1916. At twelve minutes past midnight, Barton Scott, an employee of the Dougherty Detective Agency of New York hired by the British as a watchman on the Lehigh Valley Railroad pier at Black Tom, saw the first fire on the yard's Pier 7.

"I was a short distance from the land end of the dock," he told a private investigator hired by the railroad,

> when I first caught a glimpse of a blaze. . . . The fire had started in the center of a string of cars on shore near the land end of the pier. The flames had gotten too good a start for us to do any-

thing. I ran to a telephone and called for the yard engines to come and pull the other cars away, and within a few minutes after the discovery of the fire, shrapnel shells of the smaller calibers began to explode.

These shells kept up the rattle continuously and the fire spread rapidly to other cars containing small explosives. I knew that a car in the center of the string was loaded with black powder and that once she was touched off the whole place was doomed. . . . Work of pulling the cars out began at once, but the fire was getting hot and the explosives were going off with increasing violence.

At forty minutes past midnight, a fire alarm attached to a sprinkler system in one of the huge warehouses on Black Tom sent a signal to the American District Telegraph Company in Jersey City, responsible for monitoring the system. An official in turn called the Jersey City Fire Department, which dispatched three fire engines and a fire truck to the scene.

"At eight minutes past two," Scott went on, "the biggest explosion of all came. The car of black powder had gone up. At the moment the big blast came, the ground seemed to reverberate from the concussion and the air displacement temporarily took away one's breath."

In subsequent testimony, Scott added this:

When I first saw the fire, I noticed that a piece of waste . . . had been stuffed under the door. The car started burning near the center under the door, and this seemed suspicious to me. I don't see how the fire could have started there as there were no engines passing close enough to throw sparks and it was a cool night. The fact that I found waste in the door puzzled me.

Such bits of suspicion would be examined as if they were rare gems, but not for some time to come.

Other eyewitnesses insisted the fire had started on one of the barges, or lighters, known as *Johnson No. 17*, tied up to the Black Tom piers.* It had a derrick on deck and was about eighty feet long and thirty feet

---

*The Johnson barge involved was thought at the time to be *No. 24*, and it was so reported in the newspaper accounts of the day. But it was later determined that it was *No. 17*. Attempts were made by the German government later to exploit the confusion.

wide, with a capacity of about 300 tons. The *Times* reported that the
first small flame had

> licked its way along the deck of a barge at about 12:30 o'clock.
> When the firemen arrived the deck of the barge was a furnace
> so hot that the men didn't get near to the potential inferno.
> Never was a small fire seen to burn so persistently. The water
> seemed to serve as fuel. The firemen fought hard, for there
> were cars of explosives and ammunition on the tracks and barges
> loaded . . . at the docks.

But a crew member of the Lehigh Valley tug *Geneva*, John Kilfoyle,
insisted the fire did not start on a barge:

> We were docked at Pier A in the gap about 12:30 when we
> received orders to go to Black Tom to the fire. We arrived at the
> grain docks, and, seeing we could be of no assistance there, we
> pulled around to Pier 7 where the fire was, and where the ammu-
> nition lighters were tied up. When we arrived there, freight
> cars were on fire and we hooked onto two ammunition barges to
> tow out into the stream. [They were easily identified, he said,
> by the red lights and red flags they were flying, indicating live
> explosives.]
> When we were getting away from the pier sparks from the
> burning freight cars ignited the barges and there was an explos-
> ion. . . . I was blown from the deck into the water. When I
> came up above the water, I could see nothing but sparks of all
> kinds coming down. I was then forced to submerge again, and
> when I came up again I swam over to the boat and got on board.
> We were then ordered to cut the ropes on the barges and get
> away.

Others speculated that carelessness by the watchmen on the piers
was responsible. A Standard Oil official, Joe Gordon, told of going to
Pier 7 some days earlier:

> Upon my arrival there I saw a small fire on the shore near a
> hut where the watchmen were. This was only ten or twelve feet
> from the cars of ammunition. When they saw me coming, they
> put out the fire, and I said to them, "That is dangerous to do
> such things near all that explosive," and they explained their

actions by saying they simply wanted to keep away the mosquitoes. This might be the cause of the fire.

Whatever the cause, the result was chaos.

Peter Raceta, captain of Moran lighter *No. 8*, gave this hair-raising account to the *Times*:

> I was in the cabin when the fire started. I ran up to the deck, and then the explosion occurred. I saw the cabin door blown off. I remember it flew down the length of the deck and into the water. When the explosion came, it seemed as if it was from above—zumpf!—like a zeppelin bomb. . . . I found myself going up in the air, and then I found myself in the water, a long way from the boat.

Raceta saw he was now only a short distance from the Statue of Liberty, so he swam to Bedloe's Island, now called Liberty Island, rested for a short time and then, semidelirious, swam back to Black Tom, where he was pulled out of the water and rushed to a hospital.

In the bay, tug captains braved the fusillade to cope with the peril. Captain David Findley of the Lehigh Valley tug *Sledington*, his vessel nearly lifted out of the water by the first explosion, backed the tug into Black Tom, got a line secured to four barges laden with explosives and pulled them out into the middle of the bay.

In the midst of the shrapnel bombardment and the selfless heroics, one coldly calculating tugboat captain turned the chaos to his financial benefit. Fred Bouchard was aboard the tug *Gallagher* at Erie Basin directly across Bedloe's Island from Black Tom in Brooklyn. Knocked down by the first explosion, Bouchard got to his feet and with his six-man crew headed the tug dead into the trouble.

Bouchard spotted the 4,800-ton Brazilian steamer *Tijoca Rio* lying at Black Tom without steam and saw it at once as salvage bounty. A barge loaded with building materials was in the way, so Bouchard's tug pulled it out into the river first, then went in and got the steamer. A small schooner also was tied up and Bouchard took the *Gallagher* in and got the schooner out too.

Bouchard later collected $9,000 for his work and each of his crew members got $1,200. He told an investigator that when he got the schooner out, "the tug *Geneva* came along and wanted to be on the salvage part of it. But nothing doing. My crew and I, who took our lives in our hands, were entitled to that."

On the two islands closest to Black Tom, Bedloe's and Ellis, frantic evacuation efforts started almost at once. Police boats, peppered by the flying shrapnel that continued through the night, brought twelve women and thirteen children of the Statue of Liberty staff living on Bedloe's Island to Governors Island at the mouth of the East River. Although the statue had been heavily assaulted by shrapnel, the light in Miss Liberty's torch remained lit.

The ferryboat *Ellis Island* transported nearly 500 bewildered immigrants, many of them hysterical, from the immigration center to the Battery at the southern tip of Manhattan. There, police made sure none got off the boat until all were moved to the Immigration Bureau. Included was a group of mental patients awed by what they thought was a gigantic fireworks display. One man, known for talking loud and nonstop gibberish, was stunned into silence during the crossing to the Battery, only to resume his chattering when placed safely indoors again.

Imperiling the two islands, beyond the flying shrapnel from Black Tom itself, were burning, ammunition-laden barges jolted free of their moorings and drifting close by like gunboats pouring shells and bullets into the buildings. Writing in the *New York World-Telegram* years later, A. J. Liebling described the scene:

> The shells intended to make the world safe for democracy when fired through the cannon of the czar and the mikado were knocking chips out of the Goddess of Liberty on her island in the harbor. A three-inch shell, tearing out [of] a munition car, had penetrated a barge filled with nitro-cellulose, causing the chief detonation, and now the whole harbor was having a showerbath of shrapnel. Two big barges, blown from their berths at the Black Tom piers, moved down on Bedloe [*sic*] Island with the tide, discharging broadsides as if manned by the gunners of hell. They drifted down toward Ellis Island, where 500 immigrants, fleeing war's terrors in Europe, cowered.

Repeatedly, tugboats, New York fireboats and Coast Guard cutters braved the munitions barrage to pull the flaming, exploding barges away from shore, pouring streams of water into them. But the fires and the flying shrapnel continued all night and into dawn, as thousands of onlookers lined the shoreline on both sides of the Hudson. As the hours passed, taxis and private cars clogged Manhattan's downtown streets as their drivers and passengers sought to get closer to the site of the inferno.

At the Mission of Our Lady of the Rosary in Jersey City, facing the Battery, Father A. J. Grogan held six o'clock mass before the largest early-morning congregation that had ever crowded into his church. "I can assure you," he told a reporter, "there were many praying on their knees who had not been inside a place of worship for a long time."

Only as first light came were the dimensions of the devastation realized. The Black Tom promontory was a charred ruin; thirteen huge warehouses were leveled and six piers destroyed, and fires continued to eat their way through the remains and consume hundreds of railroad cars and barges tied to the docks. At one point, a huge cavern was hewed out of the earth by the explosions of some eighty-seven dynamite-laden railroad cars. The blast excavated a hole so deep that it extended below sea level; water seeped in until a vast pond was created, strewn with the wreckage.

The barges and houseboats in the harbor, numbering more than two hundred, comprised a floating village with a population of more than five hundred persons forced to flee in the middle of the night. One who did not make it was an unidentified man about thirty-five years old found on the pier, believed to have been a watchman. Two other bodies were pulled from the river, and scores more were feared drowned.

Missing was Cornelius Leyden, chief of the private Lehigh Valley Railroad police, last seen standing where the newly created pond now existed. Martin T. Henley, the night general yardmaster for the Lehigh Valley, reported that he and Leyden had gone down to the freight cars to investigate the cause of the fire when the first explosion occurred.

The official Jersey City Fire Department report said: "Henley had his coat buttoned up. His coat was torn open and his watch and chain in his vest pocket were blown out into the river. The last he saw of Leyden was going in the direction of the river on the pier; the supposition is that he was blown into the bay and drowned." More than a month later, Leyden's body finally washed ashore in New York Harbor.

First estimates of the seriously injured at the site approached a hundred, with hundreds more hurt by the blast waves and falling debris. Miraculously, however, not a single person on the streets of New York or Jersey City was reported injured by all the shattered glass. Had the explosions occurred during the daylight hours of a business day, the casualties could easily have reached the thousands, especially in the jammed financial district of Lower Manhattan. Police reported a bizarre pattern to the glass breakage. In some buildings, hundreds of large windows were blown out completely; in adjacent buildings, not a single pane was broken—a mark of the air currents' fickleness, experts explained.

First estimates of the damages totaled $20 million, of which $12 million was assigned to the National Dock and Storage Company, owners of the warehouses. Exploded ammunition in railroad cars and on barges was evaluated at $5 million; eighty-five cars of the Lehigh Valley, plus tugs, tracks and grain elevator lost amounted to another $1 million; glass damage, including destruction of plate glass in Manhattan and Brooklyn estimated at $300,000, accounted for most of the rest.

The New York Plate Glass Insurance Company, insurers of most of the large windows in the downtown Manhattan area, made an immediate inspection of the area and came up with replacement cost estimates, which far exceeded the $200,000 annual premiums it received from clients in Manhattan and Brooklyn. Some $25 million worth of stored goods, including sugar valued at $3.4 million, was in the warehouses and much of it was set afire. Fire department officials estimated it would take a month for all the sugar to burn off.

Almost at once, authorities sought to fix the blame and, if warranted, seek criminal penalties. All day Sunday, investigators from Jersey City and Hudson County combed the wreckage and listened to eyewitness accounts. Meanwhile sporadic shell bursts continued to imperil the inspectors and crews sent in to find and remove unexploded munitions.

By Sunday night, the law-enforcement men moved. They issued arrest warrants on charges of manslaughter for Superintendent Albert M. Dickman, the Black Tom Island agent for the Lehigh Valley Railroad, and Alexander Davidson, superintendent for the National Dock and Storage Company. Theodore B. Johnson, head of the Johnson Lighterage and Towing Company, turned himself in at the Hudson County courthouse in Jersey City when he learned that a third warrant had been issued for him. Each man was released on $5,000 bail, pending a grand jury investigation.

Immediately the railroad, the storage company and the barge operator all sought to pin the blame elsewhere. Lehigh Valley officials said the fire had started on Johnson's barge and that furthermore the barge should not have been at the Black Tom pier in the first place. Johnson vehemently denied the charge.

"The barge had a perfect right in the dock," he said after his arraignment. "It went there, with the knowledge of the Lehigh Valley, to complete loading. I can prove that the fire did not start on the barge, but on the piers of the Lehigh. The Lehigh is putting out such statements to shift responsibility. . . . There have been several fires of incendiary origin on the Lehigh piers on Black Tom Island which were never reported to the Jersey City officials because the railroad succeeded in extinguishing them."

Some officials, however, were not convinced. One was the Jersey City commissioner of public safety, a short, dapper man named Frank Hague, later to become mayor and one of the nation's legendary big-city machine bosses. Hague reported he was told Johnson barge *No. 17* had tied up at Black Tom to avoid a twenty-five dollar towing charge —false economy, he noted, inasmuch as the explosions may have cost $25 million in property damages.

The Jersey City Fire Department, after its own investigation, reported that while its evidence suggested the fire had started among some freight cars and sparks had spread to *Johnson No. 17*, the barge should not have been where it was.

On that Saturday, the department reported, twelve cars of the Central Railroad, loaded with 3,125 cases of ammunition and explosive projectiles, were transferred to the Johnson barge; it was loaded up at 2:30 P.M. "and, according to federal regulations, should have gone out into the bay at New York or proceeded to Gravesend Bay, where the explosives were to be transferred to a steamer. Instead of doing that, it went to the Lehigh Valley pier and tied up there, against the express orders of the Lehigh Valley officials."

Hague also ordered the arrest of Eben B. Thomas, president of the Lehigh Valley, and William G. Besler, president of the Central Railroad of New Jersey, after checking on reports that 200 cars still loaded with explosives remained in the railroads' yards on Black Tom in violation of regulations established at the outbreak of the Great War two years earlier. Those regulations prohibited keeping explosives in the yards or on tied-up vessels for more than twenty-four hours. The railroads also were barred from storing dynamite in the yards, which they obviously had done.

The Hudson County prosecutor, Robert S. Hudspeth, likewise indicated he meant business. "I have evidence of criminal negligence of the worst sort and we will push the cases to the limit," he told reporters. "Because they have had difficulty in getting ships to transport the ammunition, the railroad and the transportation companies have allowed it to accumulate so that no one in this section of the country is safe. It was against the law for that dynamite to be on Black Tom, and I am going to find out who is to blame. . . .

"It would appear that sparks from the burning cars" set the Johnson barge on fire, Hudspeth said, and he indicated that if so, the railroad company would be in big trouble with New Jersey and federal authorities. "The ordinary storage of explosives for purposes of interstate commerce did not contemplate turning one end of this city into an arsenal. That stuff is being shipped not for purposes of interstate commerce but for purposes of war, and it is not right for millions of people to be imperiled for the benefit of foreign warring nations and for the profits of munitions dealers. It's a public nuisance of the worst kind and no body or law or power has a right to imperil millions of lives."

Other authorities were equally outraged. Governor James F. Fiedler of New Jersey noted that after a similar though not as destructive explosion of dynamite five years earlier at the Jersey Central's yards not far from Black Tom, the state legislature had enacted stronger safety laws. Now he declared:

> It does seem to me that it is barbarous to have dynamite and other explosives piled right up at the door of great cities and almost under the noses of thousands of inhabitants. I do not believe the people of New Jersey and New York will tolerate a continuance of these conditions. The custom of unloading high explosives in New York Harbor will not be permitted any longer by the public sentiment that will surely be aroused by this disaster.

But the hard fact was that the sale and shipment of war munitions was very big business in the greater New York area. Seventy-five percent of all ammunition and armaments shipped from the United States to Europe went out within a radius of five miles of City Hall in Lower Manhattan. More cartridges left New York than were sent from all other American ports put together, and more than one third of all the gunpowder.

Black Tom, through which much of this war matériel flowed, actually had been the site of three earlier explosions, two at a nitroglycerine plant built there, the second of which destroyed it. The man who built the plant of the National Dock and Storage Company, W. L. Sanders, said Black Tom had the reputation locally of being "hoodooed." That reputation was not likely to diminish now.

Although the Black Tom explosions were the most spectacular in the United States since the beginning of the Great War in 1914, they were hardly the first. The overwhelming majority of them came in factories making munitions or their chemical or metal components. The *Times* listed three in 1914, twenty-nine in 1915, and eighteen others in the first half of 1916.

Of these fifty episodes, twenty-eight took place in the New York–New Jersey area. Still, there seemed to be not the slightest notion that the Black Tom disaster was anything but a most regrettable accident, resulting from negligence by the railroads, or the storage company, or one thrift-minded barge captain.

A preliminary report to Bruce Bielaski, chief of the Bureau of Investigations of the U.S. Department of Justice in Washington, led him to say: "There is nothing in it to justify action now by the Department of Justice. Our investigator seems to think that the explosion was an accident." Bielaski did, however, promise a thorough investigation.

The *New York Times,* in reporting this statement and disclosing plans for other investigations by the Interstate Commerce Commission, Frank Hague's Department of Public Safety in Jersey City, and the Lehigh Valley and Jersey Central railroads, concluded:

> On one point the various investigating bodies agree, and that is that the fire and subsequent explosions cannot be charged to the account of alien plotters against the neutrality of the United States, although it is admitted that the destruction of so large a quantity of allied war material must prove cheering news to Berlin and Vienna.

Never, in the long and illustrious annals of the *New York Times*, was the newspaper more wrong. The chaos delivered to New York Harbor in the early hours of July 30, 1916, was the centerpiece of one of the greatest and most cunning deceptions ever perpetrated on the United States by a foreign power. It would take the next twenty-three years to unravel and prove, in a marathon manhunt and diplomatic and legal chess game played on a worldwide board spanning Europe, North and South America, and the Orient.

The story of Black Tom did not begin, however, on the night the massive munitions terminal exploded and lit up the black sky over the Statue of Liberty and millions of terrified New Yorkers. It really began with the infamous event in a distant Balkan town that plunged Europe into the Great War, and with the American government's consequent determination to stay neutral—while becoming the major arsenal for the enemies of Imperial Germany.

II: ATTACK ON NEUTRAL AMERICA, 1914-1917

3. Madness in Europe

On the late morning of June 28, 1914, an obscure Bosnian student named Gavrilo Princip stood along a cobblestone street lining the Miljacka River in the picturesque Balkan mountain town of Sarajevo, Serbia. He watched with bitterness as Archduke Franz Ferdinand, heir-apparent to the throne of the Austro-Hungarian Empire, and his wife, the Duchess of Hohenberg, motored by, en route to a reception at the nearby town hall. Princip was a member of Mlada Bosna, or Young Bosnia, a movement established in 1910 in protest against the annexation in 1908 of the Balkan states of Bosnia and Herzegovina by the Dual Monarchy of the Hapsburgs.

Only moments earlier, another member of the movement, Nedeljko Cabrinovic, had tossed a small bomb into the royal couple's open motorcar. But the alert archduke deflected it and the bomb exploded beneath the car behind his in the motorcade, injuring two aides and six spectators.

At the town hall immediately afterward, Franz Ferdinand was remarkably composed, if angry. When the mayor of Sarajevo began his welcoming remarks, the archduke interrupted him, protesting the bomb incident as "an amazing indignity." But he then permitted the mayor to continue, and insisted on returning via the same route to visit the wounded at a nearby hospital.

Young Princip, who had watched the royal couple go by the first time, did not pass up this second opportunity. At the corner of Franz Josef and Rudolf streets, he stepped quickly from the crowd and emptied the bullets from an automatic pistol point-blank into Franz Ferdinand and the duchess, killing both.

The assassination electrified Europe and the world. But in Washington, President Woodrow Wilson at that hour had a more personal matter on his mind. His beloved wife, Ellen, lay seriously ill in the White House with Bright's disease and tuberculosis of the kidney. The president's thoughts were far from the event that was to precipitate in a month's time the tragedy of the Great War.

Wilson dispatched the customary telegram of sympathy to the bereaved Emperor Franz Josef:

> Deeply shocked at the atrocious murder of his Imperial and Royal Highness Archduke Franz Ferdinand and his consort at an assassin's hands. I extend to your Majesty, to the royal family, and to the Government of Austria-Hungary the sincere condolences of the Government and people of the United States and an expression of my profound sympathy.

The assassination in the heart of the tempestuous Balkans rocked all of Europe. Vienna, already at patience's end with rebellious forces in Serbia to the south that continued to defy the 1908 annexation of Bosnia and Herzegovina, seized upon the bloody slaying as a pretext to move against Serbia.*

After a month of mounting tension, Austria-Hungary sent to the Serbian government in Belgrade an ultimatum that was so humiliating that it seemed all but certain to be rejected. And if so, it would almost surely trigger the intricate array of alliances among the European powers — Russia lining up with Slavic Serbia, Germany and Italy with Austria-Hungary, France and England with Russia — until at last the whole continent would be aflame.

But to Wilson — occupied not only with his wife's illness but also with severe foreign-policy challenges in Mexico and the Caribbean — and to the American people generally, the European turmoil seemed remote. Not until twenty-three days after the assassination of the archduke and duchess in Sarajevo did the *New York Times* feel moved to run, on page four, a brief dispatch from Berlin that said:

> Undisguised concern prevails in Berlin over the possibility of an armed conflict between Austria and Servia [*sic*] and the possible embroilment of the rest of Europe. It is stated tonight on high diplomatic authority that an Austrian note will be presented Belgrade at the end of the present week, and that unless Servia unequivocally yields the situation will bristle with grave possibilities.

---

*While Austria and Hungary remained separate entities under the Dual Monarchy, the political and military leadership clearly emanated from Vienna. In the reports of the events of the time, the Hapsburg Empire often was referred to simply as Austria, as will be seen in newspaper articles and documents quoted here.

The Berlin Stock Exchange continues to be affected by the prevailing anxiety. Another heavy drop in prices occurred today, in consequence of the failure of a Vienna bank, the movements of Austrian Army leaders and heavy selling orders from St. Petersburg. The conservative *Deutsche Tages Zeitung*, under the heading "The Situation is Very Grave," states tonight that one of the most disquieting features is the possibility that Russia will rush to Servia's assistance. That, it is asserted, would be a palpable affront to Austria and almost certainly [would] involve Germany and the rest of the European powers.

While the balance of power thus tottered precariously across the Atlantic, a sense of security engendered by three thousand miles of ocean and the distractions of concerns closer to American shores ill prepared the United States and its elected leader for the intrigues that in the end would engulf them along with Europe itself.

Four months earlier, Mrs. Wilson, already ailing, had fallen in her room and was bedridden. When she and the president vacationed at White Sulphur Springs, West Virginia, at Easter, a nurse accompanied them. In early May, Mrs. Wilson was able to perform her duties as hostess at the marriage of the Wilsons' daughter Eleanor to Secretary of the Treasury William Gibbs McAdoo. Shortly afterward, however, the first lady was obliged to retire again to her second-floor bedroom in the White House, where she now lay with what was diagnosed as a spinal injury and a nervous breakdown. She resisted doctors' suggestions that she go to the president's summer residence in New Hampshire to escape Washington's debilitating heat, choosing to stay near her husband, and she was paying the price in ebbing strength.

The president was devoted to his wife, a small woman with light brown hair and charming southern drawl, the offspring—like Wilson himself—of a Presbyterian minister. She in turn was one of her husband's fiercest defenders, firing off letters in the midst of her illness to senators who had the effrontery to attack his policies. All attention within the domestic White House centered on her health, consuming much time and even more emotional energy of the president as he tried to deal with disturbing skirmishes in Nicaragua, Haiti and neighboring Santo Domingo, and with the thorn in his side that the regime of General Victoriano Huerta in Mexico had become to him.

Ever since February, 1913, when Huerta had seized power with the murder of Francisco Madero, an idealistic reformer who himself had taken power in 1911 with the overthrow of Porfirio Díaz, Wilson had been determined to rid Mexico of the usurper. While continuing to portray himself as an apostle of peace and neutrality, Wilson in his own hemisphere sought to shape the often unruly and undisciplined states of Latin America in the democratic image, in what was then called "missionary diplomacy."

In pursuing his mission, the president did not hesitate to resort to bluster, threat and muscle to achieve acquiescence, especially in Huerta's case. Wilson backed the insurgency in Mexico of Venustiano Carranza and in April of 1914 seized upon a seemingly innocent and temporary boarding of a small U.S. Navy ship by a Huertista commander at Tampico to land American forces at Vera Cruz. The ensuing clash caused the death of 126 Mexicans and 19 Americans and the wounding of 185 Mexican and 71 U.S. troops. Formal negotiations to settle the dispute between the United States and Mexico, begun in May, were still going on at Niagara Falls, Canada, and were commanding Wilson's attention when the archduke fell at Sarajevo.

Wilson's strong and conspicuous interventionism in Mexico provided a sharp contrast to an almost religious commitment to remain neutral in the gathering storm over Europe. That this minister's son and former university president saw himself as an instrument of world peace was clear from repeated speeches and the activities of his new administration.

He approved of the ambitious plan of his secretary of state, William Jennings Bryan, to negotiate peace treaties with all the nations of the world, and in 1913 and 1914 some thirty of them were achieved. Yet Wilson's equal revulsion to the seizing of power by violent means was driving him incongruently to the most bellicose actions against Huerta short of war, and he threatened that step as well.

At the same time, economic distress at home bore down on the president. Pressures for reforms in the areas of antitrust, banking and trade were crowded out by a depression that gripped the country in the fall of 1913 and deepened as credit tightened amid increasing talk and signs of impending war in Europe. Production fell off, business failures mounted and so did unemployment, especially in the larger cities.

In a nation whose population had reached 98.6 million in forty-eight states, some 325,000 individuals were said to be without work in New York City alone. According to a police survey at the time, about 26,000 of these were sleeping each night in public places—in parks, beneath bridges, in the streets, in saloons and city flophouses. Small anarchist groups courted the unemployed, rallying them to repeated acts of public protest and disruption.

Clearly, the United States of America and its president had enough on their plate without getting embroiled in a fight that, to millions of Americans, was an obscure argument over obscure places in Eastern Europe involving even more obscure issues and matters of national pride.

Others in the United States, however, could not remain so blasé about what had happened at Sarajevo, and about the tensions that were mounting daily in all European capitals. One of these was Count Johann Heinrich von Bernstorff, since 1908 the German ambassador to the United States and Mexico, residing in the German embassy in Washington. Von Bernstorff was the London-born son of a former German minister to England, a Prussian Junker—a member of the nationalistic, landed aristocracy—married to an American, the former Jeanne Luckemeyer. A favorite in Washington social circles, he threw lavish parties at the embassy and was rumored to be a tireless womanizer. He considered as part of his mission the courting of the Washington press corps, within which he had developed many contacts.

Von Bernstorff was dining at the Metropolitan Club with the Spanish ambassador when he got the news of the assassination of the archduke. He and his companion, he observed later in a book about his tenure in America, "were not for a moment in doubt as to the very serious, peace-menacing character of the incident, but we found little interest in the matter among the Americans in the club, who, as always, regarded European affairs with indifference."

As this American attitude continued over the next three weeks, however, Germany's major ally to the east, Austria-Hungary, was tightening the screws on tiny Serbia. On July 23, Vienna sent its curt and uncompromising ultimatum to Belgrade, demanding prosecution by Austrian officials in Serbia not only of the assassins Princip and Cabrinovic but of all accomplices as well. The ultimatum also demanded an end to all traffic in arms across the Austrian-Serbian border, the repudiation and eradication of the several Pan-Serbian societies accused of fomenting unrest, an end to all anti-Austrian propaganda, and the arrests of those responsible in Serbia. Most humiliating of all, Vienna demanded that these actions be announced on the front page of the official journal of the government of Serbia.

"The Austro-Hungarian government is unable longer to pursue an attitude of forbearance, and sees the duty imposed upon it to put an end to the intrigues which form a perpetual menace to the monarchy's tranquility," read the official note, itself heavy with menace. The terms were considered to be so severe and humiliating, in fact, as to be impossible for Serbia to accept without surrender of her national honor. And so all sides girded for an invasion of Serbia by Austria-Hungary.

The partners to the great alliances that had been a buffer against a major war, finding themselves now locked into inescapable commitments, vowed their support: Germany for Austria-Hungary, Russia for her Slavic cousins in Serbia, France for Russia, England—already plagued by rebellious Irish in Ulster—for France. Only Italy of the larger powers, while part of the Triple Alliance with Germany and the Dual Monarchy, shied off, insisting its pledges applied only to defending an attacked ally, and in this case Austria-Hungary clearly would be the attacker.

The intricate network of alliances was an inevitable outgrowth of further German ambitions beyond Otto von Bismarck's establishment of the nation as a European power in triumphs over France and Austria. When Kaiser Wilhelm II took the throne of the imperial monarchy in 1888, and within two years dismissed Bismarck, all of Europe was threatened by the kaiser's continuing insistence that Germany be given her "place in the sun."

Her alliance in 1879 with Austria to establish a dominant *Mitteleuropa,* and the inclusion of Italy two years later to form the Triple Alliance, set off counterbalancing combinations—the Russo-French military alliance in 1893, the Anglo-French Entente in 1904 and finally the Anglo-Russian Entente in 1907. To the Allies, their action was defensive, but to the kaiser it was "encirclement."

Although the assassination of the archduke was a shocking incident, such episodes were not unheard of in the politically tempestuous Balkans, and hardly a justification in itself for plunging the western world into its most terrible war.

Germany's goading of her Austrian ally to deliver the ultimatum to Serbia was predicated on a gamble that Russia either would not come to the aid of her Slavic neighbor because she was unprepared, or would be unable to mobilize before Germany had disposed of France on the Western Front. Thus did miscalculation lead ultimately to disaster and a drawn-out war whose true origins would be debated for decades afterward.

In short order, the European war would spill over into Asia Minor and the Far East as well. In November, the Allies would declare war on Turkey after the Turks had permitted entry into the Black Sea of two German cruisers that proceeded to shell Odessa. And Japan would seize German territories in the Pacific, notably the province of Shantung on the Chinese mainland.

At the start, however, there seemed reason to hope the conflagration would be contained. On July 25, Belgrade replied to Vienna's ultimatum in terms surprisingly conciliatory. In fact, Serbia met all of the demands except the one to have Austrian officials conduct the investigation in Serbia of alleged Serbian involvement in the assassination. Even then the note merely inquired what the role of the Austrians would be:

> Serbia desires sincere and correct neighborly relations with the Dual Monarchy. Convinced of the necessity of maintaining such relations, the Serbian Government will readily comply with all the demands of Austria-Hungary which will serve to suppress all criminal acts, manifestations and disorders in neighboring countries. Because the Serbian Government considers it is thereby fulfilling the obvious duty of a civilized state, the Government will in all sincerity do everything possible to prove its intense desire for friendly relations with the Dual Monarchy.

But Belgrade's note again disavowed governmental responsibility for the assassination of the archduke and indicated unwillingness to leave the investigation to Austrian officials:

> The Serbian government cannot be held responsible for manifestations of a private character such as are common in all lands and escape official control. The Serbian Government has been painfully surprised by the statements connecting persons in the kingdom with the Sarajevo outrage. It expected to be invited to cooperate in the earnestness of its action against all persons concerning whom communications should be made, without regard to situation or rank.

The answer obviously was not satisfactory to Vienna, which at this point was not likely to be satisfied by any reply short of abject surrender. Serbia's note was delivered to the Austrian minister in Belgrade ten minutes before the appointed deadline of six o'clock in the evening, and as soon as the deadline passed, Vienna broke off diplomatic relations. King Peter of Serbia immediately withdrew from the capital and moved inland together with his staff and the national treasury in anticipation of the invasion, and Austrian troops massed on the Serbian border.

As word spread across Europe, the war fever hit the major capitals —Vienna, Moscow, Berlin, Paris, Rome, London. Cheering crowds poured into the streets, almost as if a great carnival was about to begin. Mobs in Berlin marched down the Unter den Linden to the Austrian embassy, singing "Die Wacht am Rhein" and Austrian national songs, pausing to cheer before the Bismarck and Molke memorials. Similar scenes unfolded on the boulevards of Paris, with speakers denouncing the Germans as instigators of the Austrian breach with Serbia.

There seemed to be little sense of the devastation that a war on such a grand scale, with a degree of mechanization never seen before in mortal combat, might bring to Europe. One after another, the military mobilizations began—in Russia, Germany, France and England, a parade of national lemmings marching into what would be a bloody sea of human carnage over the next four years.

Only in Belgrade, considered easy prey for the Austrians, did the reality appear to strike home. In the wake of King Peter's departure, much of the rest of the city fled. "The prosperous, happy, busy town," wrote the *New York Times'* correspondent, "will shortly look like a city of the dead."

The immediate catalyst for the crisis was Serbia's refusal to accept responsibility and make reparations for the assassination of Archduke Franz Ferdinand. The broader impetus, however, was the longtime determination of the Hapsburg Empire to expand southward to the Aegean Sea. Austria in 1908 had nibbled away at the Serbian population with the annexation of Bosnia and Herzegovina. But Serbia, after the Balkan Wars in 1912–13, had seized parts of Macedonia, and Greece had occupied Salonika, barring Austria's route to the Aegean. Thus Austrian expansionism and Serbia's quest to retain and if possible strengthen her national identity were on a collision course.

Count Johann von Bernstorff, German ambassador to the United States
and Mexico, 1908–1917

Above left: Captain Franz von Papen, military attaché in German embassy, later chancellor of Weimar Republic who helped pave the way for Hitler's rise to power

Above right: Dr. Constantin Dumba, Austrian ambassador to the United States, recalled in late 1915

Left: Captain Franz von Rintelen, alias Emil Gache, self-styled "Dark Invader" who was dispatched to America to impede munitions shipments to Allies

Right: Hans Tauscher, left, with American agent after arrest

Captain Karl Boy-Ed, German naval attaché, recalled in late 1915

Above left: Franz von Bopp, German consul in San Francisco who recruited two of the Black Tom suspects
Above right: Louis A. Smith, recruited by von Bopp to sabotage munitions ships at Tacoma, Washington

Left: Charles Crowley, Louis Smith's partner at attempted sabotage
Right: Present-day view of house at 123 West 15th Street in New York City where Black Tom plans were hatched   *—Manning Rubin*

S.S. *Lusitania* leaving New York Harbor on its final voyage

Wolf von Igel, Franz von Papen's deputy and later his successor

Crew of *Deutschland* upon arrival at Baltimore

Left: Horst von der Goltz, alias Bridgeman Taylor, German agent who attempted to blow up the Welland Canal

Right: Werner Horn, on the right, after arrest following attempt to blow up Vanceboro Bridge

German submarine *Deutschland* docking at Baltimore after first Atlantic crossing, July 10, 1916

On July 27, the final breach came. Austria invaded Serbia at the town of Mitrovicza, about fifty miles northwest of Belgrade. Still, the rest of Europe did not seem psychologically able to face the fact that war had begun. Sir Edward Grey, the British foreign secretary, urgently called on Vienna and Belgrade to desist and on Berlin, Moscow, Rome and Paris to confer to avoid "the greatest catastrophe."

In the United States, thoughtful and informed Americans persisted in believing that modern war would be so awful as to be deterred by that fact alone. The *Times'* lead editorial on June 28 literally implored Kaiser Wilhelm to stay his hand and in so doing avoid the inevitable escalation. Naively, the editorial then predicted that the broader war would yet be averted:

> In this time of passion and of peril the eyes of the world turn to the German emperor as the chief man of Europe, the man who more than any other has the power to provoke or to avert a great war. Undoubtedly William II [sic], by encouraging Austria in her madness and by giving to her quarrel with Servia [sic] the appearance of a menace to Russia, might bring the Czar's great armed forces into the conflict as a pretext and provocation for a German march to the front. Then France and England would be involved and the civilization of Europe would give way to savagery, [and] the greatest war of all human history would be in progress. That is too dreadful for imagining, and because it is too dreadful it cannot happen. . . .
>
> A general European war is unthinkable. With fifteen million in the field the bill of costs would be certainly not less than $30 million a day, and the waste and destruction would enormously add to it. Europe cannot afford such a war, the world cannot afford it, and happily the conviction is growing that such an appalling conflict is altogether beyond the range of possibility. . . .
>
> [Austria's] unreasonableness is so evident that the universal interpretation of her course is that she has used Servia [sic] as a pretext for the accomplishment of a purpose not avowed. No war could be more unjust, none more unholy than one provoked by such methods. But while the war which has made the whole world tremble with dread may not be averted because it

would be unjust and unholy, there is solid ground for the expectation that it will be prevented because the sober-minded statesmen of Europe, and above all the Kaiser, are not men of blood, but of peace.

The very day that editorial appeared, Austria formally declared war on Serbia and Russian forces began to mobilize and move toward Germany's eastern frontier, ignoring warnings from the kaiser. On July 30, as Vienna claimed it had occupied Belgrade, the kaiser gave Moscow twenty-four hours to cease its mobilization, and when the deadline passed, he ordered mobilization of his own forces.

"Let your hearts beat for God and your fists on the enemy," he urged his troops as he signed the order.

The Russian mobilization proceeded unrelentingly, and on August 1, Germany swiftly moved into neutral Luxembourg, signaling the German General Staff's plan to strike first at France before the Russians, requiring more time to marshal their forces, could launch an effective offensive. The move was accompanied by orders to German ships at sea to hasten to safe ports, in anticipation of the British fleet weighing in on the side of France against Germany.

One large vessel, the *Kronprinzessin Cecilie* of the North German Lloyd Line, carrying $10.6 million in gold, was bound from New York for Plymouth and Cherbourg when the word came. She was believed to be making a run for Bremen but later turned and headed back to America, eventually anchoring safely at Bar Harbor, Maine.

Two other large ocean liners of the same firm, the *Grosser Kurfuerst* and the *Friedrich der Grosse,* and another of the Hamburg-Amerika Line, the *President Grant,* turned around and raced back to New York Harbor, where with many other German steamships they soon would be interned under American neutrality laws. The return of the *Friedrich der Grosse* particularly would in due time play a major role in Germany's response to impediments to her war effort imposed by those neutrality laws.

On the same day, the urgency of the situation struck home in America. Germany declared war on Russia, whose forces responded by pouring over Germany's eastern border at several points. The madness was now totally unleashed. Wilson, however, held his regular semiweekly news conference and told the reporters assembled in his office that "so far as we are concerned, there is no cause for excitement. There is great inconvenience, for the time being, in the money market and in our exchanges," the president said, "and temporarily in the handling of our crops. But America is absolutely prepared to meet the financial situation and to straighten everything out without any material difficulty. The only thing that can prevent it is unreasonable apprehension and excitement."

Wilson cautioned the reporters against writing anything that would cause public nervousness.

"I want to have the pride of feeling that America, if nobody else, has her self-possession and stands ready with calmness of thought and readiness of purpose to help the rest of the world," he said. He urged leading members of Congress who called on him to press on with their legislative agenda. On leaving the White House, several senators said they saw no reason why they could not adjourn for the year in another few weeks.

For Count von Bernstorff, the German ambassador, it was hardly business as usual, however. Nine days after the assassinations in Sarajevo, he had sailed for Germany aboard his country's premier ocean liner, the *Vaterland*. He was a most imposing figure: tall, thin and always well-groomed, with a coldness about him underscored by a kaiser moustache, waxed ends pointing upward. But as a career diplomat of aristocratic Saxon birth, he was skilled in the social and diplomatic graces and could be ingratiating.

Von Bernstorff's return to Berlin marked the beginning of a role for him that would go distinctly beyond normal ambassadorial duties. With war rapidly approaching, the German government was aware that the United States, while determined to remain neutral, would likely become a major source of munitions, especially if the war were to last beyond the several months Berlin and Vienna hoped would be required to achieve victory. Hence a prime function assigned to von Bernstorff, and to his commercial attaché, Dr. Heinrich Albert, who was in Berlin with him and so testified later, was the buying of those American munitions. Von Bernstorff was given $150 million in German treasury notes for the purpose—and for certain other activities required, but not to be acknowledged, by a warring nation in a neutral country whose loyalties to the enemy were widely suspected in Berlin.

With the British certain to control the sea-lanes between Europe and America, it was unlikely from the start that German purchases of munitions in the United States could be transported safely to German ports. Therefore much of the money in von Bernstorff's care would have to be dispensed to find ways to limit the shipment of munitions to the British and French. Also, knowing that the practical degree of American neutrality might well depend on public and governmental attitudes toward the combatant nations, von Bernstorff was commissioned as well to generate pro-German, anti-Allies propaganda in the United States.

There was the matter, also, of German military reservists in America. Many of them responded to the prospect of war with open, frenzied fervor. The German Veterans' League in New York held patriotic parades in which its young, blond members marched to blaring German bands, singing war songs and waving German flags—much to the anger of other New Yorkers who sided with the Allies and who often scuffled with the marchers. Soon all foreign flags and parades were barred by order of the mayor.

To channel this enthusiasm properly, von Bernstorff had to see to it that a system was developed to locate German reservists throughout the United States and arrange for their safe passage home to fight for the fatherland. This he would achieve, as we will see, through an elaborate scheme of passport fraud.

The matter of the reservists in fact became an early cause of friction between Berlin and Washington. The German foreign secretary, Gottlieb von Jagow, in a heated exchange with the American ambassador in Berlin, James Gerard, warned that "if there is a war between Germany and the United States, you will find there are five hundred thousand German reservists in your country ready to take up arms for their mother country, and the United States will be engaged in a civil war."

Gerard shot back: "I do not know whether there are five hundred thousand Germans in the United States. But I do know there are five hundred thousand lampposts in my country and that every German residing in the United States who undertakes to take up arms against America will swing from one of those five hundred thousand lampposts." Such was the uneasy state of diplomatic relations between the two countries as the war began and the United States sought to follow the path of neutrality.

Among von Bernstorff's conferences on arrival in Berlin was an extremely critical one in establishing his comprehensive role in the

United States after the outbreak of the war. It took place at an office of the German General Staff, officially called "Sektion Politik des Generalstabes" but commonly referred to as "Abteilung Drei-Bai" —Section 3B. The section's prime function, however, was not politics, but military intelligence. There, the ambassador was called upon to carry out responsibilities that in effect would make him—behind the cloak of his diplomatic role—Germany's chief of espionage and sabotage in the Western Hemisphere.

As fears mounted that the unrest in the Balkans would spread to the rest of Europe, Section 3B had deployed virtually all of its experienced intelligence officers and spies to the major countries anticipated to be Germany's foes in the next war—England, France and Russia. Now, even if large numbers of trained agents could be mobilized, the chances of infiltrating any significant share undetected into the United States was slim. The only realistic solution was for Ambassador von Bernstorff to organize and oversee Germany's spy and sabotage operations in America himself—from the German embassy in Washington!

The assignment put von Bernstorff in an immensely difficult—and challenging—position. As Imperial Germany's chief diplomat in Washington, he had one obvious task: to keep the United States out of the war, and neutral. In this endeavor, President Wilson's strong pacifist inclinations—regarding Europe at least—would greatly facilitate the ambassador's efforts, and von Bernstorff would prove unstinting in nurturing those inclinations at every opportunity. That would be his public role, and he would play it convincingly and effectively within the diplomatic, social and press communities of the capital, in all of which he traveled with wide acceptance and credibility.

But in von Bernstorff's new and clandestine role, he would be obliged to practice the arts of deception and subterfuge more commonly associated with military intelligence work, though not, to be sure, totally unheard of in diplomacy. Throughout the period prior to the eventual American entry into the Great War, von Bernstorff would insist that he wore only the first, public, hat. But from the moment he got his instructions at Section 3B to oversee Germany's secret operations in the United States, and the money with which to finance them, he wore the second, private, hat as well. Secret cables later uncovered that were addressed to him and routed through him to embassy subordinates, authorizing him to disburse funds for acts of sabotage, clearly established that fact.

Among the earliest and most revealing of these secret messages, dated January 26, 1915, and intercepted by the British, dealt with the hiring of specific Irish nationals in the United States to commit sabotage. It went from Berlin to von Bernstorff, to be passed on to his military attaché for action, and will be presented later in this narrative, along with other incriminating secret messages that fell into Allied hands.

On August 2, carrying with him the $150 million in treasury notes to finance his new mission, von Bernstorff sailed to America aboard the Dutch liner *Noordam*. He was under strict orders to keep the money close at hand at all times, and in the event of British boarding or seizing of the vessel, he was to toss all of it into the Atlantic.

When a British officer boarded the ship at Dover, however, von Bernstorff was not even interrogated; he had arranged to keep his name off the passenger list. In his memoirs years later, he told of a friendly German-American fellow-passenger who said to him: "Take care that you don't expose yourself to annoyance; the people on board think you are the German ambassador in Washington." Relying on this man's discretion, von Bernstorff wrote, he confessed that he was.

On August 4, Germany, rejecting a British demand that Belgian neutrality be honored, sent her army into Belgium, clearly bound for France. The next day, Great Britain issued a declaration of war against Germany and within minutes the main thoroughfares of London were jammed with cheering, marching young men. Others crowded into Fleet Street to read the bulletins posted outside its newspaper offices.

In one of their first acts of war, the British cut the German transatlantic cable, not only severing direct communications between Berlin and its embassy in Washington but also assuring a near monopoly for the Allies on war news and propaganda from the front to the United States. This development, too, was in time to play a major role in the manner in which Germany would carry out her great deception against America.

In Liverpool, on the huge "unsinkable" Cunard ocean liner *Lusitania*, all lights that might be visible from outside were ordered darkened by the captain. Then she slid from her moorings and steamed out to sea, where the British cruiser *Essex* waited to escort her across the Atlantic.

The war declarations were now being issued wildly across the crazy-quilt map of Europe—Germany against Belgium, Austria against Russia, Belgium against Germany, even tiny Montenegro throwing in with Serbia against Austria. At the same time, German troops marched into neutral Switzerland, and all across the continent a bizarre mix of the old warfare and the new was unfurled. Russian cossacks on horseback galloped into German border towns, while farther west German troops brought down a French "aeroplane" with rifle fire and Belgian and German aviators fired revolvers at each other in midair.

Still, back in Washington, Wilson's preoccupation was with his wife, now rapidly slipping away. Lunching with his daughter Eleanor when the news first came of Austria's move into Serbia, Wilson exclaimed: "It's incredible! Incredible! But don't tell your mother anything about it."

When Eleanor asked her father whether he thought the United States would be drawn in, he is said to have stared at her for a moment, then raised his hands over his eyes and lamented: "I can think of nothing—nothing, when my dear one is suffering!"

At the White House, President Wilson continued his vigil at the bedside of his sinking wife, the gravity of whose condition was kept from the American public. Wilson did, however, take time to discuss with Secretary of State Bryan tentative plans to dispatch American army and navy transports to Europe to bring American refugees home, and to ask Congress for a special appropriation to foot the bill for as many as 300,000 stranded United States citizens.

Sitting at his wife's bedside as she slept on the day Britain declared war against Germany, the president wrote a proclamation of American neutrality and a message to the leaders of all the warring powers tendering his good offices:

> I should welcome an opportunity to act in the interest of European peace, either now or any other time that might be thought more suitable, as an occasion to serve you and all concerned in a way that would afford me lasting cause for gratitude and happiness.

But Wilson was in no mental condition to be of help to anyone. A consultation of physicians concluded that Mrs. Wilson was at death's door. While all of Europe was on the march, the president kept silent vigil at his wife's side, sometimes weeping. In one moment of consciousness, she inquired about legislation she had been championing for housing for the poor; Wilson passed urgent word to Capitol Hill, the measure was quickly enacted, and he was able to tell her the good news.

But he kept from her the bad news about the European madness, and on August 6, the day Austria declared war on Russia, as the president and their three daughters gathered at her bedside, Ellen Louise Axson Wilson died. Wilson, holding her hand, turned to the White House physician, Dr. Cary Grayson, and asked, "Is it over?"

The doctor nodded. Wilson let go of his wife's hand and walked to a window looking out to the Ellipse and the Washington Monument.

"Oh, my God!" he cried. "What am I going to do? What am I going to do?"

The funeral service for Mrs. Wilson at the White House was simple and dignified, with only the family, close relatives and friends, and representatives of Congress and the diplomatic corps present. Each of the newly warring nations sent its ambassador; von Bernstorff, however, was still at sea and could not attend.

The president's thoughts at this moment were far from the catastrophe that was descending on Europe. But von Bernstorff, as the *Noordam* headed for New York, could scarcely think of anything else —and of his new and awesome assignment as a major instrument of the German war machine, behind the facade of his diplomatic credentials and the immunity they gave him.

4. Commitment to Neutrality

The passing of Mrs. Wilson plunged her husband into a deep depression. Wearing a black armband, he continued the bare minimum of official duties, among them a speech to the American people, in Rome, Georgia, one week after his wife's burial. In it, he exhorted them to say or do nothing that would violate the spirit of neutrality to which he had already pledged the country. Wilson's wholehearted determination to observe neutral status, and in time to use it as a credential with which to play a role as mediator for world peace, was transparent in his remarks:

> The effect of the war upon the United States will depend on what American citizens say or do. Every man who really loves America will act and speak in the true spirit of neutrality, which is the spirit of impartiality and fairness and friendliness to all concerned.

Wilson took note of the natural loyalties to home countries in a polyglot nation, but reminded Americans of their first loyalty:

> The people of the United States are drawn from many nations, and chiefly from the nations now at war. It is natural and inevitable that there should be the utmost variety of sympathy and desire among them with regard to the issues and circumstances of the conflict. Some will wish one nation, others another to succeed in the momentous struggle.
>
> It will be easy to excite passion and difficult to allay it. Those responsible for exciting it will assume a heavy responsibility. . . . Such diversions among us would be fatal to our peace of mind and might seriously stand in the way of the proper performance of our duty as the one great nation at peace, the one people holding itself ready to play a part of impartial mediation and speak the counsels of peace and accommodation, not as a partisan, but as a friend. . . . The United States must be neutral in fact as well as in name during these days that are to try men's souls.

Already, however, a preponderance of partisanship seemed to lean to the British and French. The American press underscored Austria's precipitate rush to armed force rather than negotiate her differences with Serbia, and Germany's swift and callous violation of Belgian neutrality. These actions were enough for many Americans to decide which side they favored. The invasion of Belgium, whose neutrality had been guaranteed by all European powers including Germany, grated particularly on American sensitivities, especially when stories of German atrocities against the civilian population began to emerge.

In late August, German troops deliberately razed and leveled the town of Louvain as an example to Belgian civilians who had fired on the invading German soldiers. The kaiser then defended the action on grounds the civilians' conduct violated international law!

Wilson, however, was so determined to keep his country on a neutral course that he grasped at any straw that would help him do so. One was a statement by German Chancellor Theobold von Bethmann-Hollweg to the Reichstag at the time of the Belgian invasion:

> Gentlemen, we are in a state of necessity, and necessity knows no law. Our troops have occupied Luxembourg and perhaps are already on Belgian soil. That is contrary to international law. The wrong we thus commit we will endeavour to repair directly our military aim is achieved.

That surprising acknowledgment he later trumped by dismissing as "a scrap of paper" the treaty Germany had signed guaranteeing Belgian neutrality. But Wilson in his desire to play the peacemaker was only too willing at this stage to accept von Bethmann-Hollwegg's original promise of eventually righting the admitted wrong.

An exception to the growing anti-German sentiment in the United States, not surprisingly, could be found in the centers of German heritage in cities like New York, Baltimore, Chicago and Milwaukee, where so many of the eight million German-Americans of the time lived. Another surfaced among the four and one half million Irish-Americans whose hostility toward the English was particularly high at the moment of increasing clashes in Ulster. But the chargé d'affaires of the German embassy, Haniel von Raimhausen, for one, saw the greater bias against his country as the motivation for Wilson's speech.

"I suppose one of the president's reasons was the anti-German feeling which has been shown in some of the papers," he told the press in Washington. "I think it is a very good expression and a right one."

From the very start, however, Wilson himself had trouble adhering to his own advice. In an interview with the *New York Times* less than two weeks after his speech preaching strict neutrality, he allowed himself to observe that while he hoped neither side in the war would win, if Germany emerged the victor the very course of Western civilization would be changed.

Still, the president seemed not to see that prospect as warranting any particular action by the United States. When a study of American preparedness by General Leonard Wood found that the country was "pitifully unprepared should such a calamity be thrust upon us" as war against a first-class power, a preparedness movement blossomed in the country advocating compulsory military service. But Wilson came down hard against it.

"We will not ask our young men to spend the best years of their lives making soldiers of themselves," he said. Neutrality, he continued to insist, was the best protection.

Strangely, Wilson's devotion to neutrality did not extend to Mexico, where in mid-July General Huerta, under pressure from Carranza's revolutionary forces abetted by the United States, had finally abdicated. The president, even as his mourning for his departed wife continued, seemed consumed by his determination to play a major role in shaping a new democratic government of social reform in Mexico City.

But Carranza, his Constitutionalist troops now closing in on the capital, had his own ideas on a post-Huerta government, and he conspicuously let Wilson know he wanted no part of his meddling. Just when it appeared, moreover, that stability might be restored to Mexico, Carranza's most daring general, Francisco (Pancho) Villa, broke from him and launched a bloody civil war that was to grind on for the next three years.

Even before Carranza took Mexico City, however, the Wilson administration had begun secret talks with Villa, hoping to use him to depose Carranza. Villa gave assurances that once he had gained power he would initiate the constitutional safeguards Wilson wanted for Mexico and would step aside for an elected civilian president. So at the very time Wilson was urging all Americans to adhere strictly to the spirit of neutrality in the burgeoning European war, he was continuing to be distinctly unneutral in Mexico.

This ambivalent posture of the American president continued through 1914. Then the pressures of the European conflict became so demanding that he at last did embrace strict neutrality toward the Mexican conflict—in the face of demands from such as former President Theodore Roosevelt for a strong American involvement.

In dealing with the foreign-policy crises in both Latin America and Europe, Wilson relied heavily on his closest political aide and friend, Colonel Edward M. House of Texas. House was a small, thin, moustached man of unprepossessing appearance and personally self-effacing manner who had gained a reputation for political acuity in his native state. An adviser to four Texas governors, House's military title was honorary only, but it stuck to him.

House had met Wilson in 1911, only shortly before the then-governor of New Jersey made his bid for the White House. House, with some others influential in the Democratic Party, was undertaking a search for a suitable 1912 presidential candidate. Wilson called on House at his hotel in New York and the rapport was cordial and immediate. The friendship blossomed at once, probably in considerable respect because House was the antithesis of a self-seeker. He established early in the relationship that he wanted no official position nor pleaded any special case, an attitude that accommodated Wilson's own rather proper demeanor.

House was the classic low-profile political operator who, while he was regarded as an excellent mixer, at home with the mighty and the lowly alike, abhorred the public spotlight. On the day the 1912 Democratic convention opened in Baltimore, he sailed for Europe for his annual summer escape, missing Wilson's marathon nomination fight with House Speaker Champ Clark that went forty-six ballots. House returned in time for the election, however, and thereafter became the new president's prime political confidant and sounding board.

A measure of Wilson's confidence in House was the fact that the president-elect turned over to him the task of finding the best appointments to his cabinet. By most judgments, House's choices were adequate if not spectacular. The most prominent one was Bryan, whose standing in the party had more to do with his selection than did House's evaluation of his qualifications for overseeing foreign policy, which were slim. When the war in Europe broke out, however, Bryan would prove to be a crusader for peace eclipsing even Wilson in his zeal.

So obvious was House's special role at the White House that within weeks of Wilson's inauguration, *Harper's Weekly* was referring to the Texan as "Assistant President House," and others in the press dubbed him "the silent partner." The references mortified House, who acknowledged he feared Wilson would be offended. But the new president's confidence in his recently acquired friend apparently was boundless and the relationship continued unimpeded. Wilson called House "my second personality; my independent self; his thoughts and mine are one."

House was careful, however, never to overplay his role. He declined a cabinet post for himself and not only took no salary but for a time paid his own expenses on European missions Wilson asked him to undertake. He continued to reside in New York, where Wilson often stayed at his apartment, particularly in those months after the death of his wife when his grief was heaviest.

Often the president would arrive at House's place unexpectedly, as if driven from the mansion where she had left him with his memories. According to House, Wilson's depression, which he managed to hide from the public, was so consuming that he sometimes felt he could not go on.

One night when the president was visiting him, House said, Wilson suddenly announced that he intended to slip out for a walk without his Secret Service protection. House, concerned, said he would go with him, and on the way out of the apartment slipped a small revolver into his pocket. The walk was uneventful; two security men followed at a discreet distance, unobserved by Wilson and House. But on return, House said later, the president told him he wished someone would have killed him, so broken was his spirit by the loss of his wife and so doubting was he about his ability to carry on his immense responsibilities.

Wilson was determined, however, to preserve his chances to be the world's peacemaker by maintaining strict neutrality toward the warring European powers. House played an active role in trying to assist the president in this endeavor.

In May of 1914, House had met the kaiser at Potsdam, and in September he wrote to him through the undersecretary of the German Foreign Office, Arthur Zimmermann, to offer himself with Wilson's blessing as a conduit for peace talks. At Potsdam, House had struck up a friendship with Zimmermann, a large, outgoing man without the airs that often afflicted diplomats.

The kaiser was receptive to House's initiative, and von Bernstorff was dispatched to House's New York apartment to discuss how best they could communicate. In the course of their conversation, House offered the use of American diplomatic radio to send ambassadorial messages to Berlin in German code. It was a near-unprecedented offer that later infuriated State Department higher-ups when they learned of it, but House spoke for the president, and in time von Bernstorff took it up. The arrangement in fact would figure critically in 1917 in the dispatch and interception of the notorious Zimmermann telegram that eventually drew the United States into the war. House's offer of the American communications link also would play an important role in detecting the scope of the eventual German sabotage operation in America.

One other development ultimately of great significance in this same regard occurred in mid-October, 1914. Out of the blue, British naval intelligence officers were summoned to the Russian embassy in London and presented, with no strings attached, the German naval code book! In August, in the first days of the war, Russian cruisers in the Baltic Sea had sunk the German light cruiser *Magdeburg*, and the book was found on the floating body of the ship's signalman. The Russians in a burst of solidarity—and good judgment—decided to turn the code book over to an ally better equipped by training and experience to make maximum use of it against the common enemy.

Shortly afterward, in Belgium and in Persia, the British found other unlikely allies to help them penetrate the German code and cipher. The first was a young engineer born and bred in England of Austrian lineage named Alexander Szek, who had moved to Brussels with his father before the outbreak of the war. Recruited by the Austrian authorities and fluent in French as well as German and English, he was made a coding clerk in Brussels. The British secret service, learning that Szek had a sister in England who was strongly anti-German, prevailed upon her to urge him through a British emissary to obtain the German code for his native country.

Young Szek, willing to help but fearful for his life, wanted simply to steal the code and escape. But that course would not do; it would have let the Germans know the British had the code. He was persuaded to copy it painstakingly and piecemeal whenever he had the opportunity, which he did over the next several months. When the last of the code was delivered, Szek did attempt to escape, but never was heard from thereafter. The general assumption was that he was found out by the Germans and shot. After the war, however, his father accused the British of killing him themselves to make sure the Germans did not learn that their enemy had the code.

At the time young Szek was copying the code in Brussels, an older man, a German diplomat/adventurer named Wilhelm Wassmuss, was on a secret mission in Persia to cut the Anglo-Persian pipeline and to circulate anti-British propaganda in the area. Wassmuss, a dashing, elusive figure shrouded in mystery and intrigue, when finally seized by local, pro-British authorities, managed to escape. But he left much baggage behind—a circumstance about which he protested strenuously to the Persian government, officially neutral.

The baggage was routinely shipped to London, where it sat until the new head of British naval intelligence, Admiral Sir W. Reginald Hall, known less elegantly if endearingly as "Blinker" Hall because of a recurrent eye twitch, heard the story and acted on a hunch. He located Wassmuss' baggage, examined it and struck paydirt: the German code book for Code 13040, the vehicle for transmitting messages between Berlin and Washington and beyond to other German diplomatic posts in North and South America!

These tools—the *Magdeburg,* Szek, and Wassmuss code books —gave Hall and his associates in British naval intelligence three trump cards in the covert segment of the Great War. With the German cables cut, British intelligence now would be able to monitor in secret most of the important traffic between German command posts in Berlin and America, as well as much of the rest that emanated from Germany. And the remarkable offer by Colonel House to von Bernstorff to send messages in German code over American radio facilities unwittingly gave the British an additional opportunity to tune in on Berlin's innermost communications.

Through the fall of 1914 and into early 1915, House served as Wilson's personal peace emissary to both sides in the European conflict—to the continuing frustration of Bryan. He conferred frequently with von Bernstorff, who in his desire to keep the United States neutral encouraged House's aims, even to the point of suggesting Berlin would welcome a negotiated peace. House was led to believe

Germany would seriously consider withdrawing from Belgium to achieve that end, and von Bernstorff said nothing to disillusion him on the point.

On January 30, 1915, House went with Wilson's blessing to Europe to pursue his mission, sailing on the *Lusitania* from New York. But the British and French were not ready to negotiate and Zimmermann balked at any talk of evacuating Belgium without indemnity. Indeed, Germany still harbored the dream of a *Mitteleuropa* with herself dominant, with France reduced to a second-rate power and Russia thrown back into her own vast, frigid confines. House established personal relationships with all of the major players in the European capitals, but he achieved little more in the course of his European stay of more than three months.

For all the efforts of Wilson and House to pursue the role of neutral peacemakers, there nevertheless were compelling economic and financial reasons for the United States to maintain a lively commerce with Europe even as the war raged on to an uncertain conclusion. American unemployment was approaching one million; plants were operating at only sixty percent of capacity in many cities; business failures were mushrooming, eventually to total 16,769 in 1914, according to *Bradstreet's Journal* the "largest number in the country's history." And it was clear by mid-September, 1914, that there would be no swift victory in the war for either side.

Germany blunted the Russian invasion on the eastern front, but the Austrian army was in a shambles. And after the Battle of the Marne the French had thwarted the Germans' march on Paris. The invaders occupied Belgium and northeastern France. But a war of devastating attrition lay ahead—a factor that inevitably magnified the role of America as a prime supplier of munitions for the Allies, who alone could venture with relative safety across the Atlantic, thanks to British naval supremacy.

Britain and France thus were the United States' prime overseas customers. American manufacturers, bankers and farmers all were affected as panic seized the foreign markets, causing prices on the New York Stock Exchange to fall precipitously. Wilson rushed more than a quarter of a million dollars of "emergency currency" into the void in the first month after the war broke out. The move helped to stabilize the financial situation until the time, several months later, when Allied orders for munitions and other war matériel began to inundate American manufacturers, creating an economic boom that lasted through the war's end.

That boom, however, clearly depended not only on the Allies' ability to transport the purchased goods back to Europe. It rested also on their ability to borrow from American bankers—a matter of immediate consternation for Wilson. Lending money to a belligerent, it could be argued, was hardly a neutral act.

The issue came to a head almost at once, as soon as the American balance of trade deficit with the Allies was absorbed by early purchases against the American debt. The French government asked the powerful American banking firm, J. P. Morgan and Company, to float a loan of $100 million in the United States. Such a loan would have been a drain on the American gold reserve and that fact would have been grounds enough for the government to prohibit it. But Secretary of State Bryan, the neutralist's neutralist, laid down a more idealistic rationale.

"There is no reason why loans should not be made to governments of neutral nations," Bryan said in announcing the prohibition. "But in the judgment of this government, loans by American bankers to any foreign nation which is at war is [sic] inconsistent with the true spirit of neutrality." Reiterating his view in an article in his own monthly magazine, *The Commoner*, Bryan observed: "Money is the worst of contrabands—it commands all other things."

In practical terms, this seemingly neutral posture was clearly a break for Germany, countering the Allies' advantage in controlling the Atlantic's shipping lanes. Equally obvious, the no-loans policy severely restricted the prospects for great financial and economic reward for American suppliers to the Allies. In a month's time, the harsh realities had sunk in, and Bryan was obliged to give way. First, Wilson ruled that while such loans might be unneutral, he would not oppose extensions of commercial credit—an exercise in semantics. By early 1915, J. P. Morgan had won approval for a $50 million "credit" to the French government, and the door was open.

Still, in the early months of the war, the Wilson administration's major problems with the belligerents were not with Germany, but with Great Britain, which from the outbreak of hostilities set upon a course of economic strangulation of Germany.

Staples of American export were placed on the British list of contraband whose shipment into Germany from whatever source was to be prohibited. American-owned ships were being stopped, searched and detained by British naval vessels, to a point where Wilson was faced with accepting the actions or getting into a wholesale diplomatic row with the British. In the end, conciliatory notes were exchanged and Wilson elected at this stage not to go to the mat with them on the matter.

Also inflaming American-British relations was the sale of German ships in American ports to American citizens or German-controlled dummy companies for the shipment of war goods to Germany. In all of these maneuverings and disputes, both Germany and the Allies sought to conduct themselves in ways that, while possibly irritating to the United States, would not drive this new industrial giant from its ostensibly neutral posture to support of the enemy. Washington thus found itself being tugged from both sides as Wilson strove to keep his nation neutral.

Matters came to a head in February, 1915, when the British, putting all foodstuffs on its contraband list, seized the freighter *Wilhelmina*. The ship had American registry but was chartered by the German embassy's commercial attaché, Dr. Heinrich Albert, through an agent to transport a large shipment of food to Germany. The British paid the American shippers for the food at the going rate, thus denying it to the Germans.

In retaliation, the German admiralty declared a "war zone" around the British Isles in which any enemy merchant vessel found would be sunk by the new and terrible weapon, the armed submarine. The German navy had already demonstrated its lethal punch in September by the sinking of four British cruisers. Because the British were misusing neutral flags on their merchant ships, the German admiralty said, neutral vessels also might be imperiled.

The "war zone," the German propaganda apparatus in the United States insisted, was no more than a response to the British food blockade; it would be abandoned if the British refrained from trying to starve the German people into submission. But the threat that American ships might be sunk brought a sharp and threatening note from Wilson and Robert Lansing, the State Department counselor, who was much less disposed than Bryan to neutrality:

> If the commanders of German vessels of war should . . .
> destroy on the high seas an American vessel or the lives of Amer-

icans, it would be difficult for the Government of the United States to view the act in any other light than as an indefensible violation of neutral rights. . . . The Government of the United States would be constrained to hold the Imperial German Government to a strict accountability for such acts of their naval authorities . . . to take any steps it might be necessary to take to safeguard American lives and property, and to secure to American citizens the full enjoyment of their acknowledged rights on the high seas.

These were strong and even menacing words from an American president who held firm to his conviction that neutrality was both the proper and moral course for the United States. Maintaining that posture, however, clearly was becoming more difficult with every passing day.

As for Ambassador von Bernstorff, whose new mission was to frustrate by whatever means possible the advantages accruing to Germany's enemies from the American neutrality and the Allied superiority at sea, America's formal stature of nonbelligerence was irrelevant. While continuing to practice openly the art of diplomacy in Washington's most gracious and genteel salons, he was now required to perform in secret the arts of deceit on a broad scale, with only a few trusted associates to assist him. The challenge was great, but von Bernstorff was a loyal and obedient subject of the kaiser, and he set out diligently to do as he had been told.

5. Von Bernstorff's Mission

In undertaking his new, secret assignment, Ambassador von Bernstorff had three willing associates readily at hand in Washington—the three men immediately subordinate to him at the German embassy.

One, Captain Franz von Papen, the military attaché, was destined for a larger, much more unsavory, niche in history. In 1932, having risen to be chancellor of Germany and shunted aside, he helped persuade Field Marshal Paul von Hindenburg, the aged president of the Weimar Republic, to install Adolf Hitler as chancellor in 1933. The superb American chronicler of Nazi Germany, William L. Shirer, in *The Rise and Fall of the Third Reich*, labeled von Papen "more responsible than any other individual in Germany for Hitler's coming to power."

At the time of von Papen's posting to Washington in 1913, he was a thirty-five-year-old cavalry officer of down-at-the-heels Westphalian nobility who had secured the assignment in part because his wife was the daughter of a wealthy Alsatian manufacturer. That fact enabled von Papen to maintain the proper social responsibilities in diplomatic circles. He was a tall, overbearing-looking man with moustache and piercing eyes. He was known for bluster, indiscretion and intrigue, but for industriousness as well.

The second, Captain Karl Boy-Ed, was von Papen's naval counterpart, and often at odds with him over methods and style. A large, stocky, clean-shaven man, more convivial and less impulsive than von Papen, Boy-Ed was of German-Turkish parentage. He had been a prodigy on the staff of Grand Admiral Alfred von Tirpitz and a naval attaché at other posts before landing the choice Washington assignment.

The third principal collaborator was Dr. Heinrich Albert, the embassy's commercial attaché. As paymaster for all German diplomatic activities in America, Albert became as well the chief dispenser of most of the funds von Bernstorff brought from Berlin to finance his secret mission. Albert and von Bernstorff held a joint account in the millions of dollars at the Chase National Bank in New York, where Albert also maintained an office, at 45 Broadway.

Albert, a tall, thin man, was more soft-spoken and cordial than the two military men and the least suspect of the trio—for a time, anyway—of any underhanded activities. Albert, it will be recalled, was in Berlin with von Bernstorff when the Section 3B meeting was held and the $150 million secret bankroll was given to the ambassador, and Albert so testified later. They returned to the United States on the same ship at the war's outbreak, together with Dr. Bernhard Dernburg, a former Germany secretary of state for colonies, assigned to oversee German wartime propaganda in America.

Together, these three embassy subordinates gave von Bernstorff the time-honored diplomatic dodge of "deniability." When each eventually was caught in extra-diplomatic activities, von Bernstorff denied any knowledge of what the subordinate had been up to. But cable traffic from Berlin directly to the ambassador governing such activities, later made public, established that he knew full well what they were doing, and indeed oversaw the funding of their operations.

Another individual, though personally of little importance, provided a valuable and at times colorful setting for the activities of the principals and many of their associates even before the outbreak of the war. This was the robust German opera singer Martha Held, already mentioned. Sometime in 1912, at the commission of the German government, she leased the fashionable brownstone row house at 123 West Fifteenth Street in Manhattan, establishing what came to be a safe house for German diplomats, sea captains and other officers, spies and a variety of other agents of intrigue.

Martha Held, also known as Martha Gordon, was a character right out of central casting—busty and buxom, with shiny black hair, dark blue eyes, a pointed chin and a voice that could shatter china. She frequently regaled her guests with German operatic arias as well as national songs that often filled the house through the late evening and early morning hours, as wine flowed and feelings of patriotism mounted. Photographs of the hostess in opera costumes adorned the walls, looking down on festive occasions that came to calendar each German success in the war—and especially activities in the United States designed to hasten the day of German victory.

Because the well-dressed visitors usually called at night and entered through a basement door covered by an iron grill, and because shapely young women were often seen to arrive unescorted, the impression endured in the fashionable neighborhood that Frau Held was the proprietress of a high-class bawdy house. Among the callers once the war began were von Bernstorff, von Papen and Boy-Ed, as well as the masters of German vessels interned in the ports of New York, Baltimore and elsewhere along the East Coast.

The German safe house on West Fifteenth Street was a subject of neighborhood gossip even before Martha Held rented it. The landlord, J. Irving Walsh, told the New York police much later that "the house had a very unsavory reputation. I remember going into the house shortly before the previous tenant's death in about July, 1912. I recall that in looking over her goods I ran across a notebook which had several notations reading as follows: 'Inspector so-and-so called, gave him $200, or Officer so-and-so called, gave him $250.'"

After Martha Held moved in, Walsh recalled:

> Everything was kept spotless and clean, and she told me she had "everything rented," referring to the rooms of the house. . . . I happened to look in the closets of the different rooms and noticed that there were no clothes hanging in them, and I was somewhat suspicious of her statement that she had "everything rented." In view of the nature of the use of the house during its prior occupancy I was somewhat suspicious of these circumstances and I remember that I warned Martha Held that she "be careful" with regard to her use of the premises. . . . I noticed there was a great deal of wine and liquor about and it [the house] always had quite a German atmosphere. Mrs. Held told me on several occasions that the sea captains on the German boats were accustomed to coming there and she said that she would give them little dinners at night.

When the war began, von Papen was in Mexico City, where he also served as military attaché at the German legation there. He hastened back to Washington and got his orders along with Boy-Ed from von Bernstorff. The two military men went immediately to New York, each establishing a special wartime office in the Wall Street area near the New York Custom House and close by Albert's office in the Hamburg-Amerika Building.

One of von Papen's first visitors was a German intelligence agent named Horst von der Goltz. When Germany plunged into the war, he was plying his trade in the guise of a soldier of fortune in the Mexican army. As a German, he was discharged and went immediately to see the German consul at Chihuahua, who sent him on to von Papen.

Von der Goltz had big ideas about how to help the fatherland. For openers, he proposed to von Papen the secret mobilization of German reservists in the United States and German warships in the Pacific for an invasion of Canada through British Columbia. The action, he argued, could tie down Canadian supplies and troops otherwise destined for the European front. If successful, it would give Germany a base from which to buy munitions and other matériel from neutral America—a circumstance that might persuade the United States to stop supplying either side, a great gain for Germany. Von Papen was intrigued and, according to von der Goltz later, passed the scheme on to von Bernstorff. The ambassador recognized the notion as farfetched and squelched it. But von Papen encouraged von der Goltz to come up with something more practical.

Within weeks, in September, 1914, the agent returned with a plot more to von Papen's liking—a plan to blow up the Welland Canal linking Lakes Ontario and Erie in the Canadian province of Ontario, just across the American border west of Buffalo. Von der Goltz was commissioned by von Papen to proceed, with the objective of disrupting the shipment of raw materials from Canada to makers of munitions and other commodities of war in the United States.

Using the alias Bridgeman H. Taylor, von der Goltz rounded up several accomplices from the seafaring and German communities in New York. One of them, Friedrich Busse, testified later he had met von der Goltz while reading war bulletins in Herald Square. They discussed the war and went to dinner at the Hofbrau House at Broadway and Twenty-ninth Street. From the start von der Goltz marked himself as a big talker.

"The conversation turned to how we could get back to Germany," Busse reported. "Von der Goltz spoke of buying a large motor boat and taking several men over to Germany with him." Other dinner meetings ensued with other German nationals or sympathizers. Von der Goltz, Busse said, talked of:

> A plan of raiding Canada and organizing an expedition of Germans for that purpose. . . . About one week after I had met von der Goltz, he suggested that we take a trip to Niagara Falls, New York, saying, laughingly, that we would conquer Canada.

He proposed to us that it would be of great advantage to Germany to damage the Welland Canal, and at the same time made an appointment to meet all of us at 137th Street and the Hudson River to get materials, which we did. He rented a small motor boat and [the group] went down the Hudson and up the East River to a point near the Bowery around Chambers Street or Park Row.

At the ringleader's instruction, Busse said, he and the others went to a Bowery pawn shop and bought several three-dollar brown suitcases and filled them with bottles of beer. The beer presumably was required as a courage-booster for the would-be saboteurs.

"We then went to the powder boat of the Dupont Powder Company lying in the Jersey Flats off the Statue of Liberty," Busse said, "and secured therefrom two cases of dynamite weighing fifty pounds each, and containing sticks about eight inches long. These we packed into the suitcases and we then returned to 137th Street and the Hudson River."

The dynamite was supplied by Captain Hans Tauscher, New York representative of Krupp, who obtained it from Dupont under the guise that he required it to blast out tree stumps on his farm in New Jersey. The suitcases were turned over to von der Goltz. He took them to Martha Held's house on West Fifteenth Street and stored them in a closet—with her full knowledge, he testified later, of their contents.

Within the next few nights, the party of aspiring saboteurs left for Buffalo by train—trailed now by suspicious Secret Service agents. Von der Goltz had the dynamite-laden suitcases under his seat, and he recounted later how "several men entered the car, two of which hurriedly left it when they saw us smoking. As I never smoke cheap cigars it cannot have been the flavor of the leaf we were smoking which caused their hurried exit."

In spite of this evidence that the American authorities were onto them, von der Goltz and his accomplices proceeded to Buffalo. Busse testified later, however, that he got cold feet when von der Goltz ordered him to go up the Welland Canal in Canada as far as St. Catherines "and get all the information I could concerning the shipments of . . . munitions to the Allies, how the canal was guarded, etc." He balked, as did others in the party, because the canal was too closely protected, and the scheme fizzled.

There was never any question, though, who had bankrolled the plot. "From what von der Goltz told me," Busse said in a later affidavit, "we all knew before leaving New York that Captain Franz von Papen had directed von der Goltz to go into Canada and do some service there in the interests of Germany—in other words, that von Papen was behind the whole scheme and was paying our expenses. If we had not known von Papen was back of it, we would not have entered upon the enterprise."

After von der Goltz' failure in the Welland Canal project, von Papen recommended that he be shipped to Turkey. Instead, he was called back to Berlin for consultation and further orders in October, 1914. On his way back to the United States via England he went to Scotland Yard and offered information on projected German air raids on Britain from Holland, but was arrested.

Von der Goltz testified later that "I came not to England in order to spy, it being my intention to throw myself on the protection of England, my life not being safe on the continent, and to revenge myself on Papen for his treachery by divulging what I knew to His Majesty's Government, on the condition that I should be allowed to proceed to Mexico."

He claimed he could provide proof "that I willfully and deliberately prevented the blowing up of important points in Canada, that I was not in German employ when I came to England, that I tried to inform His Majesty's government of attempted outrages in Canada at the time, informing it [also] of the means employed by spies in German pay in sending their dispatches to Holland."

For all of his trouble, however, von der Goltz eventually was extradited to the United States, where he told all about the Welland Canal attempt, implicating his accomplices as well. Tauscher was acquitted on grounds he didn't know what the dynamite was to be used for, but von der Goltz and the other minor players were convicted and jailed.

Before being imprisoned, however, von der Goltz in May of 1916 led Justice Department agents to Martha Held's safe house, telling them he had stored dynamite there in two suitcases. Frau Held, professing not to know what was in them, told the agents that a man whose name she did not know had picked up the suitcases about nine months earlier. So the Justice Department knew about the house on West Fifteenth Street well before the American entry into the war but never moved against it, even afterward.

Justice Department files later revealed this report from "Justice Operative 85": "It is reported also that the Held woman ran a house of easy virtue at the above address frequented by several German sea captains and others of the same caliber, and that she is constantly in touch with the alien enemy of the better class. Von Papen and Boy-Ed were in her place there on many occasions."

Other than von der Goltz' grandiose Canadian schemes, a more elemental task occupied the diplomats-turned-saboteurs, von Papen and Boy-Ed, in those first months of the war. As already noted, thousands of Germans residing in the United States who were reservists in the German army or navy were eager to return home to join their units. Under pressure from Britain and France, the United States tightened its previously very loose passport requirements to include more extensive proof of American citizenship and a photograph of the applicant. The move obliged von Papen and Boy-Ed to establish an elaborate system of passport forgery, and to concentrate on getting back to Germany upwards of a thousand military reserve officers sent to New York by German consulates throughout North and South America.

Von Papen and his chief aide, Wolf von Igel, and Albert recruited a man in New York named Hans von Wedell, the nephew of a German Foreign Office official, Count Botho von Wedell, to head the project. An American citizen, a lawyer and onetime newspaper reporter in New York, von Wedell knew his way around the city and particularly the seamy waterfront areas frequented by German-American seamen and the flotsam of other men willing to turn a quick dollar.

Setting up shop in Lower Manhattan, he recruited hundreds of longshoremen, sailors and assorted Bowery and Hoboken bums to apply for passports and then sell them to him for ten to twenty-five dollars apiece—funds supplied by von Papen. Soon reserve officers, their photos affixed to the passports bearing the names of the sellers, were being dispatched regularly by von Papen and Boy-Ed to ports in Italy, Holland and Scandinavia, from whence they would make their way to Germany.

The scheme went forward swimmingly until some of the streetwise sellers began to blackmail von Wedell. Soon the Department of Justice was on to him and he fled to Cuba. Before doing so, however, he wrote an incriminating letter to von Bernstorff that later fell into American hands. Defending his departure, von Wedell insisted that he had delayed leaving until he could train his replacement, a clerk named Carl Ruroede, "and in order to hold in check the blackmailers thrown on my hands by the German officers until the passage of my travelers through Gibraltar."

He was forced to flee at last, he wrote, because "the State Department had, for three weeks, withheld a passport application forged by me" and because a German for whom he had forged another "had fallen into the hands of the English. That gentleman's forged papers were liable to come back any day and could, owing chiefly to his lack of caution, easily be traced back to me."

Von Wedell's replacement, Ruroede, didn't last long. A Justice Department agent named Albert Adams, playing the role of a Bowery bum with pro-German sentiments, signed on with him to round up American passports from waterfront derelicts. Several days later Adams checked in at Ruroede's office with four passports—made up for the purpose by the State Department.

The delighted Ruroede proceeded to take one of the passports, of a man named Howard Paul Wright. He selected another passport photograph of a German reserve officer whose physical description approximated that of Wright. He pasted it over Wright's picture and then, using a bone knitting needle, rubbed until the seal on Wright's photo could be seen on the overlaid photo of one Arthur Sachse, a German army reserve lieutenant. Ruroede repeated the process with the three other passports, using the photos of three more German reserve officers.

It so happened that Howard Paul Wright, and the three other men in the passports, were all Justice Department agents. Adams quickly ascertained that the four Germans would be sailing in a few days on a Norwegian ship, the *Bergensfjörd*, for Bergen, Norway. On January 2, 1915, as the ship left New York Harbor, Ruroede was arrested. The Justice Department agents boarded a small boat and overtook the *Bergensfjörd*, ordering it to halt. All male passengers aboard were interrogated and Sachse and his three colleagues were quickly seized.

The same day, the Justice Department agents in a stroke of luck established the complicity of the German embassy beyond doubt. As they were collecting papers in the arrested Ruroede's office, a German naval captain named Wolfram von Knorr, until recently the German naval attaché in Tokyo, walked in. Without fanfare, he handed a

letter of introduction from von Papen to an FBI agent he apparently
mistook for Ruroede.

The agent, Joseph Baker, did not disabuse von Knorr of that impression. In conversation, the German captain acknowledged that he had
been sent by von Papen to obtain one of the phony passports. Confronted with this admission, Ruroede confessed and was sentenced to
three years in jail. The four Germans with the forged passports got off
with fines of two hundred dollars each.

The most luckless of all, however, was von Wedell. He had slipped
back into New York and was aboard the *Bergensfjörd* when it was
stopped and searched by the Justice Department agents. They did
not spot him and he seemed to be safely on his way when Ruroede
identified him in his confession. Nine days at sea, a British patrol
boat took von Wedell, posing as a Mexican named Rosato Spiro, off
the *Bergensfjörd* and headed for port. En route, the patrol boat struck
a German mine and sank with von Wedell aboard.

Even this calamity did not end the traffic in phony passports. Only
a few days after Ruroede's arrest, von Bernstorff sent a coded cable to
Berlin assuring his superiors that although the American government
was investigating the frauds "there is no reason to fear that the embassy
will be compromised. State Department informed me definitely that
this [U.S.] Government attached no importance to the rumors that
the [German] Embassy had been concerned."

However, von Bernstorff reported, the consul general in New York
was raising "pedantic objections" to the scheme. The ambassador
urged his transfer to somewhere in South America. Actually, President Wilson himself had been informed of the passport fraud but,
determined to preserve America's neutral posture, he ordered that
no public disclosure be made.

Von Papen and Boy-Ed found new recruits to obtain passports, but
the documents were more difficult to come by now. Reservists who
made it back safely to Germany turned the passports in to German
intelligence and they were reused to send spies into Britain, France
and Russia. American authorities tightened up application requirements and procedures, and in time the Germans were obliged to
develop their own forgery facilities from scratch.

A German document captured later underscored the difficulties
and the need for caution by reservists making the crossing with fake
passports. It instructed:

Reservists must be tested in advance by examinations as to ability in language, knowledge of the country, readiness to adapt themselves. Their physical characteristics must agree exactly with passport. They must be able to tell a suitable story of their life which will tally with their passport, trunk, clothing, etc. Swiss passports are the least adapted to their purpose. North American passports must correspond to the latest regulations. Paid spies are to travel on the steamers in each class.

The rules [to avoid detection aboard ship] drawn up in New York are to be observed with the utmost possible precision. Simulated seasickness is the safest. The foregoing was not sufficiently emphasized with those sent by S.S. *Rotterdam*. Behavior of majority of reservists so incautious that only special weather conditions made success possible. The enemies know that reservists are going to Europe on passports and unless all petty details tally, there is no prospect of sending any more.

Meanwhile, efforts to inhibit the traffic in men, munitions and other matériel from the United States and Canada to the Allies had been intensifying. On November 11, 1914, the German General Staff dispatched a message to military attachés in certain neutral countries, including von Papen in the United States, suggesting "hiring destructive agents among members of anarchist organizations." The communication, signed by General Army Counselor Dr. E. Fischer and sent specifically to von Papen, advised him of German funds set aside for such recruitment and authorized him "to avail yourself in unlimited amounts of these credits for the destruction of the enemy's factories, plants and . . . setting incendiary fires to stocks of raw materials and finished products" in neutral America.

Also, on November 28, 1914, a directive went out from the "Intelligence Bureau of the General Staff of the High Sea Fleet" to all German "marine agencies and naval societies" that read:

You are ordered to mobilize immediately all destruction agents and observers in those commercial and military ports where munitions are being loaded on ships going to England, France, Canada, the United States of North America and Russia, where there are storehouses of such munitions, and where fighting units are stationed.

It is necessary to hire through third parties who stand in no relation to the official representatives of Germany agents for arranging explosions on ships bound for enemy countries, and for arranging delays, embroilments and difficulties during the loading, dispatching and unloading of ships. For this purpose we are especially recommending to your attention loaders' gangs, among whom are to be found a great many anarchists and escaped criminals, and that you get in touch with German and neutral shipping offices as a means of observing agents of enemy countries who are receiving and shipping the munitions. Funds required for the hiring and bribing of persons necessary for the designated purpose will be placed at your disposal at your request.

A key figure under von Papen in all this activity in New York was a man named Paul Koenig, who before the outbreak of the war had been in charge of a small bureau of detectives for the Atlas Line, a subsidiary of the Hamburg-Amerika Line. This Koenig, not to be confused with the man of the same name who was captain of the German merchant submarine *Deutschland,* was a physical brute known and feared among the waterfront hands. He was also a sometime investigative collaborator before the war with New York police and Justice Department agents. Within weeks of Germany's declared belligerency, von Papen assigned him to recruit and supervise saboteurs.

A note in Koenig's memo book dated August 22, 1914, and obtained later by police read: "German Government, with consent of Dr. Bunz, entrusted me with the handling of a certain investigation. Military Attache von Papen called at my office later and explained the nature of the work expected. (Beginning of Bureau's service for Imperial Government.)"* Koenig over the next year established a network of agents and saboteurs in New York. With offices at 45 Broadway, he provided bodyguards for von Bernstorff and others through a special detail division of his bureau and kept watch on the docks through a pier division.

But it was the third part of his operation, the secret service division or "Geheimdienst," that performed the brunt of the illegal work.

---

*Karl Bunz, the managing director of the Hamburg-Amerika Line and Koenig's superior, earlier had been German consul in New York and was well acquainted with von Bernstorff, von Papen and Boy-Ed.

Koenig operated this division in utmost secrecy, barring its agents from his Lower Manhattan office and instead meeting with them at locations coded in a "safety block system."

Describing it in his memo notebook, Koenig explained: "A street number in Manhattan named over a telephone means that the meeting will take place five blocks further uptown than the street mentioned. Pennsylvania Railroad Station means Grand Central Depot. Kaiserhof means General Post Office in front of P.O. Box 840. Hotel Ansonia means cafe in Hotel Manhattan (basement). Hotel Belmont means at the bar in Pabst's, Columbus Circle." Designated locations were changed by Koenig every few weeks.

Koenig's notebook also listed cases performed by agents, with a sabotage case designated "D-Case," and contained a full list of Koenig's aliases, including his prime designation, "Triple X."

Still other efforts at disruption went forward under the general direction of von Bernstorff. A sidelight of the cataclysm in Europe was an opportunistic Japan, which had a mutual-defense treaty with Britain and now cast a covetous eye on the Chinese province of Shantung, where Germany by force of arms in 1897 had seized valuable railway and mining rights. Now, after sending Berlin an ultimatum on Shantung in the first week of the European war, the Japanese sent troops in. Berlin feared that Japan, to cement its relationship with Britain, also would send troops to Europe by way of Canada. On December 12, 1914, the Foreign Office sent this ciphered telegram No. 357 to the German ambassador:

> Secret: The transportation of Japanese troops through Canada must be prevented at all costs, if necessary by blowing up Canadian railways. It would probably be advisable to employ Irish for this purpose in the first instance as it is almost impossible for Germans to enter Canada. You should discuss the matter with the Military Attache. The strictest secrecy is indispensable.

The reference to the Irish clearly was to the Irish agitators in America who were fomenting strikes to impede the British war effort, in the hope that battlefield setbacks on the Continent would force the granting of Irish independence.

Three weeks later, on January 3, 1915, von Bernstorff received another telegram in cipher, No. 386, signed by the German foreign undersecretary, Arthur Zimmermann:

Secret: The General Staff is anxious that vigorous measures should be taken to destroy the Canadian Pacific in several places for the purpose of causing a lengthy interruption of traffic. Captain Boehm [another agent] who is well known in America and who will shortly return to that country is furnished with expert information on that subject. Acquaint the Military Attache with the above and furnish the sums required for the enterprise.

These two ciphered telegrams, later uncovered, constituted the first authoritative confirmations that von Bernstorff personally, and not von Papen or some other subordinate, was the ultimate overseer of the sabotage operations in America. Both telegrams specifically instructed the ambassador to convey the orders to "the Military Attache," von Papen, and provide him with the money he needed to implement those orders.

The second order produced the desired result, but with embarrassing consequences. Von Papen recruited a German reserve officer named Werner Horn, who made his way from Guatemala to New York, and dispatched him to Vanceboro, Maine. His mission was duly noted in Koenig's records as "D-Case 277," and for a fee of seven hundred dollars from von Papen, on February 2, 1915, Horn attempted to blow up the international bridge of the Canadian Pacific Railway, which linked American munitions suppliers with the Canadian port of Halifax.

Horn, informed erroneously by von Papen that if he pinned the German flag on his sleeve and was caught, he would merely be interned as a prisoner of war, did indeed pin a small red, white and black flag to his coat. Then, getting off a train with a suitcase loaded with dynamite, he set it down at the bridge, lit the fuse and walked off.

But the suitcase bomb failed to explode and a few hours later Horn was picked up on the American side—still wearing the telltale flag. He was promptly arrested by American authorities, who in turn were immediately pressed by the Canadian government for the man's extradition. Von Bernstorff, interested in seeing that Horn not reveal the embassy's complicity, wired Zimmermann:

Most secret: The carrying out of your telegram, No. 386, for Military Attache was entrusted to a former officer, who has been arrested after an explosion on the Canadian Pacific Railway. Canada demands his extradition. I request authority to protect him;

according to the laws of war, the decision ought presumably to be: non-extradition, provided that an act of war is proved. I intend to argue that, although the German Government has given no orders, the Government regarded the causing of explosions on an enemy railway as being, since it furthered military interests, an act of war.

Von Bernstorff, obviously, was no mere unknowing bystander in this episode. Zimmermann agreed with his recommendation and instructed him to fight Horn's extradition as far as the Supreme Court if necessary, ordering that "adequate legal assistance should be provided and the cost will be borne by the Imperial Exchequer." In the end, Horn pleaded guilty, was convicted in this country of transporting explosives from New York to Vanceboro—there being no sabotage law at the time—and was sent to the federal penitentiary in Atlanta. Horn never directly implicated von Papen. Later on, however, the military attaché carelessly let his bank checkbook fall into British hands and it showed a check stub for the seven-hundred-dollar payment to Horn.

Horn's fate demonstrated that the war against neutral America at this early stage was very ragged and mostly ineffective. But it had begun; as the effort developed it would improve in imagination, daring and destructive achievement. And sabotage was only one part of this seemingly contradictory effort to violate American neutrality without destroying it. On other fronts as well, the effort was going forward.

6. Blockades, Submarines, Subversions

While the early, mostly failed acts of sabotage were being attempted, Berlin and its embassy in Washington aggressively pursued all legal means to block the growing shipments of munitions to the Allies. Von Bernstorff himself explicitly acknowledged that a clause in the Hague Convention permitting munitions traffic by neutrals had been inserted at Germany's specific suggestion. Still, his embassy encouraged leaders in the German-American community in the United States to pressure their members of Congress to introduce legislation that would impose a flat embargo on such arms traffic.

In addition, the ambassador notified Berlin by telegram on December 15, 1914, that he was committing a portion of his special funds to the effort:

> A strong agitation is being developed by the Germans and Irish with a view to carrying these resolutions. In view of the great importance of the matter, I considered myself authorized to assist the agitation financially and so I gave as a provisional measure the five thousand dollars for which I was asked by a trustworthy quarter.

Von Bernstorff argued that while it was one thing to protect existing industry in a neutral country, the blossoming of a vast new arms industry in the United States, all of it supplying the only side that could safely transport the munitions to the front, was not honorable behavior by a neutral state.

"The readiness, in theory, to do the same for Germany, even if the transport were possible, does not alter the case," he said in an official memorandum.

Wilson at first seemed disposed to support this view. He had, after all, enunciated it a year earlier in imposing an arms embargo toward the belligerents in the Mexican civil war.

"I shall follow the best practice of nations in the matter of neutrality," he had told Congress then, "by forbidding the exportation of arms or munitions of war of any kind from the United States to any part of the Republic of Mexico."

But now a ban on munitions traffic was opposed by those who intellectualized that it would favor the side—the Central Powers—that had prepared for and launched an aggressive war, as well as by the merchants of war matériel whose profits from the traffic were growing by leaps and bounds. Robert Lansing, the State Department counselor, was among those who persuaded Wilson that government intervention to prohibit arms sales would be an unneutral act clearly benefiting one side. For once the prime peace advocate, Secretary of State William Jennings Bryan, agreed. By February of 1915, the so-called embargo bills were laid to rest.

Also rejected were proposals for the United States, desperately in need now of a merchant fleet of its own, to buy German ships interned in American ports and sail them under American registry and flag. The British, whose navy had effectively bottled up these German ships, vigorously and outspokenly objected.

The dispute reached a peak in early January of 1915 when an enterprising German-American in Michigan named Edward Breitung bought the Hamburg-Amerika Line cargo ship *Dacia*. He transferred it to U.S. registry, bought a cargo of cotton, and asked the State Department to clear the ship to sail for Rotterdam, where the cargo obviously would be shipped on into Germany.

The State Department in turn asked the British Foreign Office to permit the voyage, and the British unsurprisingly balked. The British navy, they said, would seize the ship but would buy the cotton at the same price it would have brought in Germany. With the impasse unsettled, the *Dacia* finally sailed anyway but was seized by a French cruiser off Brest in late February. The ships-purchase bill was defeated, amid British sighs of relief.

Although it is difficult to grasp now in a world grown used to total, no-holds-barred warfare, the world of Europe, 1914, was one in which war was still looked upon as an exercise among clearly defined military forces on clearly identified military fronts. Civilians and the cities and towns in which they lived were to be protected by common decency and civilized behavior on both sides of the fight. This attitude explained the outrage generated by the German razing of the Belgian town of Louvain and the reprisal shooting of civilians who fired on the invading troops.

In an attempt to codify behavior in warfare after the Crimean War, international lawyers in 1856 wrote the Declaration of Paris, an effort to draft rules in prize law—the seizing of ships of belligerents in war—and in general warfare as well. The second Hague Peace Conference in 1907 set out to establish definitions of contraband, one of which was that while food intended for use by military forces could legitimately be seized, food for the civilian population could not.

Two years later, the major powers wrote the Declaration of London for the same purpose. But it was full of reservations—later seized upon by the British to bend the definitions of contraband. Still, that declaration did in general reinforce the attitude at the outset of the Great War that while all might be fair in love, the view that anything goes ought not to prevail in war among civilized nations and people.

For this reason, two naval decisions in the first months of the war—one by the British, one by the Germans—triggered tormented cries of foul play and even "barbarism" from their targets. Only weeks after the outbreak of the war, the British instituted a total blockade on goods, including foodstuffs, destined for Germany aboard ships of neutral countries. The justification offered was that the German government was mobilizing the entire country to pursue the war to a swift and victorious decision; therefore the old differentiation between food for civilians and for fighting men no longer applied.

"Experience shows," a British note said,

> that the power to requisition will be used to the fullest extent in order to make sure that the wants of the military are supplied, and however much goods may be imported for civil use, it is by the military that they will be consumed if military exigencies require it, especially now that the German Government have taken control of all the foodstuffs in the country.

Berlin charged that the British were setting out to inflict defeat on Germany through a policy of starvation by blockade, and the allegation was clearly valid. But the Germans weren't the only ones complaining. Many in the United States saw the blockade as an unwarranted infringement on the rights of this country as a neutral nation.

Shippers of food and raw materials, especially the cotton growers in the American South, were angered at the British policy. Indeed, in the early phase of the war the British drew considerably more protest in Washington for their interference with the neutrality of the United States, and "freedom of the seas," than did the Germans.

Sir Edward Grey, the British foreign secretary, later wrote that the "blockade of Germany was essential to the victory of the Allies, but the ill will of the United States meant their certain defeat. . . . The object of diplomacy, therefore, was to secure the maximum of blockade that could be enforced without a rupture with the United States."

Berlin, for its part, instituted its own more limited blockade of the British Isles on the very first day of the war by laying mines thirty miles off the coast of Suffolk. In "civilized" warfare, such minelaying was supposed to be accompanied by clear notification of where the mines were, so that ships of nonbelligerents and other "peaceful shipping" would not be imperiled. Also, the nation laying the mines was to be responsible for destroying any that floated free.

On August 6, 1914, the British cruiser *Amphion* hit a mine and sank with 151 men aboard, all of whom perished. The next day the Germans gave notice of the minelaying, but only in the vaguest of terms and then went on to lay others indiscriminately in the North Sea.

Soon merchant ships were going to the bottom as well. The British cabinet complained that Germany's "manifest behaviour must call down upon its authors the censure and reprobation of all civilized peoples." But in a short time the British navy also began laying mines, though identifying their locations with more precision than did the Germans.

Minelaying, however, was not a major weapon for a nation with a superior navy. Besides, many British naval leaders considered all mines a danger to their own ships and a complication to their deployment. As German minelaying spread, the British took the then unusual step of declaring all of the North Sea a war zone. They specified safety lanes into which merchant ships would have to sail, thus facilitating the search of their cargoes.

Much more important in Germany's effort to blockade the British and French was her use of the submarine. Just as military strategists on both sides failed at first to grasp the military applications of the airplane and how it would revolutionize war on land and extend it into the air, so the potential of the submarine as an offensive weapon was unappreciated at the outset. Indeed, a heated debate took place within the German navy and among Kaiser Wilhelm's key advisers about the wisdom of submarine warfare on any great scale, for the same reason that gave the British pause in imposing their blockade —fear of driving the United States out of its neutrality and into alliance with the enemy.

In the first weeks of the war, an expedition of ten of the twenty-eight German submarines then in commission returned with no sinkings of enemy ships and the loss of one sub by ramming. But several weeks later, U-boats sank four old British cruisers out on patrol without destroyer escort, and the awareness that Allied merchant ships would be similar easy prey quickly spread.

Admittedly, the German submarine fleet at the time was small and generally regarded as experimental. But the surface fleet was large, and for the most part it was being held in German ports out of respect for the superior British fleet, producing widespread frustration among German naval officers. They argued that a few sinkings could intimidate shippers of Allied goods into staying off the seas, and the German navy would at least have some offensive role in the war.

Before the war's outbreak, American trade with the Allied countries had been ten times greater than it was with the Central Powers, and the disparity certainly would multiply without some effort to impede it. While the intimidation of the German submarine presence doubtless occurred to some degree, American trade with the Allies nevertheless continued to climb rapidly before the United States' entry into the war. From an estimated $3.44 billion in 1911–13 it rose to nearly $9.8 billion in 1915–17.

Reducing that kind of trade obviously was an imperative for Germany. Political advisers to the kaiser, however, had great concern that use of unrestricted submarine warfare might so outrage the neutral United States as to trigger its entry on the side of the Allies. For months, Chancellor von Bethmann-Hollweg persuaded Wilhelm against employment of that weapon, but the German public was demanding a more forceful response to the British "starvation blockade."

In an interview with Karl von Wiegand, an American journalist,

Admiral von Tirpitz had fueled the impatience by saying: "What will America say if Germany declares submarine war on all the enemy's merchant ships? Why not? England wants to starve us. We can play the same game. We can bottle her up and destroy every ship that endeavors to break the blockade."

Finally, the British declaration of a war zone in the North Sea and a British admiralty authorization for British merchant ships to fly a neutral flag to escape enemy attack—a "ruse de guerre" approved by international law—turned the kaiser around. On February 4, 1915, he signed this declaration:

> The waters around Great Britain, including the whole of the English Channel, are declared hereby to be included within the zone of war, and after the eighteenth inst. all enemy merchant vessels encountered in these waters will be destroyed, even if it may not be possible always to save their crews and passengers. Within this war zone neutral vessels are exposed to danger since, in view of the misuse of the neutral flags ordered by the Government of Great Britain . . . and of the hazards of naval warfare, neutral vessels cannot always be prevented from suffering from the attacks intended for enemy ships.

Von Bernstorff had the duty of delivering the declaration personally to a chagrined Bryan. Its effect, however, was not immediately or deeply felt among many others in Washington or in the country at large. Not until the policy began conspicuously to exact a price in American lives did the negative sentiment in the United States start to switch from the British to the Germans as the prime culprits.

In the context of this war of blockades, and the companion tug-of-war over the sympathies of Woodrow Wilson and the American public, the covert work of Ambassador von Bernstorff and his associates in Washington and New York took on increasing significance. If the war was to be won or lost as much in the Atlantic Ocean as on the battlefields of France, the effectiveness of the British blockade had to be countered. And the task would fall not only to the torpedoes of German U-boats lurking in and around the major sea-lanes; also on the firing line would have to be the coterie of German agents now being recruited in America, the ostensibly neutral great provider of the essentials of war to Germany's enemies.

On the surface, von Bernstorff was no more than the diplomatic representative of the kaiser in Washington, working single-mindedly to preserve American neutrality and to encourage President Wilson to play the role of peacemaker. Unless the unrestricted submarine warfare could achieve a swift victory over the Allies, he argued later in his book, *My Three Years in America,* it would indeed drive the United States to the Allied side:

> If, as I personally believed, the U-boat war did not guarantee a victory, it ought . . . under all circumstances to have been abandoned; for by creating American hostility it did us more harm than good. I, as the German Ambassador, in the greatest neutral State, with the evidences of American power all about me, could not help feeling it my duty to maintain our diplomatic relations with the United States. I was convinced that we should most certainly lose the war if America stepped in against us. And thus I realized ever more and more the supreme importance of preventing this from taking place.

Von Bernstorff did not write, obviously, about his distinctly nondiplomatic activities. Rather, he expressed the view that at this juncture Woodrow Wilson represented the best hope for a negotiated peace, adding: "I therefore pursued the policy of Peace with undeviating consistency."

This observation was among the least of his deceptions in the course of the war. Under his direction, more acts of sabotage continued in the first months of 1915, of necessity conducted by the ragtag collection of relative amateurs that could be culled from the German reservists and more adventurous of German-Americans at hand.

Von Bernstorff unwaveringly insisted that he was a full-time diplomat and nothing more, and that to have been involved in the conspiracies of which he was later accused would have been directly counter to his single-minded efforts to keep the United States neutral:

> In any case, I myself was never a partner to any proceedings which contravened the laws of the United States. I never instigated such proceedings, nor did I consciously afford their authors

assistance, whether financially or otherwise. I was in no single instance privy to any illegal acts, or to any preparations for such acts. Indeed, as a rule I heard of them first through the papers. . . .

Such offenses against the laws of America as were actually committed were certainly reprobated by none more sincerely than by myself, if only because nothing could be imagined more certain to militate against my policy [of pursuing peace] than these outrages and the popular indignation aroused by them. . . . It is thus obviously absurd to accuse me of being responsible in any way for the acts in question, seeing that any such instigation, or even approval on my part, would have involved the utter ruin of my own policy!

But the cables from von Bernstorff to Berlin, intercepted by the British or obtained after the war, underscored that von Bernstorff was involved in a great deal more than mere ambassadorial functions. Another, dated October 18, 1914, said in part:

No answer has ever been given to my telegram of 10th September, in which Albert, in complete accordance with myself, advised the purchases of an option on the output of American artillery and munitions. The matter is of utmost importance. But it may perhaps be possible to secure the same result in a less costly way.

In another cable of the same date, von Bernstorff wired:

The American steamer *Sun* is bound for Amsterdam. She is calling at Rotterdam for homeward cargo on the twenty-second. Get the refining works [Scheider Anstalt] at Frankfort to ship one thousand tons cyanide by the *Sun* and to instruct their representative here to pay Kuhn, Loeb; payment of the refinery works to take place on my confirmation that the money has been paid. My name is never to be mentioned.

The cable added: "By a misunderstanding a sum of one million dollars has been remitted to me instead of Boy-Ed. I am using it. Settle the question with the Navy Office."

Von Bernstorff wrote in his postwar book that his two attaché-accomplices, von Papen and Boy-Ed, took no orders from him regarding anything beyond diplomatic duties. In fact, he wrote, "Captain von Papen and Commander Boy-Ed frequently held back from me the instructions they had received from Berlin in order not to embarrass the Embassy by passing on military or naval information." It was the deniability dodge, in full flower.

However, a cable from the German General Staff on January 26, 1915, addressed to von Bernstorff from Zimmermann in the Foreign Office, brought to light later, established that instructions on sabotage activities were routed through the ambassador. It said:

> For Military Attache. You can obtain particulars as to persons suitable for carrying on sabotage in the United States and Canada from the following persons: one, Joseph MacGarrity, Philadelphia, Pa.; two, John P. Keating, Michigan Avenue, Chicago; three, Jeremiah O'Leary, 16 Park Row, New York. One and two are absolutely reliable and discreet. Number three is reliable but not always discreet.

> These persons were indicated by Sir Roger Casement [the Irish insurrectionist leader]. In the U.S., sabotage can be carried out in every kind of factory for supplying munitions of war. Railway embankments and bridges must not be touched. Embassy must in no circumstances be compromised. Similar precautions must be taken in regard to Irish pro-German propaganda.

This particular message was to take on tremendous significance after the war in the effort to prove that the Germans had indeed carried out sabotage against the United States while the country was still neutral. It became, in fact, a cornerstone of charges that Germany not only was guilty of such acts but had used outright fraud to refute the allegation. And it went through von Bernstorff, with the explicit instruction that there be no embassy fingerprints on any sabotage carried out by the listed Irishmen.

Furthermore, the curt and unqualified manner in which the phrase "carrying on sabotage in the United States" was used at the very outset of the message clearly suggested previous discussions or communications had taken place on the matter between Berlin and the recipient of the cable, von Bernstorff.

In the first months of the war, the threat to the Central Powers' effort from the American munitions industry was not fully perceived, for a good reason. Armaments and ammunition from the United States were not in exceptional demand prior to the outbreak of the Great War, and it took months for American manufacturers to gear up for the new trade opportunity.

As von Bernstorff correctly noted in his appeal for arms embargo legislation in Congress, a whole new industry in effect was being created. So while that was happening, the neophyte saboteurs had their eyes focused more intently elsewhere; on Canada, which was at war with Germany and was an obvious target for troublemaking from within the United States, and somewhat surprisingly on the other major British colony, India.

As early as December 27, 1914, Zimmermann sent a cable in code to von Bernstorff advising him to provide money to Indian nationalists at the University of California at Berkeley and elsewhere who were planning revolution. One of their leaders, a postgraduate student named Har Dyal, facing deportation as an undesirable alien, went to Berlin. There he helped organize a plot in India aimed at tying down Indian regiments that otherwise would be made part of the British expeditionary force in France, possibly drawing British troops to India as well.

"A confidential agent of the Berlin Committee, Heramba Lal Gupta, is shortly leaving for America," Zimmermann wired, "in order to organize the importation of arms and the conveyance of Indians now resident in the United States to India. He is provided with definite instructions. You should place at his disposal the sum which he requires for this purpose in America, at Shanghai and Batavia, viz., 150,000 marks."

In a second cable to von Bernstorff four days later, Zimmermann added: "You should in conjunction with Gupta—but without attracting attention—take steps to have such Indians as are suitable for this purpose instructed in the use of explosives by some reliable person." This was a clear order to the ambassador, not to the military attaché.

In three months' time, with the aid of German agents in San Francisco, a small ship, the *Annie Larsen*, was chartered. The vessel was loaded with ten carloads of freight, including eight thousand rifles and four million cartridges, and sent on its way to the island of Sorocco in the South Seas. There it was to rendezvous with an oil tanker, the *Maverick*, bought by the Germans through an intermediary, whose crew was to hide the armaments in the ship's oil tanks, then sail to

India. But the *Maverick* was late in arriving and the *Annie Larsen*, running short of water, was obliged to depart.

The whole fiasco cost the German government several hundred thousand dollars without the desired result. When the Secret Service about a year later raided the office of von Igel, von Papen's chief assistant, agents found evidence connecting the German consulate in San Francisco with the two ships, refuting a denial by von Bernstorff that his government was in any way involved.

In fact, in the spring of 1915 von Papen himself became involved in other attempts to recruit Indians in the United States and Canada to commit acts of sabotage in Canada, and in the process impede the British war effort. One involved organizing a community of Hindu coolies in Vancouver to dynamite bridges and tunnels of the Canadian Pacific railroad in the West, but it too failed.

Other activities overseen at the time by the German consul in San Francisco, Franz von Bopp, were more successful, including the placing of time bombs on four ships loading gunpowder destined for Russia at Tacoma, Washington. The resulting explosions shook Tacoma and nearby Seattle and obliterated the whole cargo of powder. Two of von Bopp's agents in this act, Louis Smith and Charles Crowley, fled east where they visited the Chicago stockyards and Detroit railroad yards to plan the bombing of trains taking thousands of horses to ports of embarkation for Europe.

Through all this, von Bernstorff insisted Germany had nothing to do with the destructions. He cited a cable sent by him in the spring of 1915 to all the German consulates in the United States specifically prohibiting them from engaging in any acts of sabotage against American property. But such messages, American investigators would learn in time, more often than not were dispatched as a cover for undertaking those very activities.

More than a year later, one of von Bopp's saboteurs, Smith, turned himself in to American authorities in Detroit, and eventually they cracked the San Francisco operation. Von Bopp and other officials of the German consulate in San Francisco were charged with "conspiracies to interfere with the transportation of munitions of war and supplies needed by the Allied Governments by dynamiting and blowing up factories, railroad bridges and tunnels, trains, docks and steamships." After a long postwar trial, they were convicted and sentenced to jail terms of one to two years.

Two of von Bopp's best German agents, however, eluded the Justice Department's investigation and went on to play significant roles in the German secret war against the officially neutral United States.

One was Kurt Jahnke, a moderately tall man in his early thirties weighing about 160 pounds, with blond hair and a swarthy complexion, described by another German saboteur as having "light weasly eyes, small and ratty," and "a rough dresser." He had become a naturalized American citizen before the outbreak of the war and for a time was in the U.S. Marine Corps.

The other was Lothar Witzke, a handsome and athletic fellow in his early twenties, a German naval academy cadet on the cruiser *Dresden* off South America when the ship was sunk and he was interned in Valparaiso, Chile. He escaped and made his way to San Francisco, where von Bopp teamed him with Jahnke to form what later proved to be one of Germany's most effective sabotage teams.

Although Germany's effort to mount an effective campaign of disruption in America was severely inhibited in the first months of the war by the shortage of professionally trained saboteurs, a pattern began to emerge that should have raised official American suspicions.

On New Year's Day of 1915, an incendiary fire of undetermined origin broke out at the John A. Roebling wire-cable manufacturing plant in Trenton, New Jersey. Two days later, an explosion wracked the S.S. *Orton* in Erie Basin, Brooklyn. Subsequent fires and explosions over the next four months damaged factories manufacturing munitions or powder in Haskell and Pompton Lakes, New Jersey, and Allon, Illinois, and in April one munitions-carrying ship caught fire at sea and bombs were found in two others.

Still, the German sabotage campaign sorely needed a specialist who could operate outside the confines of the embassy. That need was addressed on March 22, 1915, when a man traveling with a Swiss passport under the name Emile V. Gache calmly obtained visas at the American and British consulates in Christiania (Oslo) and boarded the S.S. *Kristianiafjörd* for New York.

Much later, after the completion of his mission, he came to be known to the Allies and to the United States as Captain Franz von Rintelen, or as his subsequent self-congratulatory account of that mission for his London publisher put it unabashedly, "The Dark Invader." With von Rintelen's arrival in America, Germany's sabotage campaign sought to graduate from its early amateurish poking about to a level somewhat more in keeping with the German reputation for discipline, precision and ingenuity.

7. Enter "The Dark Invader"

By the time Captain Franz von Rintelen, a junior officer of the German admiralty staff in Berlin, was dispatched to the United States, Berlin well understood that the American version of neutrality provided a lopsided advantage to the enemy. As von Rintelen later put it in his extravagantly melodramatic and self-serving account:

> I was inwardly certain that the dice were cast, that America had to be attacked! American capital had flung itself upon an opportunity to make immense profits. It was thrown into the scales of war and began to send up in a dangerous manner the balance which held Germany's fate. That was what was happening in America.
>
> In Berlin and at the General Headquarters this new invisible enemy was the cause for the deepest gloom. It was no opponent who could be faced in the open field, it was no foe whose trenches could be taken by storm; it was a spectre, an intangible phantom, against which strategy, tactics, and all the courage of the German soldier were helpless. These shipments of American munitions were the ghost which haunted the corridors of the Army Command in Charleville. A powerful and sinister hand was raised against the soldiers of Germany and hurled them back with ghastly wounds.

After diplomatic appeals had failed, including an offer in which von Rintelen himself was involved to permit America to send food for the Belgian civilian population in return for an end to Allied munitions shipments, Berlin turned to more drastic methods. A German sympathizer in the United States named Malvin Rice, claiming to be an official of the DuPont deNemours Powder Company, conveyed word that he could arrange sufficiently large German purchases of explosives to make a severe dent in Allied battlefield firepower. Von Rintelen, who had worked for a London banking house in New York and spoke impeccable English, was given half a million dollars and instructed to contact Rice, even though it was well-nigh impossible to ship explosives to Germany. Once purchased, they could be destroyed and thus kept out of Allied hands.

Von Rintelen, fired by patriotism—and burning career ambition —seized the assignment as a golden opportunity to make his mark. With a bravado that came to be his trademark, he claimed to have told Zimmermann during a briefing at the Foreign Office: "Ich kaufe, was ich kann; alles andere schlage ich kaput!"—"I'll buy up what I can, and blow up what I can't!" That was the kind of talk Berlin liked to hear; von Rintelen set off with the wholehearted support of his superiors.

He took the name Emile V. Gache because a fellow naval officer had a Swiss brother-in-law by that name who was willing to coach him in family history, the better to carry on his subterfuge. Von Rintelen had a wife and small daughter, but he left them readily, not realizing at the time it would be six years before he saw them again.

As matters turned out, he never met his contact, Malvin Rice, at all. On arrival in New York, von Rintelen found not a soul awaiting him. In his most excessive manner, he wrote later: "So I stood there on that pier in New York, entirely alone, left to my own wits, but bent upon going through with what seemed ill-starred at the beginning. Single-handed I now ventured an attack against the forty-eight United States!"

As part of his assignment, von Rintelen was instructed to deliver to von Papen and Boy-Ed a new top-secret code for the transmission of messages to Berlin, a protection against the possible Allied breaking of the code then being used. He carried the miniaturized code in two small capsules that he was to swallow if captured by the enemy.

Neither of the attachés was pleased to see von Rintelen; they took his presence as an indication that Berlin felt the performance of their additional duties had left something to be desired. In addition, he was a man of dubious aristocratic lineage, and his use of the "von" in his name irritated many of those who came by it without challenge. To them this affectation was the crowning example of the airs he put on, although unlike many of them he was clean-shaven, with neither the flamboyant moustache nor beard that many other Germans of the day flaunted. Many fellow German officers contemptuously made certain to refer to him simply as "Rintelen." This contempt, however, did not overcome Berlin's confidence that this man could supply the imagination and daring that the sabotage operation had lacked up to this point.

Perhaps anticipating the cold reception he would receive from von Papen and Boy-Ed, von Rintelen buttered them up with good news from home: von Papen had been awarded the Iron Cross and Boy-Ed the Order of the House of Hohenzollern. The news seemed to placate the two somewhat. Von Rintelen proceeded about his business of establishing himself in New York, moving into the Great Northern Hotel on Fifty-seventh Street.

Within several days, von Rintelen met with Ambassador von Bernstorff at the Ritz-Carlton on Madison Avenue. Von Bernstorff insisted after the war that von Rintelen had merely "presented himself to me during one of my periodical visits to New York" and had "declined at the time to give any information as to his official position in the country, or the nature of his duties." When he wired Berlin for details about von Rintelen, von Bernstorff said, he received no reply, and eventually, "as his continued presence in New York was considered undesirable by both von Papen and Boy-Ed, they took steps to have him sent back to Germany."

Von Rintelen, however, claimed that von Bernstorff sent for him and that he told the ambassador why he had come to the United States. Although von Rintelen in time proved himself to be a master spinner of tall tales, there was little doubt that the three ranking German embassy officials well knew what his mission was. In fact, shortly after von Rintelen's arrival, von Papen wrote a letter to General Erich von Falkenhayn, chief of the German General Staff, expressing his appreciation that "at last someone had come to America to take steps to hamper the shipment of munitions by all means."

Once von Rintelen arrived in New York, he saw no reason not to operate aboveboard in a neutral country—at least as long as his endeavors could be justified as entirely legal. A member of the New York Yacht Club—one of only three Germans, the others being the kaiser and his brother Prince Heinrich—von Rintelen cut a smooth swath through social circles all along the Eastern seaboard. He wrote after the war:

I began to lead a dual existence. In the evening I went about as "myself" in dress suit and white tie; I had decided that it was much more dangerous to go out about New York under a false name. For, if one of the numerous English agents should find out anyhow who I actually was, he would know instantly that I had something nefarious up my sleeve. If, however, I did not conceal my identity, it would be assumed that I was in America on some peaceful economic mission. Otherwise, it would be argued, I should have kept behind the scenes.

Through his banking connections, von Rintelen knew where and how to pursue the most likely leads on the purchase of large amounts of munitions. In short order, however, he realized the hopelessness of his task:

> I went to several firms and told them I was a German agent anxious to purchase powder, but within a few days I was satisfied that it would be quite impossible to buy up the vast quantities of explosives that were by now available in the American market. The daily production was so great that if I had bought up the market on Tuesday there would still have been an enormous fresh supply on Wednesday.

In the course of his pursuits, von Rintelen learned that the government of Italy was also buying heavily in the American munitions market, through French agents. Before the war, Italy was bound to Germany in a mutual-defense treaty, but had begged off on grounds Germany initiated hostilities by invading Belgium. The information about the arms purchases convinced him that Italy was preparing to join the Allies, and he so informed Berlin. He was right; in the secret Treaty of London in late April, 1915, Italy succumbed to a host of territorial inducements and finally sided with Britain and France.

Von Rintelen also learned in making his way about the German community in New York that many German reservists off the interned ships and German-American sympathizers regarded von Papen as a disaster. They widely criticized him for the arrest of Werner Horn in the Vanceboro bridge affair and for general carelessness.

Beyond that, von Papen and Boy-Ed fell to feuding between themselves. On one occasion von Papen fired off a telegram to his colleague warning him that he was getting careless. Boy-Ed replied in another telegram that a "secret agent" just returned from Washington had informed him that "the Washington people are very much excited about von Papen and are having a constant watch kept on him. They are in possession of a whole heap of incriminating evidence against him," but that "they have no evidence against Count B. and Captain B-E." Von Papen, Boy-Ed and their associates came to be known on the docks and in the waterfront saloons frequented by German reservists as "the Kindergarten."

The Eastern seaboard docks at this time were an exceedingly ripe environment for von Rintelen's mischief. More than eighty German merchant ships were now pinned down in American ports by the dominating and alert British fleet. In addition to the many German seamen left idle by this circumstance, the docks from Boston, New York, and Baltimore down to New Orleans were swarming with men of all nationalities looking for work loading ships bound for European ports.

The old, traditional daily shape-up for hiring prevailed on a first-come, first-taken basis, though unions did function in the major ports. It was not hard to find men interested in turning an extra dollar or two to load cargo, and no questions asked. Many Irish longshoremen, intensely hostile to the British cause as their countrymen struggled and plotted for independence, were particularly tempting targets for German recruitment.

The New York Police Department, alert to the inherent threat to security in the situation, immediately after the outbreak of the war had created a special bomb squad under Inspector Thomas J. Tunney, a strapping Irishman with a special knowledge of explosives. At first it focused on the anarchists and immigrant crime groups that operated in New York. But it soon branched out and was renamed the Bomb and Neutrality Squad.

Even before von Rintelen's arrival in New York, numerous dock workers were brought into service for the German war effort by Dr. Bunz of the Hamburg-Amerika Line and his chief detective, Paul Koenig. Koenig was a familiar figure on the waterfront and his activities soon drew the suspicions of Tunney's squad. The plainclothesmen tailed him constantly but he was cunning and elusive. Tunney wrote of him after the war:

Koenig, a man of keen animal senses, was unusually quick in discovering his shadower. It used to confuse certain agents considerably to have him disappear around a corner, and when the agent quickened his pace and swept around the same corner after him, to have Koenig pop out of a doorway with a laugh for his pursuer, which meant that the day's work had gone for nothing.

Among the activities of Bunz and Koenig, in league with von Papen, was the chartering of ships that were then loaded with coal. Their captains were bought off, the ships taken over by German crews and dispatched under neutral flags to sea, where they rendezvoused with and fueled German cruisers.

Bunz struck on the idea of having these German crews engage in a bit of sabotage while they were at sea. While awaiting the arrival of the cruisers, they would intercept any tramp steamer carrying munitions to the Allies that might come along, run up the German flag and board the ship with an armed party, take the crew as prisoners and blow up the vessel. But Bunz needed explosives and he turned to von Rintelen for help.

In league with a down-and-out German export merchant named Max Weiser, von Rintelen concocted a phony export firm as a front, enabling him to establish a sabotage operation while appearing to be legitimately soliciting goods for export. They called the firm "E. V. Gibbons, Inc.," using the same initials of von Rintelen's Swiss pseudonym. They opened a small office on Cedar Street in the Lower Manhattan financial district, and while Weiser busied himself writing scores of purchase orders, von Rintelen set about obtaining explosives.

Weiser was so conscientious in constructing a believable front for von Rintelen's real work that goods began to come in and had to be accepted to maintain the credibility of the operation. In one case, Weiser somehow contracted for the purchase of a trainload of whiskey and had to receive and pay for it or blow the cover. He tried frantically to sell it, to no avail. Weiser finally contacted a shady lawyer, one Bonford Boniface, a two-bit operator along the waterfront, who for a fee and some bribe money managed to squash the deal without a public fuss.

Von Rintelen described Boniface as "tall and lean, wore pince-nez which kept on slipping down his nose, and gave one on the whole the impression of a mangey hyena seeking its daily prey on the battlefield." But Boniface was the sort who for the right price was always able to come up with some legal rationale for whatever outrage von Rintelen had in mind. He came in handy in the weeks ahead.

In this endeavor at least, von Papen also proved to be of major assistance. He sent to von Rintelen a German chemist named Dr. Walter Scheele, a onetime German field artillery lieutenant who since 1893 had been Imperial Germany's first and only paid spy in America, in the industrial field. In that year, Berlin dispatched him to America to do "chemical research." For twenty years he reported periodically to the German military attaché on advances in the development of explosives and applications of chemistry to warfare.

Scheele now had his own cover as president of something he called the New Jersey Agricultural Chemical Company, which he set up at von Papen's instruction in 1913. "Von Papen told me," Scheele recounted later, "that the German government needed lubricating oil. . . . I had to produce oil in such a way that the United States officials would be deceived, and the same shipped in some way to the other side."

Scheele came to the office of E. V. Gibbons, Inc. with precisely what von Rintelen needed for his own assignment. After being assured of von Rintelen's true identity and mission, Scheele withdrew from his pocket a long tube of lead about the size of a large cigar. The tube was divided into two compartments by a copper disc. Into one of them Scheele had poured picric acid, and into the other, sulphuric acid. Then each open end had been plugged with wax. The copper disc functioned as a timing device. The two acids on either side would eat their way through; the amount of time it required for them to do so and mix, causing an intense flame, depended on the thickness of the disc.

What Scheele had invented was an inexpensive, dependable, easily concealed incendiary bomb that would burn itself away, leaving no trace. Scheele's "cigar" was perfect not only for Bunz' mission but for another more ambitious sabotage scheme von Rintelen already had in mind. Together Scheele and von Rintelen found a wooded spot and Scheele loaded a "cigar" with a very thin copper disc, laying the device on the ground. As von Rintelen described the scene later:

We stood nearby. If the detonator worked, I could put my scheme into operation. I knew what use could be made of this "diabolical" invention; and all that was necessary was that it should function. Heaven knows it did! The stream of flame which suddenly shot out of the confounded "cigar" nearly blinded me, it was so strong; and the lead melted into an almost invisible fragment.

Von Rintelen immediately commissioned Scheele to start producing his "cigars." Meanwhile, the captain began to round up German skippers and Irish longshoremen who were easily recruited with a promise of good pay and a chance to strike a blow against England. Von Rintelen's idea was simple: take Scheele's "cigars," armed with copper discs thick enough to keep them from firing for several days or even weeks, and have them placed aboard ships carrying cargo—preferably munitions—to the Allies. Ideally, the ships would be set ablaze while on the open sea, in international waters, and no one would be the wiser as to the cause.

Von Rintelen's recruits quickly embraced the scheme and were ready to go into action at once. But Scheele had been working only in his own small quarters; he needed a full-scale assembly operation. But where could a safe metalwork shop be created that would be free of prying eyes, and if possible outside the jurisdiction of the United States and its bothersome neutrality laws?

Von Rintelen discussed the matter with Boniface, the waterfront lawyer, a man who had a reputation for familiarity with the neutrality laws and how to get around them. Boniface came up with the perfect answer: make the "cigar" bombs on one of the interned German ships berthed in solitude along the New York and New Jersey waterfronts!

Boniface produced a retired German ship captain of von Rintelen's acquaintance, Karl von Kleist, then living in Hoboken, to supervise the effort. They quickly set about creating a bomb workshop on the *Friedrich der Grosse*, which had dashed to the safety of New York Harbor at the outbreak of the war. They recruited all the ship's officers into the scheme—under the very noses of the New York port authorities and federal agents who were keeping a casual eye on the interned vessels and crews.

Von Rintelen, recounting the moment later, wrote: "We were to transplant ourselves, with all our schemes, devices and enterprises, on board one of the German ships and thus place ourselves in a most admirable situation. Germany within American territorial waters! What possibilities!"

Von Kleist, now nearly seventy years old and champing for a chance once again to serve the fatherland, had spent a lifetime at sea, starting as a boy on an old windjammer and moving up to mate and finally captain. Knowing as he did a great many of the German merchant mariners whose ships were interned, he proved to be a valuable and discerning recruiter of men to manufacture the casings for Scheele's "cigars" and then to plant them. Von Kleist, too, was a movie casting director's dream for the part: a balding man with a thin face and a pointed nose and goatee to match.

Through the ersatz firm of E. V. Gibbons, Inc., Weiser bought the required lead pipe and copper, and the materials were easily slipped aboard the *Friedrich der Grosse*. As von Rintelen recalled the bizarre scene later, "during the following nights the great dark ship was the scene of ghostly activity." When the pipe had been cut to the proper length and the copper discs placed inside in various thicknesses, they were carried by night to the laboratory of Dr. Scheele at 1133 Clinton Street in Hoboken. There, he filled them with the copper-eating acids, sulphuric and picric, or sulphuric and potassium chlorate, or a combination of sodium peroxide and urotropin, depending on availability.

Members of the ship's crew were ready recruits for the work, for a few extra dollars a week under the table. The ship's electrician, Ernest Becker, later gave police this account of the first time Scheele showed him the product:

> He took a small copper vessel about two inches in diameter. . . . He poured powder in it. He took a bottle with acid and let a drop fall on it. . . . It burst into flames. . . . I was astonished and I said, "That's grand!" I was wonder-struck. . . . He laughed and said, "That's chemistry." . . . I thought it was for experimenting purposes. . . . I did not think anything more about it. I thought Dr. Scheele was a doctor of chemistry and wanted to invent something.

Most of the initial batches of tubes were timed to flame out in fifteen days, a period deemed sufficient to have the "cigars" placed on ships before they left port and have them ignite before they arrived at their destinations. By von Rintelen's own testimony later, the first success was a British ship, the S.S. *Phoebus*, that sailed from New York with a cargo of shells bound for Archangel and the Russian army. According to von Rintelen, Irish dockhands loading the ship took six of Scheele's "cigars" and hid two of them in each of the vessel's three holds. He recalled:

> I walked unobtrusively past the steamer while my men were at work, looked down the opened hatchways through which the cases of shells were being lowered, and saw the British agents who were standing guard on deck, carbines slung across their arms ready to prevent anything suspicious from approaching their valuable cargoes. That evening my assistants came to my office. They were in good humour, and reported that the *Phoebus* was to sail on the next day, and that they had placed detonators in some other ships too, which were to leave harbour a few days later. . . .
>
> We sat in our office and waited for the first success. We had subscribed to the *Shipping News*, which printed the daily reports of Lloyd's in London concerning everything to do with shipping and shipping insurance. We had calculated the date on which the accident was to take place, but a few days passed and there was still nothing about the *Phoebus* in the paper. Suddenly we saw: "Accidents. S.S. *Phoebus* from New York—destination Archangel—caught fire at sea. Brought into port of Liverpool by H.M.S. *Ajax*."

More successes followed, with the ships either exploding or their captains obliged to flood the holds to put out the fires, also dousing the explosives and rendering them useless. Soon von Rintelen was thinking about expanding his operation, not only in New York but in other major ports such as Baltimore and New Orleans, from which munitions and other valuable cargo were being shipped to the Allies.

Among the most important recruits to the effort now was Captain Frederick Hinsch, master of the S.S. *Neckar*, a North German Lloyd steamer, and later to be overseer of the Baltimore docking of the merchant submarine *Deutschland*. We met Hinsch briefly at the beginning of this narrative, as the *Deutschland* prepared to dash down the Chesapeake Bay to freedom only hours before the destruction of the Black Tom terminal.

After months of dodging British cruisers in the South Atlantic in order to supply German warships, the *Neckar* had developed engine trouble and had been forced in late 1914 to put in at Baltimore. Hinsch was a corpulent, brutish man with a reputation for daring, intelligence, toughness and an ability to handle the coarse but loyal German seamen now stranded on American waterfronts. Von Rintelen enlisted him to supervise the actual placing of Scheele's bombs on ships along the Eastern seaboard.

Von Rintelen's contact with Hinsch was the North German Lloyd representative in Baltimore, Paul Hilken, whom we also briefly met at the pier of the *Deutschland*. The suave, aristocratic son of the German consul in Baltimore, Hilken also was brought directly into the effort by Berlin to collaborate with Albert, the commercial attaché, as paymaster for the sabotage ring.

Next, in New Orleans, von Rintelen recruited Erich von Steinmetz, a captain in the German navy who had managed to enter the United States by way of Vladivostock disguised as a woman. In addition to helping place bombs on ships, von Steinmetz played an initial role in another and even more bizarre scheme to cripple the fighting ability of the Allies.

In his woman's garb, von Steinmetz smuggled into the country cultures of glanders, the highly contagious disease that attacks the nose and air-passages of horses. The intent was to inoculate horses and mules purchased in the United States by Britain and France and bound for the European front. He injected the cultures into some horses but they had no effect. Then, in an act of considerable daring, von Steinmetz posed as a researcher and took the cultures to a prominent American laboratory for testing. He was told they were dead. The scheme, however, was not; other saboteurs in a short time were to pick it up and carry it out with devastating effect.

According to the ever-boastful von Rintelen, there was no end to his own ingenuity in service to the fatherland. In one instance, he claimed, he actually obtained loans from New York banks to buy supplies for the Russians, sold the supplies to them, had bombs placed that destroyed the cargo and then paid off the loans with the Russians' money before they got wise. The scheme, he bragged, worked this way:

He persuaded a German-American woman of his acquaintance in New York who had lived in Paris to write to the Russian military attaché there, Count Ignatieff, an old friend known as a connoisseur of fine wines. The woman wrote that an American importer she knew named Gibbons (von Rintelen) wanted to import claret into the United States and she wondered if he could help. The flattered Ignatieff replied speedily in the affirmative. Weiser, using the count's name, proceeded to purchase a large consignment of the wine from France, paying by cable promptly. Weiser easily sold the claret.

Next, Weiser wrote the count suggesting that his import-export company, which had proved itself to be so competent and prompt in the wine transaction, was in a position to provide many of the Russian army's needs. Would it be possible, did the count think, for the Gibbons firm to obtain a large military contract? Ignatieff suggested that the firm contact several stipulated Russian purchasing agents in New York, by all means using his name as a reference. Von Rintelen did so, posing as Gibbons, an American citizen. After handing Ignatieff's letter to one of the recommended purchasing agents, an impressionable Russian army officer of low rank, "Gibbons" landed a handsome order. The requisition included horses, mules, saddles, bridles, field kitchens, boots, shoes, underwear, gloves, tinned meat and small-arms ammunition. Von Rintelen then took the contract to the New York bank that handled the E. V. Gibbons, Inc. account and quickly obtained a loan of three million dollars, which he deposited secretly in another bank.

Von Rintelen and Weiser obviously were in no position to deliver on an order of such magnitude and variety, so they simply sat on the money. Delivery according to the contract was to be made in forty-five days, but in a couple of weeks the Russian agents phoned the Gibbons firm and asked for earlier delivery, for which they would pay a bonus. Fearful of giving the scheme away, von Rintelen promised delivery of the most important items as specified by the agents —the tinned meat and small-arms ammunition. Weiser set to work to fill that small portion of the order, and did so. The Russians were elated and immediately chartered a ship to take the emergency cargo to Archangel.

Von Rintelen later recounted what happened next: "I summoned my [dockhand] captains, and although I did not tell them exactly what I had done, I gave them to understand that we had been able to arrange for Allied supplies to pass through our hands, and that we should be handling the cases of ammunition and tinned foods on the way from the brokers to the ship. They knew what they had to do."

What they had to do, obviously, was to slip some of Dr. Scheele's "cigars" in with the cargo. Von Rintelen ordered that thirty of them be placed, to be sure there was no failure. "It was quite simple," he wrote later, "for we only had to put them in the provision cases. They were laid among wood shavings to ensure their effect."

Von Rintelen was paid off at the dock before the sailing, with a handsome bonus for delivering early. In four days, the *Shipping News* duly reported that the ship had caught fire and foundered, with the crew taking to lifeboats, from which they were rescued by an American vessel.

The Russian agents were beside themselves, not because they suspected von Rintelen, but rather because the cargo had been needed so desperately. Von Rintelen, demonstrably sympathetic, offered to help. He and Weiser this time managed swiftly to round up enough tinned meat and small-arms ammunition to fill the holds of two ships, and again they were loaded by the collaborating German and Irish dockhands, including once again the deadly cigars.

This time, to avert any suspicion and to further confound the Russian agents, von Rintelen actually hired detectives from a reputable agency to guard the ships "to see that nobody should sneak on board without authority." The ships set to sea and, lo and behold, met the same fate as the first.

Still, von Rintelen was not suspected. After all, other ships were catching fire whose goods were being supplied by many other export firms, and why would an exporter set fire to his own cargo?

The Russians continued to deal with E. V. Gibbons, Inc. until several barges of munitions purchased through the firm suddenly sank as they moved from the terminal on Black Tom Island toward waiting ships in New York Harbor. The Russians still suspected nothing but demanded immediate delivery of the rest of their large order.

Von Rintelen now realized he had played the string as long as he could. So, he said, he simply told the Russians:

that I had no intention of delivering the goods. The Russian officers were struck speechless. I shrugged my shoulders; they grew wild, I remained calm. They began to abuse me, so I took my hat and left them. . . . I went to the bank to pay back my advances; and the bonuses I had earned on the three sunken steamers sufficed to pay the interest. I went home with the conviction that I had done a good job. By the time the Russians were ready to take legal proceedings, the firm of E. V. Gibbons, Inc. no longer existed.

Von Rintelen's operation, even by his own self-congratulatory lights, had its problems. The heavy use of Irish stevedores entailed certain risks. So zealous were they in their determination to do harm to the British that von Rintelen and Weiser feared they would lose control over them. Although von Rintelen was operating independently of other aspects of the German war effort, he was mindful of the overriding concern in Berlin that no action be taken so harsh, and so clearly traceable to German agents, as to bring the United States into the war on the Allied side.

The danger that America might abandon her neutrality and go to war against the Central Powers remained ever present, for a reason that overshadowed von Rintelen's handiwork: Germany's intensified submarine warfare. Even as "The Dark Invader" was sailing for New York aboard the *Kristianiafjörd* as Emile V. Gache, Washington had been jolted by the sinking in the Irish Channel of the S.S. *Falaba*, a small British liner bound from Liverpool to West Africa. Among those killed was an American engineer. His fate angered Wilson and the American public and intensified the growing debate between Bryan and Lansing on the neutrality question.

Bryan sought to minimize the incident, questioning "the right of a citizen to involve his country in war when by ordinary care he could have avoided danger." Lansing on the other hand pressed Wilson for a tough response to "an atrocious act of lawlessness." Wilson temporized, but it was clear that the threat to American lives posed by German submarines attacking passenger ships had the potential of dragging the United States into the war.

The danger was brought home vividly to von Rintelen when Weiser informed him one morning that an Irish dockhand had just bragged to him that he had placed two "cigars" in the mail room of the *Ancona*, a large English mailboat carrying only passengers. A fire on this ship, which carried no explosives, almost certainly would have triggered a close investigation by members of the New York bomb squad, which was already getting close to von Rintelen's trail. Weiser, by bribing a postal official, was able to get into the mail room before the ship sailed from New York and retrieve the cigars, wrapped as parcel post, before the sailing.

Still another problem cropped up in Dr. Scheele himself. The importance of his invention had not been lost on him, and he began to feel emotions beyond the purely patriotic. He called on von Rintelen and demanded ten thousand dollars at once, threatening to go to the police if he didn't get it. Von Rintelen gave him a check, but then put two burly German ship captains onto him. They followed him home and intimidated him into surrendering the check.

Von Rintelen remained concerned, however, that Scheele might try his blackmail stunt again or, out of spite, simply turn von Rintelen in. So von Rintelen hired a young woman to befriend Scheele, then snared him in an elaborate seduction "sting." Threatened with exposure by Boniface, von Rintelen's shady waterfront lawyer, Scheele agreed to toe the line and continue making his cigars.

It was not possible, nevertheless, for the scheme to go on forever. Some days earlier, dockhands had placed cigar-bombs in the hold of the S.S. *Kirk Oswald*, bound for Archangel with a cargo of sugar. The ship's orders were changed, however, and instead it was routed to Marseilles, a shorter trip. The bombs had been timed to flame out as the ship approached Archangel, and the acids had not yet eaten through the disc dividing the two compartments when it docked in Marseilles. The cargo was removed without incident, and as the empty hold was being swept out, [some] peculiar lead pipes resembling cigars were found.

The ship's British captain, Frederick Williamson, testified later that "hatch No. 2 was three parts full of sugar and when they got one third of it out, that is when they found these bombs. They all fell out of one bag. The bag broke right in the center and out they came."

The French government in short order figured out what they were, emptied the acids and sent them on to Inspector Tunney in New York. Another crew member, ship's carpenter Karl Gustafson, recalled that on the way to Marseilles a fire had broken out in the port bunker of the *Kirk Oswald* but was put out with minimal damage. He recalled as well that "before we left on that trip to Marseilles when we found the bombs, we were docked over in South Brooklyn, in 31st Street. The *Friedrich der Grosse* was at the other shed. We could see it from where we were."

The trail was getting hot behind von Rintelen, and he decided to lie low for a while. He liquidated E. V. Gibbons, Inc. and headed for a quiet retreat he knew near Stamford, Connecticut, until the situation cooled off.

Police, however, eventually bagged von Kleist, the aging go-between with German dockhands, with a time-honored ploy. It so happened that Scheele owed von Kleist $134 in back pay and wouldn't come up with the money. Angered, von Kleist wrote to the German military attaché's office requesting an interview with von Igel, von Papen's deputy. The New York police intercepted the letter and an officer, Henry Barth, phoned von Kleist, posing as a German agent. He told von Kleist that he had been ordered to find out what the letter-writer wanted before an interview could be granted. They met for dinner and von Kleist spilled the beans. He named names of all those who made the bombs on the interned ship and said two of them "were going to lick the chemist, Dr. Scheele," for making bombs that failed to explode.

Von Kleist then took the German "agent" to the back yard of his home in Hoboken and dug up the proof of his story—an empty bomb container that was an exact duplicate of the one found on the *Kirk Oswald* in Marsailles. Barth next set up another dinner meeting with a man described to von Kleist as the military attaché's secretary. Von Kleist, lavishly dining and drinking at his host's expense, willingly repeated his story while the "secretary"—detective George Barnitz —took it all down.

Then, when von Kleist had dutifully signed the notes, he was whisked off to—he thought—von Igel's New York office to get paid the money Scheele owed him. Instead, he found himself at police headquarters, confronting not von Igel, but Tunney.

There von Kleist was shown one of the bombs taken off the *Kirk Oswald* and he identified it as one of the duds for which Scheele was almost given a beating. After this failure, von Kleist said, the partition between the two chambers in the "cigar," made of paraffin in those placed on the *Kirk Oswald*, was henceforth made of aluminum filed down so that it eroded and let the combustible materials flow together at precisely the time desired.

"I see now," Tunney recalled von Kleist saying when he realized where he was, "why you have been so good to me."

Von Kleist had been good to the detectives too, and—unwittingly—did not stop being good to them. At one point during his interrogation of the old man, Tunney stepped out of the room, leaving him alone with an "electrician" working on a light fixture. The man spoke fluent German and von Kleist, now desperate, asked the man whether he would deliver a couple of notes for him. They were warnings to accomplices, but in the hands of the "electrician"—detective Henry Senff—they became calling cards for the bomb squad. Others involved in the *Friedrich der Grosse* caper were rounded up and jailed, but Scheele escaped to Florida and then to Cuba.*

Meanwhile, another skilled German saboteur had arrived in the New York area in late April of 1915. He was Robert Fay, originally an infantry lieutenant who took part in some of the fiercest early trench warfare against the French on the Western Front. An engineer, Fay appreciated that the shells being fired on his positions by the Allies, manufactured in the United States, were of a superior quality, and that unless the flow was somehow arrested, Germany would lose the war. He hit upon an idea for a device for blowing up munitions cargo ships by fastening a container of TNT and a metal rod to the ship's rudder. The rod would wind up a firing mechanism with each turn of the rudder blade.

Fay told his commanding officer, who passed him and his idea on to German military intelligence, which obtained a neutral passport for him and sent him on to contact von Papen in New York. Fay was set up in an apartment in Weehawken, New Jersey, just across from Manhattan, and he began work in a nearby garage perfecting his new device.

While these schemes of direct sabotage were going forward, von

*Another worker on the shipboard bomb factory, ship's engineer Charles Schmidt, when charged by an arresting officer, took a philosophical view. "I am better off here than being in the trenches," he told his captor. Schmidt, Scheele, von Kleist, Becker and most of the other defendants were convicted in 1918 and given eighteen months at the federal penitentiary in Atlanta, their activities having occurred while the United States was still neutral. Scheele was not captured until March of 1918, courtesy of the Havana police. He testified at his trial that about five hundred "cigar" bombs were made on the interned ship, and that he had been part of an 'executive committee" of German agents that met regularly in the back dining room of the Hofbrau Haus at Broadway and West Twenty-seventh Street to plot strategy. Scheele said he had received between $25,000 and $28,000 from von Rintelen for the work. But he insisted that about seventy-five percent of the bombs made were never placed aboard ships. Many of the men hired to put them in cargoes, he said, merely threw them overboard and collected their pay.

Bernstorff's chief embassy subordinates were also employing certain nonviolent means to impede the export of American munitions to the Allies. Dr. Albert as paymaster was funding extensive purchases of basic materials required in the manufacture of armaments—not with the intention of shipping them to Germany, for that was impractical considering the British control of the Atlantic, but merely to deny them to the Entente Powers. In a report dated April 20, 1915, for example, Albert cabled the state secretary of the interior in Berlin:

> By issuing an order for two million shrapnel, contracts for powder and [other materials] for the manufacture of shrapnel cases have been made, by which the whole output-capacity of the powder and machine factories here is tied up. . . . The conclusion of the agreements has, to our great joy, produced a result hardly hoped for by ourselves. The large Russian orders for many millions of shrapnel in the market here . . . have not yet been placed . . . because the factories concerned were compelled to learn the truth that it is not possible to get the necessary powder. . . . No doubt exists that our timely intervention has, if not entirely prevented, yet delayed large orders of our enemies by many months.

Neither these nonviolent schemes nor the ship fires and other explosions held center stage in the United States or were among the concerns of its president, however. Wilson had more pressing matters on his mind. The sinking of passenger ships by German submarines increasingly challenged American neutrality. And once again, the exigencies of the president's personal life intruded on his concentration.

It had been scarcely seven months since the passing of his beloved wife Ellen, but Woodrow Wilson was not a man meant to live alone, without the companionship and consolations of a loving woman. One day in mid-March of 1915, a cousin of the president, Helen Bones, brought a friend, the widowed Mrs. Edith Bolling Galt, to the White House for tea. Wilson was supposed to be out on the golf course, but he and the White House physician, Dr. Cary Grayson, returned early from their weekly game and they all had tea together.

The president obviously was taken with Mrs. Galt from the start. He asked her to stay to dinner, but she declined. Soon, though, they were taking afternoon motorcar drives and dinners at the White House. Only six weeks after their first meeting, he professed his love and proposed marriage. She did not say yes at once, but she did not say no either, and so the courtship continued.

Woodrow Wilson, however, did not have the luxury of such personal pursuits. He was the leader of a great nation threatened by the greatest war yet conceived by the ambitions and folly of man, and was striving mightily to remain above it. He had now managed to do so to a remarkable degree for nine months, but events were drawing him ever closer to the edge.

Now came a development that would test his patience, and his ability to rationalize away reality, as none other since the start of the war. At shortly after two o'clock in the afternoon of May 7, 1915, off the south coast of Ireland, a German U-boat fired a single torpedo into the side of the pride of the Cunard fleet, the majestic passenger liner *Lusitania*, sinking her within minutes. Some 1,201 passengers and crew went down with her, including 124 Americans. Surely now, Woodrow Wilson could no longer simply turn the other cheek.

8. The *Lusitania* and Other Dark Deeds

The sinking of the *Lusitania* electrified the world, and the United States in particular. It brought home as never before the manner in which warfare had moved from battlefield and combat between naval vessels of war into the routine lives of peaceable neutral citizens.

Although it was not routine, certainly, for most Americans to sail for Europe on the luxurious *Lusitania*, doing so had been the stuff of which average Americans' dreams were made. Newspapers and newsreels on the silver screen glamorized Atlantic crossings of the time, with accounts and images of famous statesmen, writers, stage actors and movie stars dancing starry nights away. But then came the shocking news of American women and children, along with hundreds of Europeans, suffering horrible deaths as a German torpedo without warning ripped a lethal hole in the supposedly unsinkable leviathan, within sight of the Irish coast.

Immediately, von Bernstorff became embroiled in the furor. It so happened that on the very day the *Lusitania* left New York Harbor, May 1, the German ambassador had run a paid notice in the shipping columns of the *New York Times* that in retrospect seemed coldly calculated:

> Travellers intending to embark for an Atlantic voyage are reminded that a state of war exists between Germany and her Allies and Great Britain and her Allies; that the zone of war includes the waters adjacent to the British Isles; that, in accordance with the formal notice given by the Imperial German Government, vessels flying the flag of Great Britain or any of her Allies are liable to destruction in those waters; and that travellers sailing in the war zone in ships of Great Britain or her Allies do so at their own risk. [signed] Imperial German Embassy, Washington.

Von Bernstorff insisted after the *Lusitania* went down that the advertisement was to have appeared a week earlier but was inadvertently delayed, and that in any event he had no foreknowledge that the great liner would be a U-boat target. He intended the notice to be of a general nature, he said, not a specific warning against sailing on the *Lusitania*.

The ambassador was on a train going from Washington to New York on May 7 when he heard the news of the sinking. On arrival he went directly to the Ritz-Carlton Hotel and closeted himself as reporters flooded the lobby. He canceled plans to attend a play being performed that night by a German company for the benefit of the German Red Cross, and he returned to Washington the next day. In his book, von Bernstorff wrote of the intense American reaction:

> On my departure from New York I found myself at once face to face with this immense popular excitement. I left my hotel by a side door, but did not manage to escape notice; several cars filled with reporters followed me to the station, and pressed round me so persistently that I was unable to shake them off. I could only refuse to make any statement, which only increased the excitement of the reporters; but had I said anything at that time, I should but have added fuel to the fire which was already raging in the minds of all. Finally I succeeded in forcing my way through the infuriated and howling mob of pressmen and reaching the train.

Some German authorities—but not von Bernstorff—insisted initially that the *Lusitania* was armed and was carrying munitions of war and hence was a legitimate target. Dernburg, Berlin's propaganda chief in the United States, in a Cleveland speech made the allegation that there had been large antisubmarine guns aboard. But the charge came in the wake of a disclosure that Boy-Ed through Koenig had paid a private investigator two thousand dollars to swear he had seen four such guns aboard. The investigator subsequently confessed that he had lied, and he was jailed for perjury. As for munitions, ship manifests revealed that 4,200 cases of Remington rifle cartridges, 1,000 to a case or 4.2 million .303-caliber bullets, 1,250 cases of empty shrapnel shells, and eighteen cases of nonexplosive fuses had been in the cargo.

Von Bernstorff wrote later that "the rapidity with which the ship went down and the resulting heavy death-roll can only be attributed to the explosion of the masses of ammunition which formed part of the cargo." But in his official statement to the State Department, he merely expressed his country's regrets that American lives had been lost as a result of "the events of the war." Because England was pressing her "starvation blockade" with dire effect against the fatherland, the Germans saw nothing particularly horrible in the *Lusitania* sinking.

As von Bernstorff also wrote:

> We, accustomed as we have been to daily reports of battles and casualties, were little impressed by the destruction of a solitary passenger ship. America, however, execrated us wholeheartedly as murderers of women and children, oblivious to the fact that the victims of the submarine campaign were far less numerous than the women and children killed by the English blockade, and that death by drowning was no more dreadful than slow starvation.

Still, von Bernstorff well appreciated the impact on American public opinion of the shocking episode. "Our propaganda has completely collapsed," he cabled Chancellor von Bethmann-Hollweg at one point. "Another event like the present one would certainly mean war with the United States."

Dr. Albert, writing to his wife at the same time, told her:

> Liebste Ida: I believed I knew the American people somewhat, but I am completely at a loss to understand this outbreak. . . . Everything we have done to enlighten the Americans is as though wiped out. . . . The German-Americans have completely lost their nerves. There are people who are changing their names and deny all connection with us. . . .
>
> I find myself like a healthy man who sees a great strong lout suffering from shrivelling of the brain, and is watching with a certain uneasiness to see whether the patient himself is again well, or whether he is not in the course of his illness bringing to those standing near him or living together with him to harm. . . .
>
> I am still as formerly of the opinion that one should not lose one's nerves, should continue the submarine warfare and refuse the demand of the Americans; only in manner, one should be as calm, friendly and even cordial as possible, incredible though the latter may sound. Germany ought to treat the United States like a great big child, point to the fact that the greatest experts

could not reckon upon such a rapid sinking of the Lusitania, and then . . . discuss the whole situation from the point of view of right and humanity, including the munitions question, and talk in this connection a good deal about courts of arbitration and the like, without committing oneself, and as a matter of fact refuse all demands with quiet firmness. Finally, if it comes to the worst, namely to war, still that is never the worst. On the contrary, the United States would still in the long run probably have come in.

Colonel House, in a cable from London where he was winding up another fruitless peace mission, tried to impress upon Wilson the significance of the tragedy as a test of American will and honor:

America has come to the parting of the ways when she must determine whether she stands for civilized or uncivilized warfare. We can no longer remain neutral spectators. Her action in this crisis will determine the part we will play when peace is made, and how far we may influence a settlement for the lasting good of humanity. We are being weighed in the balance, and our position amongst nations is being assessed by mankind.

But Wilson continued to see nonintervention and nonbelligerency as essential to his role as the world's peacemaker, to be maintained even at the cost of public taunts of cowardice and appeasement. Once again, in his determination to maintain the American neutrality from which he felt he could most effectively mediate, the president three nights after the tragedy permitted himself to make a remarkably naive speech to a group of newly naturalized American citizens in Philadelphia.

"The example of America must be a special example," Wilson said. "The example of America must be the example not merely of peace because it will not fight, but of peace because peace is the healing and elevating influence of the world and strife is not. There is such a thing as a man being too proud to fight. There is such a thing as a nation being so right that it does not need to convince others by force that it is right."

Although there was certainly no consensus in the United States to plunge into war with Germany over the *Lusitania* affair, neither were Americans in a mood blithely to turn the other cheek, as Wilson's unfortunate phraseology suggested. He insisted afterward that he was not thinking specifically of the *Lusitania* when he made these remarks. He was merely reiterating what he had said on another occasion three weeks earlier, that maintaining neutrality required "absolute self-control and self-mastery."

Still, such observations did nothing to discourage those Germans, like von Bernstorff, striving to find the safest middle ground between the committing of acts of sabotage and the preservation of American neutrality.

Neither did a series of diplomatic notes Wilson sent to Berlin in the wake of the *Lusitania* sinking. The first, dispatched six days after the great liner went down, defended the right of neutral Americans to travel on unarmed merchant ships and called on Germany to make a "disavowal" of any policy of unrestricted submarine warfare. But it did not explicitly threaten either a breaking of diplomatic relations or a declaration of war.

Wilson treated Berlin to one of his high-minded lectures, instructing the German authorities that

> rights of neutrals are based upon principle, not upon expediency, and the principles are immutable. Illegal and inhuman acts . . . are manifestly indefensible when they deprive neutrals of their acknowledged rights, particularly when they violate the right to life itself. If a belligerent cannot retaliate against an enemy without injuring the lives of neutrals, as well as their property, humanity as well as justice and a due regard for the dignity of neutral powers should dictate that the practice be discontinued.

Such presidential lectures to Germany chagrined most members of Wilson's inner circle, who thought him too soft. Secretary of State Bryan, however, ever the pacifist, frowned on this one as too tough. Determined even more than Wilson to keep the country on the peace track, Bryan sought to minimize the significance of the tragic event. He argued that because the *Lusitania* was carrying 4,200 cases of cartridges, American passengers had been used, ineffectively, as a shield for the ammunition. They should be warned by Washington not to travel on belligerents' liners, he said, and a softer note should have been sent to Berlin.

More than two weeks passed before Berlin replied. When it did,

Germany said only that she had already expressed regret at the loss of American lives on the *Lusitania* and that she wished the United States would examine the facts of the ship's cargo, alleged armament and past use of neutral flags in assessing the incident.

A frustrated Wilson called in von Bernstorff, urging him to persuade his government to address the issue of unrestricted submarine warfare raised in his first note. He told von Bernstorff privately that if Germany would abandon that U-boat policy he would press the British to lift their food blockade. Wilson thereupon sent Berlin a second note substantially the same as the first, obviously hoping to force Berlin to respond directly to the protest he had raised in the first note.

Pursuing this point, which seemed a reasonable and even modest approach by other cabinet members, was too much finally for Bryan. Convinced it would lead to a break in relations with Germany and American entry into the war, and champing at House's special role that rendered almost meaningless his already hollow stewardship of the State Department, Bryan resigned.

Wilson without enthusiasm appointed Lansing to replace him. He regarded the man he was promoting as essentially a technician; Lansing would not unduly intrude on the conduct of foreign policy by the president and House, who continued to insist on serving only as a personal adviser to his friend in the White House.

A full month passed before Berlin replied to the second note. In the intervening time, von Bethmann-Hollweg—along with von Bernstorff and other diplomatic and political leaders much more fearful of American entry into the war than were the German military men—had temporarily regained the upper hand over the militarists.

Secret orders already had gone out to U-boat commanders after the *Lusitania* sinking not to attack passenger liners. But Berlin was not prepared to make the orders public. It feared doing so would acknowledge wrongdoing in that celebrated torpedoing, and would be a voluntary erosion of the legality of unrestricted submarine warfare as retaliation for the British "starvation" blockade. The second German note said submarines would permit safe passage of American liners with special markings, plus four specific enemy liners placed under the American flag.

Two weeks later, Wilson sent a third *Lusitania* note, in which in effect he accepted as legal the so-called "cruiser rules" governing submarine warfare. That is, a submarine was to function as a surface cruiser except in its ability to approach a target undetected. Torpedoes were to be reserved for submerged firing against armed vessels. If a submarine encountered an unarmed enemy ship, it was to surface, search the ship if possible, but in any event permit the crew and passengers to abandon the vessel before sinking it. Wilson's third note observed only that repetition of U-boat behavior in contravention of Americans' neutral rights would be regarded "as deliberately unfriendly."

Wilson obviously was now more than ever in a mood to let the bitter *Lusitania* cup pass. Indeed, the day after the dispatch of the second German note, in spite of all of Berlin's assurances, a U-boat had fired a torpedo at another large Cunard liner, the *Orduna*, headed for Europe from New York with 227 passengers including 21 Americans. Fortunately, the torpedo missed and Wilson rather incredibly decided to look the other way.

Berlin ultimately treated all three of Wilson's notes as toothless, acknowledging Germany's right to conduct submarine warfare short of a *Lusitania* repetition. Von Bernstorff, writing to his superiors in Berlin, observed that "the president has definitely come close to our position, for he now considers the submarine war as legitimate, while he earlier thought that it could not be executed at all according to international law."

All this diplomatic jockeying, meanwhile, did not seriously inhibit the covert war Germany was conducting against the United States through von Bernstorff's shadier agents. Between April and July of 1915, eight ships caught fire at sea under suspicious circumstances and bombs were found on at least five others.

In addition, explosions ripped munitions and powder plants in Wallington, Carney's Point (three times), and Pompton Lakes, New Jersey; Wilmington, Delaware (twice); Philadelphia, Pittsburgh and Sinnemahoning, Pennsylvania; and Acton, Massachusetts. Also, a munitions train was wrecked at Metuchen, New Jersey, and an incendiary fire destroyed a railroad grain elevator at Weehawken, New Jersey.

Some of these episodes doubtless resulted from von Rintelen's operation and Scheele's "cigar" bombs, but others probably were the work of Koenig's agents. Hinsch in Baltimore apparently was working for both von Rintelen and Koenig, because one of Hinsch's agents later confessed to having planted another kind of incendiary device variously described as resembling a lump of coal or an egg. Koenig's records later indicated he had made payments to an unidentified man for such a device.

For some of the most difficult, dangerous and distasteful tasks, the German agents often sought out black dockhands, who were generally treated as second-class workers on the waterfront. Prominent among them was the foreman of a black stevedores' gang in Baltimore named J. Edward Felton, an employee of the North German Lloyd Line. He told authorities long after the war that he was first recruited by Hinsch to pass out circulars among dock workers in Norfolk inciting them to strikes, and then was given jobs of much higher risk. Felton testified:

> After I had been working on this strike matter for about a month Captain Hinsch told me that he had some other kind of work that he wanted me to do in helping set fire to some of the supplies that they were getting ready to ship to Europe. This was in early 1915. There was a lot of grain and horses, cotton and other supplies at and near Baltimore, Norfolk and Newport News.
>
> Captain Hinsch gave me some things to start fires with. They were about the size of a small egg. Captain Hinsch told me that some of his men were making these on the Neckar. He showed me how to fill them with acid and gave me instructions as to how they would cause a flame and start fires. They did not explode. They merely sent out a big sissing flame and set fire to things around them. . . . After we put in the acid we closed up a little spout and then they were ready to work. I gave them to my men who were working for me to put around among the wheat and cotton and other supplies on the docks and in warehouses and on the ships, which was what Captain Hinsch told me to do.

It was dangerous work, and not simply because of the possibility of being caught. Felton told of how, on one occasion in Newport News, one of the egg bombs he was carrying in his pocket went off by mistake. "It burned my overalls badly and burned me before I managed to put the flame out," he said. For this work, Felton said he received expenses and about $150 to $200 a week for paying off others in his gang who planted the bombs.

In addition to such organized efforts at mayhem, individual acts of sabotage were carried out by Germans or German-Americans whose patriotism was aroused by the war, by the propaganda spread by Dr. Albert, and by what seemed increasingly to be a pro-Allied, anti-German bias in American actions. The most celebrated of these occurred on July 2 and 3, 1915, perpetrated by a professor of German at Cornell University and earlier at Harvard named Eric Meunta.

On the morning of July 2, at the beginning of the Independence Day weekend, Meunta boarded a train from New York to Washington, took a room near Union Station and assembled a time bomb. He then walked to the United States Capitol and into the deserted Senate wing. He placed the bomb near a telephone switchboard, timing the device to explode eight hours later. Then he went back to his room and wrote a letter protesting the shipment of American munitions to the Allies, signed it "R. Pearce" and mailed it to a Washington newspaper. It said, in part:

> In connection with the Senate affair, would it not be well to stop and consider what we are doing? . . . Sorry, I too had to use explosives (for the last time I trust). It is the export kind, and ought to make enough noise to be heard above the voices that clamor for war and blood money. . . . By the way, don't put this on the Germans or Bryan. I am an old-fashioned American. . . . P.S. We would, of course, not sell to the Germans if they could buy here, and since so far we only sold to the Allies, neither side should object if we stopped.

Meunta then checked out of this room and caught the midnight train back to New York. While it sped north through the night, the bomb he had planted in the Senate went off, shattering the telephone switchboard, wrecking a reception room and its expensive chandeliers and tearing gaping holes in the walls and ceiling.

When Meunta's train arrived in New York in the early hours of the morning, he transferred to another to Glen Cove, Long Island. From the station he went directly to the home of financier J. Pierpont Morgan, whose loans and other dealings with the Allies were enabling them to buy American munitions. He identified himself to the butler with a calling card that said "Summer Social Directory, Represented by Thomas C. Lester." When the butler asked for better credentials, Meunta pulled a revolver from his coat and forced his way inside.

At that moment, Morgan and members of his family were at the breakfast table. The butler ushered the intruder into the library, but as he did, Meunta saw that the room was empty, and he turned suspiciously. The butler, still looking into the barrel of the revolver, cried out to Morgan to get up to the second floor. Morgan bolted up a rear stairway, his wife behind, and began to search the second-story rooms to determine what the trouble was.

Mrs. Morgan was now in the lead, and as they approached the main stairway they saw Meunta, who had just come up, brandishing a revolver in each hand. Morgan brushed his wife aside and charged at him. Meunta fired twice, hitting the financier in the abdomen and left thigh. But the portly Morgan, a man of well over two hundred pounds, fell on his attacker, pinning him to the floor. Morgan seized one of the guns and his wife wrenched the other from Meunta's hand, and the butler knocked him unconscious with a large lump of coal.

At the Glen Cove jail, Meunta gave police an alias, "Frank Holt," and the following sworn statement:

> I have been in New York City about ten days and had made a previous trip to the home of Mr. Morgan last week. My motive in coming here was to try to force Mr. Morgan to use influence with the manufacturers of munitions in the United States, and with the millionaires who are financing the war loans, to have an embargo put on shipments of war munitions, so as to relieve the American people of complicity in the death of thousands of our European brothers.
>
> If Germany should be able to buy munitions here we would of course positively refuse to sell to her. The reason the American people have not as yet stopped the shipments seems to be that we are getting rich out of this traffic, but do we not get enough prosperity out of non-contraband shipments? And would it not be better for us to make what money we can without causing the slaughter of Europeans?
>
> I am very sorry I had to cause the Morgan family this unpleasantness, but I believe that if Mr. Morgan would put his shoulder to the wheel he could accomplish what I have endeavored to do. I wanted him to do the work I could not do. I hope that he will do his share anyway. We must stop our participation in the killing of Europeans, and God will take care of the rest.

Morgan was not severely injured. Meunta continued to insist he was "Frank Holt" and would say nothing more of substance. A search of a room he had taken at the Mills Hotel in New York revealed a supply of dynamite and other explosive materials. Meunta owned up to planting the bomb in the Senate and to writing the letter to the Washington press. When asked by Inspector Tunney of the New York bomb squad where he had obtained the explosives, however, he would only say he would tell him on the following Wednesday, July 7.

The police learned, however, that Meunta had bought a large trunk of dynamite, and that his wife a few days earlier had received a letter from him saying that "with God's help a ship that sailed from New York July 3 will sink on July 7." They immediately alerted all ships that had sailed on that day to make thorough searches, and to be prepared for the worst.

Sure enough, on the next Wednesday, a ship that had left New York on July 3, the *Minnehaha*, was rocked by an explosion in mid-ocean, but managed to get to port without casualties. Police rushed to Meunta's cell to interrogate him about it, but they found him dead. He had climbed to the top of the high-ceilinged room and dived head-first to the concrete floor below, crushing his skull. It was never established whether he had indeed placed a bomb on the *Minnehaha*. But the episode demonstrated the strong pacifist, if not pro-German, sentiment that existed among many in the United States at this time.

During much of this period, von Rintelen had been lying low at his Connecticut hideaway as police sought to locate the men behind the "cigar" bombs found in the hold of the ship detoured from Archangel to Marseilles. He was registered at the small hotel as a Mr. Brannon, an Englishman, and he received daily reports by mail from subordinates in New York on the progress of the search of which he was the prime target.

Because von Rintelen was such a celebrated spinner of self-serving tales, his own account of what persuaded him it was safe to return to New York and his sabotage activities is suspect. Nevertheless it does warrant recounting if only to illustrate the man's colossal ego and capacity to gild his own lily.

In his wartime autobiography, von Rintelen told of how one afternoon at a nearby hotel he came upon two young women who had met him once in New York without knowledge of his real identity. In the course of casual conversation, they invited him to a party at the hotel the next night. Among those who would be present, he was told, was the naval attaché of the British embassy, who von Rintelen had been informed was in charge of the search for him.

"I looked out over the sea," von Rintelen wrote of the scene. "The orchestra was playing softly. My two companions began to devour pastries in large quantities. On the spur of the moment I decided to take a great risk in order to find out what I wanted to know."

On meeting the British naval attaché the next night, von Rintelen daringly introduced himself as a British commander sent to the United States to study "a new torpedo invention," but who had come across some intelligence he wanted to share. He told the Englishman that he had heard about a group of men in a motor boat loading "mysterious cases" on a munitions-laden ship in New York harbor—just enough to elicit from him what von Rintelen wanted to know.

The British officer said he was on to a man named von Rintelen but "the American police stick to their statement that he is a gentleman who is not doing anything criminal." From this report von Rintelen deduced that the trail toward him had cooled off, and that he could return to New York.

Not content with weaving this tale of his own cleverness, von Rintelen wrote that the British officer, now completely gullible, told him of how British intelligence had just definitely pinpointed the location of the German cruiser *Karlsruhe* in the Atlantic and how British warships were now closing in for the kill. Whereupon von Rintelen confided to him that several large German steamers in American ports had been secretly armed and were preparing to break out and make a run for Germany.

"I could see that this information had startled him," von Rintelen wrote. "There was not a word of truth in it, though the idea had once been on the tapis. Attachés resemble each other all over the world. They would rather let their ears be cut off than admit that there is anything connected with their job that they do not know."

Sure enough, the British officer swallowed the fish story and told von Rintelen he was cabling it to his superiors so the cruisers could be diverted from the *Karlsruhe* to these more appetizing targets. Or so von Rintelen said.

"I had achieved more than I dared to hope," von Rintelen crowed in the retelling, "for I knew that the English had no more inkling of the shady paths that my agents and I had been pursuing in New York, and I believed that I had saved the *Karlsruhe* from the guns of the British battleships. It had been a good evening. Next morning all the king's horses could not have kept me in the place, and I left for New York as soon as I could." He subsequently reported that in spite of his efforts, the *Karlsruhe* was indeed sunk. But that fact clearly did not take away from him his sense of personal achievement.

On returning to New York, von Rintelen learned that the New York police had mistaken for him a waterfront alcoholic engaged in nothing more subversive than trading illegally in liquor and tobacco. He located the man, von Rintelen wrote, and paid him to keep the police busy while he resurrected his operation, now called the "Mexico North-Western Railway Company," with Weiser and the new bomb-making recruit, Robert Fay, who had arrived in New York just prior to von Rintelen's forced vacation.

Von Rintelen insisted in his book that Fay went out into New York Harbor under cover of night in a motorboat and attached his explosive devices to the rudders of two munitions-bearing vessels. At sea, von Rintelen said, the devices exploded, destroying both rudders, leaving one of the ships a drifting wreck in the Atlantic and requiring that the other be towed to port. After that, von Rintelen said, Fay had to be more careful and was obliged to swim out to the ships at night and fasten the devices.

"A number of further successes were recorded," von Rintelen wrote after the war,

> and numerous Allied shells failed to reach the guns for which they had been destined. With the help of Fay's new invention, which he used not only in New York but in other ports, we were able to give our undertaking a new turn. What the incendiary bombs could not achieve was reserved for Fay's machines.

American officials said later, however, that although Fay worked at assembling his devices in the garage in Weehawken from late April until late October, 1915, when he was arrested, they never could prove he actually put any of them on a ship's rudder. Fay himself said he had never put a single one of his rudder bombs in place. He bought and equipped the small motorboat to go out to the ships at anchor, he said, but he never received a go-ahead from his superiors in the German embassy, von Papen and Boy-Ed.*

Inspector Tunney, in a book about his experiences later, expressed his frustration at the time, not simply about Fay but about other unnamed saboteurs who took up Fay's work after his arrest:

> There was a maddening certainty about it all that suggested that every ship that left port must have nothing in her hold except hungry rats, parlor matches, oily waste and free kerosene. Never in the history of the port had so many marine fires occurred in a single year. Marine insurance was away up and our patience as away down. . . . The steamship companies put on special details of guards to watch the vessels from the moment they entered port until they sailed again. We resumed patrolling the river in various disguises. Fay's swift motorboat had disappeared but there were plenty of others, and the men of the Bomb Squad suffered real hardship in all sorts of inclement weather.

Not until October, 1917, six months after the American entry into the war, Tunney wrote, did his bomb squad make more arrests relating to the ship bombings.

In any event, the rapid growth in munitions traffic by now convinced von Rintelen that the piecemeal bombing of transports, however successful, could not keep pace. The American economy was booming on the strength of its trade with the Allies, boosted by the gradual loosening of the official United States policy against foreign loans to belligerents.

In August of 1915, Secretary of the Treasury William McAdoo, Wilson's son-in-law, pleaded with the president to make a clean break and permit all loans, if only for purely self-serving economic reasons. He called the original prohibition "most illogical and inconsistent," adding: "We approve and encourage sales of supplies to England and others but we disapprove the creation by them of credit balances here to finance their lawful and welcome purchases. . . . To maintain our

---

*Fay, convicted and sent to the federal penitentiary, escaped and was spirited out of the country with the assistance of Paul Koenig. Near the end of the war, in September, 1918, when it was clear Germany would be defeated, he turned himself in to the American consul in Spain. He offered to help the American military develop jet propulsion for ships and planes. "In the case of the aeroplane," he advised the Justice Department, "I propose to do away with the propeller altogether, using a reaction machine instead which results in very much higher pushing force per motor horsepower." His offer was ignored.

prosperity we must finance it. Otherwise it may stop and that would be disastrous."

Lansing, too, pressured the president to permit outright foreign loans. American exports for 1915 were going to outrun imports by $2.5 billion, he told Wilson, and if the Allies couldn't get the dollars to pay for what they wanted from America "they will have to stop buying and our present export trade will shrink proportionately. The result would be restriction of output, industrial depression, idle capital and idle labor, numerous failures, financial demoralization and general unrest and suffering among the laboring classes."

Besides, Lansing argued, obviously with a mind to Wilson's fixation on appearing to remain neutral, "popular sympathy has become crystallized in favor of one or another of the belligerents to such an extent that the purchase of bonds would in no way increase the bitterness of partisanship." The rationale worked; Wilson yielded and in October of 1915 a joint loan of $500 million was floated to the British and French.

Critics such as Harry Elmer Barnes later argued that such loans were responsible for the German decision to engage in unrestricted submarine warfare and, ultimately, American entry into the war. "By abandoning his neutral financial and industrial policy in favor of the Allies," Barnes wrote after the war, "President Wilson made it possible for the Entente Powers to enjoy an enormous advantage in getting war supplies. The only way for the Central Powers to overcome it was to resume unlimited submarine warfare and try to sweep from the seas the ships that were carrying these supplies to the Allies."

Von Rintelen, however, was not waiting for that development, or relying on it. As his next contribution to the fatherland's cause, he hit upon the idea of fomenting widespread strikes at American ports that would tie up the whole shipping industry. His ace card in this endeavor was the burning hostility toward the British of the Irish dock workers who constituted such a major share of the waterfront work force.

But a severe impediment to this scheme proved to be the American Federation of Labor and its president, Samuel Gompers, who was strongly pro-British and would stomach no strikes that might hurt the Allied war effort. Gompers also steadfastly resisted the efforts of some other trade union leaders who objected to the export by a neutral country of munitions. Strikes accordingly were short-lived, because Gompers controlled the strike funds without which no dock worker could long afford to be idle.

"An idea occurred to me," von Rintelen wrote later,

> which struck me at first as being fantastic, and that was to found my own "union." A union which was properly registered could proclaim a legal strike, and the law could not interfere. If, in addition, we could pay strike benefits, it might be possible to achieve something, and I certainly had the money to do so.

Knowing he could not lay his cards on the table, von Rintelen posed as a wealthy American humanitarian. He sought out several lower-echelon labor leaders of Irish and German extraction and socialist bent who "held the point of view that it could not be in the interest of the workers in other countries to supply munitions with which their brothers were to be shot down." He added a good mix of neutralist and pacifist members of Congress, lawyers, professors and theologians and guided them all unobtrusively into the formation of a new union, called "Labor's National Peace Council."

The effort appeared doomed until a group of Irish stevedores, some of whom had joined the fledgling union, initiated a wildcat strike against loading a ship with munitions bound for Russia. They struck because they were refused hazardous pay and because the ship was guarded by armed British. Weiser at von Rintelen's order withdrew large sums of money from German accounts and began to pay strike benefits, leading to a temporary rush of dock workers to join the union and then strike.

The scheme made considerable headway, and along with it there developed a strong lobbying effort for arms embargo legislation. But munitions makers backed counterefforts by Gompers and the AFL, and suspicions of German involvement rose. Von Rintelen's venture into union organizing eventually crumbled.

Not to be deterred for long, the ambitious von Rintelen next turned to a brazen foreign-affairs gambit that he calculated could draw American munitions away from Allied hands. In Mexico, Pancho Villa was still challenging the rule of Venustiano Carranza, and the deposed Victoriano Huerta was still nursing his ambition to return to power —two vexing distractions for Wilson.

Learning that Huerta was in New York to raise money for his comeback, von Rintelen boldly confronted him in the lobby of the Manhattan Hotel. They discussed a deal: German U-boats would land weapons along the Mexican coast, loans would be provided for their purchase, and as soon as Huerta had matters in hand he would attack the United States. Like many of von Rintelen's other extravagant schemes, however, this one proved to be all bluster and amounted to nought. So much for the German-Mexican connection—until more than a year later, when a somewhat similar German initiative at a much higher, more responsible level came to have an infinitely greater effect on German–United States relations.

Shortly after von Rintelen's Mexican caper fell through, he received an urgent phone call from Boy-Ed. "The Dark Invader" was being ordered home. By this time American agents were hot on his trail. Among other acts of carelessness and pomposity, he had told a young woman he met at a hotel in Maine during the summer that he was a secret German agent and in fact had planned—the sinking of the *Lusitania*!

The young woman, Anne Seward, happened to be acquainted with the new secretary of state, Lansing, and passed the boast on to him. Lansing in turn advised the president, who ordered an investigation. In doing so, however, Wilson cautioned that there be no public disclosure, lest the shaky ground of neutrality be further disturbed under his feet.

Returning to Germany again as Emile V. Gache of Switzerland aboard the Holland-America Line's *Noordam*, von Rintelen did not make it back. British naval intelligence, using the German code that had fallen into British hands, intercepted the cable calling him home, and when the ship called at Dover on August 13, 1915, British security men arrested him.

Still professing he was Swiss, von Rintelen was taken to Scotland Yard. There, Admiral "Blinker" Hall, the British naval intelligence chief, confronted him. Hall knew all about von Rintelen, having read most of the German cables discussing him that had passed between Berlin and Washington.

In a scene straight out of a "B" movie, Hall engaged von Rintelen in a casual conversation in English, then suddenly barked out a sharp order in German. Von Rintelen without thinking quickly snapped to attention, clicking his heels! Realizing that he had fallen for an incredibly old trick, he confessed, not without considerable pride and bombast, that he was indeed "The Dark Invader."

In December of this same year, 1915, the United States indicted von Rintelen for fomenting strikes in American munitions plants and the British eventually extradited him. He was tried, convicted and sent to the federal penitentiary in Atlanta until war's end.

For all of von Rintelen's exaggerations, boastings and failures, Berlin regarded him as a valuable operator. Two weeks after the United States entered the war, the German government through the Swiss offered to trade him for an American convicted by the Germans as a spy, one Siegfried Paul London. The United States refused.

Von Rintelen was not by any means, however, essential to the continuation of the German sabotage and disruption effort in America. Other individuals and other schemes were at hand to carry on the work, with comparable ingenuity and daring.

9. The Recall of von Papen and Boy-Ed

Around the time of von Rintelen's departure, the Germans undertook an exceedingly ambitious project, bankrolled sub rosa by Dr. Albert, the commercial attaché and sabotage paymaster. They set out to establish from scratch, without revealing German ownership, a complete munitions manufacturing plant. The plan was to buy up vital raw materials, manufacturing equipment and tools, then obtain armaments and powder contracts that would never be fulfilled, and pay unusually high wages in an effort to cause labor unrest and foment strikes among other munitions plants in the area.

The firm was called the Bridgeport Projectile Company, in Bridgeport, Connecticut. Buildings and factory workshops were constructed starting in April, 1915, with a target date for operations to begin in September. The scheme as conceived would deny other, bona fide munitions plants the materials they needed as well as the orders they sought and, in the process, create severe labor headaches. It was a plan audacious in its concept and objectives. But it failed, ironically, as a result of a bizarre case of absentmindedness on the part of its architect and bankroller, Dr. Albert.

On the warm Saturday afternoon of July 24, 1915, George Sylvester Viereck, editor of the *Fatherland*—a notoriously pro-German publication—and a man under suspicion as a violater of American neutrality laws, walked into the Lower Manhattan offices of the Hamburg-Amerika Line at 45 Broadway. A Secret Service agent named W. H. Houghton was tailing him and another agent named Frank Burke joined in the stakeout.

In midafternoon, Viereck came out with none other than Dr. Albert. The two of them walked to nearby Rector Street and boarded the Sixth Avenue elevated train—with Houghton and Burke discreetly behind. Viereck got off at the Thirty-third Street stop, with Houghton following. Burke stayed on, keeping an eye on Albert, who was toting a large portfolio.

In the humid afternoon and close quarters of the train, Albert dozed off. As the train jerked to a halt at Fiftieth Street, he woke with a start. Seeing that he was at his stop, he jumped up and dashed off the train—leaving his portfolio behind.

Realizing at once what he had done, Albert turned and raced back into the car before the doors closed. But the briefcase was gone. Burke, having seen the German embassy official depart hurriedly and leave the portfolio on the seat, had grabbed it and dashed off himself, hopping a streetcar before Albert could catch up with him.

Burke immediately notified his superior, William Flynn, who took one look at the papers in the briefcase and called his boss, Secretary of the Treasury McAdoo. McAdoo ordered Flynn to bring him the portfolio at once. When he saw its contents, he in turn took the papers to the president, who instructed him to consult Lansing and House on what to do with them.

The decision was a sticky one; the United States did not want to acknowledge that a government agent had seized the private papers of a fully accredited diplomat. So House suggested the next best thing. McAdoo slipped the documents to Frank Cobb, editor of the *New York World*. The paper promptly published a series of embarrassing stories spelling out the best of Albert's schemes—including the creation of the ersatz Bridgeport Projectile Company, fully detailed in his papers.

The stories themselves created a sensation, as well as profound ridicule of Albert. He henceforth became known in Washington's diplomatic salons and in public print as "the minister without portfolio." Still, the evidence was not deemed substantial enough for Washington to demand his recall or von Bernstorff's, although McAdoo favored that step. Wilson continued to avoid at all costs any incidents or actions that might push him out of his neutral posture and into the war. The episode did, however, cast a veil of suspicion over the German ambassador.

"I do not feel that Bernstorff is dealing frankly with us somehow," Wilson wrote House a few days after Albert's portfolio was seized. Under the circumstances, Wilson's remark was, to say the least, a prize of understatement. Nevertheless, von Bernstorff in his official capacity and functions pressed on in his determination to keep Wilson on his chosen, neutral course. And the State Department and the president continued to deal with him with all the correct protocol that his position commanded.

That correctness of protocol, however, was undergoing strain for other reasons. Only a month after the third Wilson note on the *Lusitania*, a German U-boat sank another British passenger liner, the westbound 16,000-ton White Star *Arabic*. Forty-four persons, including two Americans, perished off the south coast of Ireland.

The submarine's commander claimed he had mistaken the liner for a 5,000-ton cargo ship. Only four days earlier, he said, he had been fired upon by such a vessel and he assumed the *Arabic* was the same menacing armed ship. But if this act was not "deliberately unfriendly," it seemed, none was. How an experienced submarine commander could fail to distinguish between a cargo ship and a liner three times as large was incomprehensible.

Still, amazingly, Wilson waffled. He declined even to call a cabinet meeting, and two days after the sinking he wrote to House:

> I greatly need your advice what to do in view of the sinking of the *Arabic*, if it turns out to be the simple case it seems. . . . Two things are plain to me: one, the people of this country count on me to keep them out of the war; two, it would be a calamity to the world at large if we should be drawn actively into the conflict and so deprived of all disinterested influence over the settlement.

Wilson added that he felt he must write to the British suggesting they rescind their food blockade. House was aghast at the indecisiveness of his friend. "I am surprised at the attitude he takes," he wrote in a diary. "He evidently will go to great lengths to avoid war." House sent the president this prodding reply:

> Our people do not want war, but even less do they want to recede from the position you have taken. Neither do they want to shirk the responsibility which should be ours. Your first note to Germany after the sinking of the *Lusitania* made you not only the first citizen of America, but the first citizen of the world. If by any word or act you should hurt our pride of nationality, you would lose your commanding position overnight. Further notes would disappoint our own people and would cause something of derision abroad. In view of what has been said and in view of what has been done it is clearly up to this government to act. The question is when and how?

Von Bernstorff was equally distressed that the careless free-lancing of a single U-boat commander might undo his diligent efforts to keep

America out of the war. He encouraged the State Department to send a note to Berlin urging once again a complete abandonment of German submarine warfare and promising that the United States would enter negotiations with the British to lift their blockade.

But Berlin needed no such bait; the Foreign Office was equally chagrined at the *Arabic* sinking. It fanned von Bethmann-Hollweg's suspicions that the German navy was guilty of insubordination toward the political authority. "Unhappily, it depends on the attitude of a single submarine commander," the chancellor wrote chidingly to the chief of the German naval cabinet, "whether America will or will not declare war."

If the German navy felt the benefits of unrestricted submarine warfare were worth the risk of American entry into the war, the German army clearly did not. General von Falkenhayn, then planning an offensive against Serbia, wrote:

> There can be no more doubt that our enemies, after realizing that they cannot defeat Germany with weapons, will now try to reach their goal by a war of exhaustion. It will be up to us to prevent this with military measures. . . . At any rate, our situation is so serious that it would be irresponsible to make it worse. An open allying of the United States on the side of our enemies would mean just such a worsening, and a very serious worsening, indeed. . . .
>
> In order to break this war of exhaustion, we need the help of the neutrals. If, therefore, the responsible leader of German policy makes demands regarding the conduct of submarine war in order to maintain peace with the United States, then according to my conviction there is no other choice but to oblige him unless one could prove that the assumption that the United States would go to war was wrong.

Von Bernstorff accordingly was ordered to pursue the American proposal: an end to the submarine war in exchange for the abandonment by the British of their "starvation blockade." And while Berlin felt it could not say flatly the commander who sank the *Arabic* had knowingly acted against orders, von Bethmann-Hollweg instructed von Bernstorff to advise Lansing confidentially that secret orders had gone to U-boat commanders that passenger ships were not to be attacked without warning.

Von Bernstorff did so, but Lansing insisted that the statement be made public, and on his own, the ambassador agreed. He gave Lansing a text that came to be called "the *Arabic* pledge," and Lansing released it on September 1, 1915.

It said: "Liners will not be sunk by our submarines without warning and without safety of the lives of non-combatants, provided that the liners do not try to escape or offer resistance." There was no reference to the negotiations with the British on their blockade, and so the pledge was hailed as a diplomatic triumph for the relentless Wilson.

The cheering, however, was premature. Berlin dragged its feet on a specific admission or disavowal of responsibility for the *Arabic* sinking. On September 4, 1915, the bubble burst with the torpedoing without warning of the British liner *Hesperian*, killing eight persons. One American crew member was aboard but was unhurt.

Berlin immediately insisted no U-boat had been operating in the area, though later—after the war—a German commander reported he had attacked the ship under the impression it was an auxiliary cruiser, since it had a six-inch gun mounted astern. The commander was Captain Walter Schwieger, who four months earlier in the same submarine, U-20, had sent the *Lusitania* to its watery grave.

To make matters even worse, just two days after the *Hesperian* went down, there surfaced a sensational development directly tying the Central Powers, and by clear implication von Papen, to disruptions of the American munitions industry.

On the very night of the *Arabic* torpedoing, von Bernstorff was dining on the roof terrace of the Ritz-Carlton in New York with Dr. Constantin Dumba, the Austro-Hungarian ambassador to the United States, and an American journalist of open German sympathies named James J. Archibald. Archibald was planning a trip to Europe and during the evening Dumba handed him a packet of documents to take to Vienna for him.

It so happened that among the waiters in the restaurant was a Bohemian of strong anti-German sentiments. He overheard the conversation and, witnessing the transfer between Dumba and Archibald, he notified the American authorities. They in turn cabled the British in London.

Eleven days later the Dutch ship on which Archibald was sailing stopped at Falmouth, England. The British promptly arrested him on charges of functioning as an enemy courier. Among the documents seized was a memorandum from Vienna to Dumba outlining a plan for bribing and agitating workers at American munitions plants, fomenting strikes and otherwise undercutting production.

Attached to the memo was a copy of a letter from Dumba to the Austrian foreign minister advising him of good prospects for such a plan at Bethlehem Steel plants around the country and at others in the Midwest—and that the German military attaché, von Papen, was highly enthusiastic and encouraging.

There were other embarrassing letters in the seized packet as well. One from Dumba denigrated Wilson and another from von Papen to his wife made less than diplomatic references to his host country. Commenting on the progress of the war against the Russians, von Papen wrote: "How splendid on the Eastern Front! I always say to these idiotic Yankees that they should shut their mouths and better still be full of admiration for all that heroism."

On September 6, 1915, Wilson demanded Dumba's recall "by reason of the admitted purpose and intent of Ambassador Dumba to conspire to cripple legitimate industries of the people of the United States and to interrupt their legitimate trade." The president also protested "the flagrant diplomatic impropriety in employing an American citizen protected by an American passport as a secret bearer of official despatches through the lines of the enemy of Austria-Hungary."

Wilson wanted to recall von Papen and von Bernstorff as well but the State Department felt there were insufficient provable grounds. Instead they stepped up surveillance on von Papen and Boy-Ed. Von Bernstorff, so importantly involved in the peace maneuvers of Wilson and House, again was spared.

Von Papen not surprisingly became a target of public ridicule in the United States. That fact, however, did not stop him in his supreme arrogance from traveling openly, generating local press attention wherever he went. A German acquaintance wrote Boy-Ed later about encountering von Papen and a companion at Yellowstone National Park and in Denver, dodging the inevitable questions about his "idiotic Yankees" remark. He wrote:

> The reporters from San Francisco, instructed to do so, had sworn to compel Papen to an utterance, and followed the two gentlemen everywhere. Both held newspapers in front of their

faces in order not to be snapshotted, and a whole series of laugh-
able photographs resulted, which circulated through the States.
On papers held up in front of them appeared printed in German, "Wir haben nichts zu sagen" (We have nothing to say). A
mad comedy at our expense!

Meanwhile, the acts of sabotage continued on land and at sea.
Explosions occurred at plants in Wilmington; Trenton; Eddystone,
Pennsylvania; at several Bethlehem Steel factories. At least a dozen
more ships caught fire at sea under mysterious circumstances. In several other cases unexploded bombs were found on contraband-laden
ships or under their piers, and a train loaded with dynamite was
blown up at Pinole, California. Von Rintelen was long gone by now,
but the work for the fatherland was being carried on effectively by
Paul Koenig, Paul Hilken, Frederick Hinsch and other loyal agents of
von Papen and Boy-Ed.

Among the more bizarre activities was another assignment given to
Edward Felton, the black stevedores' foreman from Baltimore who
had been helping Hinsch incite dock strikes and plant "egg bombs"
on munitions-bearing ships. Hinsch called Felton to New York in the
late summer or early fall of 1915 and enlisted him in a revival of the
scheme to inoculate Europe-bound horses with glanders and anthrax
bacilli. Hinsch dispatched Felton to Van Cortlandt Park north of Manhattan, where a great number of the horses were penned in. Felton
later described the operation this way:

> The germs were given to me by Captain Hinsch in glass bot-
> tles about an inch and a half or two inches long, and three-
> quarters of an inch in diameter, with a cork stopper. The bottles
> were usually contained in a round wooden box with a lid that
> screwed on the top. There was cotton in the top and bottom to
> protect the bottles from breaking. A piece of steel in the form of
> a needle with a sharp point was stuck in the underside of the
> cork, and the steel needle extended down in the liquid where
> the germs were. We used rubber gloves and would put the germs
> in the horses by pulling out the stopper and jabbing the horses
> with the sharp point of the needle that had been down among
> the germs. We did a good bit of the work by walking along the
> fences that enclosed the horses and jabbing them when they
> would come up along the fence or lean over where we could get

at them. We also spread the germs sometimes on their food and in the water that they were drinking.

Captain Hinsch gave me the instructions as to where I would find the horses and also gave me the bottles of germs and the money [to pay his associates]. I used a good many of the same men on this work that I did in starting the fires. I had about ten or twelve men working on these matters with me. We would work at it sometimes at night and sometimes in the daytime. A good many of the men were also doing other work and they made this extra money on the side. Captain Hinsch was accustomed to giving me brown paper bags filled with these tubes and with the fire things. . . . Captain Hinsch spoke often when I met him of different fires that had occurred and of outbreaks of disease among horses and would make remarks about how well things were going.

Meanwhile in New York, Koenig enlisted the covert services of a German reservist named Frederick Schleindl, a clerk at the National City Bank in New York, heavily engaged in contracts between American manufacturers and the Allies. Every night from May to December of 1915, Koenig or an associate would meet secretly with Schleindl and obtain from him the day's traffic in cables and letters, revealing what goods were being transported and by what method. Schleindl would replace the papers each morning before the bank opened for business.

Not satisfied with the results he was achieving in the United States, Koenig continued to consider targets in Canada, including the Welland Canal. In September of 1915 Koenig and his wife went to Niagara Falls, where he recruited a distant relative named George Fuchs to spy on the canal. Fuchs later moved to New York and became a Koenig agent for the magnificent sum of eighteen dollars a week. But Fuchs was a heavy drinker and Koenig fired him after a disagreement over an expense account item of less than three dollars.

Koenig would have been wise to pay him out of petty cash. New York police were tapping Koenig's phone by now and they picked up the name of the estranged Fuchs, who confessed in mid-December of 1915 and implicated Koenig. When police arrested Koenig they found in his room the black looseleaf memo book meticulously chronicling all of his agents' assignments, right up to the previous day, and marking those in which destructions were to be undertaken as "D-Cases."

The notebook was one of the most valuable pieces of evidence against the Germans seized up to this time. "A fanatic on office efficiency might have conceived it," Tunney wrote later, "but none but a German would have kept it posted up. For it told the story of his Bureau of Investigation with a devotion to detail almost religious."

Among those convicted in part as a result of having been listed in Koenig's notebook assigned to a "D-Case" was Werner Horn for the Vanceboro Bridge job in Maine. The book also helped finger Gustav Stahl, the man paid by Koenig to give a false affidavit that he had seen guns on the *Lusitania*.

Also arrested in the fall of 1915 was Robert Fay. He caused the German embassy even more trouble, because he explicitly identified von Papen as the man behind his bomb manufacturing. On top of the reference to the military attaché in the Dumba papers, Fay's confession was the last straw for Wilson, and for American public opinion.

On December 1, Lansing summoned von Bernstorff to the State Department. The secretary of state told the German ambassador that the President of the United States considered Captains Franz von Papen and Karl Boy-Ed personae non gratae, and demanded their recall.

Although these two men were von Bernstorff's two top agents in the sabotage activity, the ambassador himself again dodged the bullet. As he wrote later:

> On the day Secretary of State Lansing requested me to call upon him to take up with me the question of the request to have both Messrs. von Papen and Boy-Ed recalled, I at once put the question to him whether I was in any way compromised by the acts attributed to these two gentlemen. I stated that if the American Government was of the opinion that I had been compromised by these dealings, I would at once request my Government to recall me, since it was impossible for an ambassador to remain at his post who did not have the confidence of the government to which he was accredited.
>
> Secretary of State Lansing gave me the following categorical answer: "You are in no way included in this episode, and we should look upon it with extreme regret were you to leave us,

because you are at present entrusted with these important negotiations." This announcement of Secretary Lansing's was reiterated to me by Colonel House two days later in still more emphatic terms.

Von Bernstorff added concerning his relationship with von Papen and Boy-Ed: "They operated completely on their own responsibility during the war; they were not authorized to apply to the embassy for money but had their own funds. . . . Similar relations were the general rule for, in the course of my diplomatic experience of many years, I have on numerous occasions come into contact with a situation where military attachés were recalled by their government on account of espionage or similar reasons and where, by no possibility, would anyone have dreamed of connecting the ambassadors with the matter in question." Good old deniability again.

Astonishingly, the State Department seemed to buy von Bernstorff's complete disavowal of involvement. Addressing Congress several days later, Wilson confessed that the United States had been remarkably gullible in dealing with the sabotage threat, and now needed to take legislative action to deal with it.

The president particularly castigated German-Americans who assisted in the intrigues:

> I am sorry to say that the gravest threats against our national peace and safety have been uttered within our own borders. There are citizens of the United States . . . who have poured the poison of disloyalty into the very arteries of our national life; who have sought to bring the authority and good name of our government into contempt, to destroy our industries wherever they thought it effective for their vindictive purposes to strike at them, and to debase our politics to the uses of foreign intrigue.
>
> Their number is not great as compared with the whole number of those sturdy hosts by which our nation has been enriched in recent generations out of virile foreign stocks. But it is great enough to have brought deep disgrace upon us and to have made it necessary that we should promptly make use of processes of law by which we may be purged of their corrupt distempers. A little while ago such a thing would have seemed incredible. Because it was incredible, we made no preparation for it. We would have been almost ashamed to prepare for it as if we were

suspicious of ourselves and our comrades and neighbors. But the ugly and incredible thing has actually come to pass and we are without adequate federal laws to deal with it. I urge you to enact such laws at the earliest possible moment and feel that in doing so I am urging you to do nothing less than save the honor and self-respect of the nation.

Wilson, indeed, seemed more outraged at the cooperation of German-Americans with von Papen and Boy-Ed than at the conduct of the two diplomats who had used their official positions as a cover for their illegal activities and as a shield against American prosecution.

There are some men among us and many resident abroad who, though born and bred in the United States and calling themselves Americans, have so forgotten themselves and their honor as citizens as to put their passionate sympathy with one or the other side in the great European conflict above their regard for the peace and dignity of the United States. They also preach and practice disloyalty. No laws, I suppose, can reach corruptions of the heart; but I should not speak of others without also speaking of these and expressing the even deeper humiliation and scorn which every self-possessed and thoughtfully patriotic American must feel when he thinks of them and of the discredit they are daily bringing upon us.*

Berlin categorically denied any culpability in the deeds to which Wilson referred. An official note said:

Apparently the enemies of Germany have succeeded in creating the impression that the German government is in some way morally or otherwise responsible for what Mr. Wilson has characterized as anti-American activities . . . attacks upon property and violations of the rules which the American government has seen fit to impose upon the course of neutral trade. This the German government absolutely denies.

It cannot specifically repudiate acts committed by individuals over whom it has no control, and of whose movements and inten-

---

*German-Americans were not the only persons who were the focus of suspicion, or vengeance, in the outbreak of disruptions to the manufacture of munitions. When a DuPont plant in Hopewell, Virginia, was wracked by explosions and fire on December 10, 1915, a black workman was summarily lynched.

tions it is neither officially nor unofficially informed. It can only say . . . that whoever is guilty of conduct tending to associate the German cause with lawlessness of thought, suggestion, or deed against life, property and order in the United States is in fact an enemy of that very cause, and a source of embarrassment to the German government. . . .

For all that, however, there was ample evidence of the sort of collaboration by American sympathizers with the Central Powers to which Wilson referred. One example was a letter, found later among the papers of von Papen and his deputy, von Igel, sent to von Papen from one Otto B. Block in Shippensburg, Pennsylvania, dated August 14, 1915. It read:

Your Excellency: I trust that my frequent communications are not looked upon as an intrusion or imposition. I assure you they are prompted by the thought of doing at least a little, for the country of my birth, Austria, and her brave partner, Germany.

I have noticed of late that quite a large number of cars, marked explosive, pass over the Cumberland Valley Railroad in a southern direction. The number of such is so unusually large that the thought occurred to me that ammunition may be sent from the various manufacturers over this course to Southern seaports, rather than by way of New York, Philadelphia or Boston, and may be shipped through steamers from the Southern ports, over a southern sea route, by way of Spain or the Mediterranean, in order to easier escape our submarines or other war craft. If the suggestion is of any material benefit to you or not, I do not know, but it is given with the best of wishes for His Royal Majesties Emperor William I [*sic*] and Emperor Francis Joseph I, and his people.

I further learn that the same firm which I called to your attention in my recent communications is about to manufacture shrapnel for the Allies, but at this point I am without any further particulars. If at any time I can be of service to you, I shall be only too glad to do all in my power. Very sincerely yours.

For all of Wilson's harsh rhetoric to the contrary concerning von Papen, Boy-Ed and German sympathizers in the United States, the president remained at the end of 1915 in basically the same posture as when the year started—determined to remain neutral and out of the war. To those in the American government who were intimately aware of the mountain of evidence now chronicling German duplicity, Wilson's attitude was both unfathomable and maddening. His idealism and his desire to play the unbiased referee, they felt, could only be sustained for so long when one side was behaving so contemptuously toward him. Yet with the matter of satisfaction for the *Lusitania* sinking still unsettled, and with other incidents testing the durability of American neutrality, the president still clung to his course.

Shortly after the Germans gave the "*Arabic* pledge," another liner, the Italian 8,000-ton *Ancona*, was sunk with nine Americans perishing. According to witnesses, the commander surfaced his submarine and, giving the crew and passengers no time to escape, opened fire. The surfacing submarine flew the Austrian flag.

Lansing, adopting with Wilson's approval a tougher posture toward Vienna than was customary against Berlin, threatened a break in diplomatic relations with Austria and hence an end to American neutrality. Vienna, as aware as Berlin was of Wilson's great reluctance to take that step, stalled for more than a month. In the end, however, she accepted liability and pledged indemnification.

Von Bernstorff for his part was not unhappy at this capitulation by his Austro-Hungarian ally. He had feared an American diplomatic break with Vienna would inevitably lead to a similar break with Berlin. As for Wilson, he particularly welcomed Vienna's answer because this latest crisis had come at a most unpropitious time for him personally.

On December 18, 1915, the president married Edith Galt at a small evening ceremony in the White House and they went off to Hot Springs, Virginia, on their honeymoon. There continued to be talk about the short interval between the passing of the first Mrs. Wilson and the president's marriage to the second. But those closest to him, such as Colonel House and Dr. Grayson, knew the heavy toll that loneliness had extracted from him as a widower. In the year ahead, they also knew, he would need all the support and companionship he could get as he sought to maintain his pledge to keep the country out of war—a pledge that would become the centerpiece of his 1916 campaign for reelection.

It was a promise Woodrow Wilson had made to himself as well as to the American people, but no one hoped he would be able to deliver on it more than did Count Johann von Bernstorff. Wilson, in fact, in a most ironic way was von Bernstorff's best ally in this regard. No matter what Germany did that the German ambassador feared would push Wilson over the edge—most notably the continuing U-boat outrages—the president clung to the precipice.

Still, von Bernstorff could not count on Wilson's neutrality-at-all-costs determination forever. If there were more serious breaches of security of the sort that had just sent von Papen and Boy-Ed packing, and more sinkings costing more American lives, Wilson might well at last be forced into breaking his promise to keep America out of the war. That in turn would mean, von Bernstorff fully believed, ultimate defeat for Germany.

And so the German ambassador approached 1916 like a man on a tightrope. He continued to walk a taut, shaky line between the legalities of his official diplomatic duties and the illegalities of the shadow world of sabotage that constituted his dual mission in America—all the while depending on Wilson's seemingly inexhaustible patience.

10. More Talk, More Trouble

Although the end of 1915 brought the indictments of von Rintelen and Koenig and the recall of von Papen and Boy-Ed, these actions did not come before the Germans had chalked up another six months of successful sabotage. From August, 1915, through the end of the year, at least thirteen more ships caught fire or suffered explosions at sea. A like number of mysterious blasts damaged or destroyed munitions and powder plants at Trenton, Carney's Point and Gibbstown, New Jersey; Turtle Creek, Eddystone and Callery Junction, Pennsylvania; Wilmington (twice) and several Bethlehem Steel Company plants in the East.

Von Papen and Boy-Ed each sailed for home still vowing innocence. "I leave my post with no bitterness," von Papen said, "because I know too well that when history is once written it will stand by our clean record despite all mispresentations and calumnies spread and broadcast at present." And Boy-Ed: "Of course I refrain at the hour of my departure from again refuting all the stories which were told about me in the American newspapers." Most of them, he said, "were invented" by the press.

But von Papen's carelessness quickly provided evidence that disproved his protestations. Granted along with Boy-Ed personal safe conduct back to Germany under diplomatic protocol, von Papen either naively or stupidly assumed that the safe conduct extended to his papers as well. He methodically packed them in a trunk and took them with him.

When his ship reached Falmouth, British authorities seized the papers. They immediately confirmed many of the activities of von Rintelen, then under arrest at Donington Hall, a British detention center, and other saboteurs and spies. Von Rintelen later described von Papen's blunder with scathing sarcasm and bitterness in his own book:

> His training in diplomacy misled him once more: whilst traveling, for his own all-important person, under British "safe con-

duct," his trunks did not; and they were unkind enough in
Falmouth to send to Whitehall whatever letters, codes, copies,
documents, counterfoils the enlightened diplomat saw fit to carry
across the seas. The results were: a trail of ruin and misery for
dozens and dozens of Germans and others in America sympathetic to the German cause; and a foaming with rage on the part
of untold men interned in England, of the two hundred officers
interned in Donington Hall. . . .

This incident—by far more serious than Geheimrat Albert's
nap in the New York "Elevated". . . was soon to prove, for me
personally, nothing short of a disaster. Whatever links were still
missing, where proof or at least alleged proof was required by
the American authorities to bring me and my helpmates to trial,
Papen had been graciously pleased to furnish them!

Among the papers seized were von Papen's checkbooks listing in
detail the various receipts and payments made to agents for acts of
sabotage. These included von der Goltz' aborted Welland Canal caper,
Horn's plot against the Vanceboro Bridge and von Rintelen's elaborate
network for the manufacture and planting of bombs on munitions-
carrying ships. It was determined in time that von Papen had received
more than three million dollars from his embassy colleague, Dr.
Albert, for such purposes. Von der Goltz subsequently confessed in
Scotland Yard that von Papen was directly involved in the arrangements to obtain the dynamite he transported to Niagara Falls for the
Welland Canal job.

Although the capture of von Papen's documents set off a furor
within the intelligence communities of both belligerent camps, he
and Boy-Ed received decorations and promotions on their return to
Berlin. Boy-Ed was assigned to the admiralty staff and von Papen to
an important military post in Palestine.

Albert, "the minister without portfolio," writing to his wife shortly
after von Papen's letters and checkbooks were seized, told her of a
newspaper editorial that

> speaks of "bovine stupidity." This of course is the way they
> get even for the "idiotic Yankees" [of von Papen's letter], which
> they curiously enough have not got over yet.
>
> People here have a crazy touchiness which for my part I utterly
> fail to comprehend. I for instance do not feel at all insulted at

"bovine stupidity." I am obliged rather to admit frankly that this reproach is not so entirely unjustified, applying not to von Papen alone but myself too. For no matter how valid [the] excuses you may give for the disappearance of a briefcase or a few carrying letters which get seized, it is the result after all which determines and marks such things as "bovine stupidity." So what's the use of being touchy? This excitement will calm down too and be as quickly forgotten as all the rest.

Von Papen's papers, while creating a furor in the United States, did nothing to deter Section 3B, the German intelligence headquarters in Berlin, from pressing on with new agents and new sabotage schemes and devices for use in America.

In the first days of 1916, Paul Hilken, the Baltimore representative of the North German Lloyd Line now also functioning as a sabotage paymaster, was called to the Bremen headquarters of the firm. He was summoned ostensibly to discuss a plan to launch a commercial submarine run between Germany and the United States as a limited means of combating the British blockade. The plan was to employ the U-boat *Deutschland* to carry vital foodstuffs and raw materials from the port of Baltimore back to Germany.

After conferring with his superiors in Bremen, Hilken went on to Berlin to arrange for the necessary credits to buy the materials, and there he encountered the just-returned von Papen. It was determined that Hilken could play a larger role in the sabotage work beyond bankrolling his Baltimore colleague Frederick Hinsch.

At a meeting at the Section 3B headquarters in early February, Hilken met Anton Dilger, the man who was manufacturing glanders and anthrax germs for Hinsch's horse-inoculation project, and Fred Herrmann, a twenty-year-old Brooklyn-born son of a naturalized American father from Germany. It was a meeting that in time would be crucial in the postwar legal wrangle over German responsibility for sabotage against neutral America.

Dilger was an American-educated surgeon who had specialized in wound surgery at Johns Hopkins University. To obtain field experience, he volunteered as an army surgeon during the Balkan wars and then joined the German army at the outbreak of the Great War. He was assigned to an army hospital in Karlsruhe that was severely bombed in an air raid by the French. Many children were killed and wounded and Dilger suffered a nervous breakdown in the experience. He was sent to the United States to recuperate at the country home of his parents at Front Royal, Virginia.

At his government's instruction, Dilger took with him strains of anthrax and glanders germs—code-named "E and B cultures"—to begin the horse-inoculation project. Eventually Dilger and a brother, Carl, opened what came to be known inside the German sabotage operation as "Tony's Lab" in the Washington, D.C., subdivision of Chevy Chase. Periodically, one or the other of the Dilger brothers would deliver tubes of the germs to Hinsch at the Hansa Haus at Charles and Redwood Streets in Baltimore, a quaint Old-World structure whose third-floor attic served as the sabotage operations headquarters.

As new cultures of the germs were developed in Germany, they were sent to Dilger to manufacture, using couriers such as von Rintelen traveling on neutral ships with phony passports or, when the *Deutschland* went into service, as part of her westbound cargo. Dilger later went to St. Louis to establish a second lab there for the inoculation of Europe-bound horses and mules raised in the Western states. But the plan was abandoned when it was found that the St. Louis winter was so severe that the germs could not survive exposure to the cold.

The second man Hilken met at Section 3B in Berlin, Fred Herrmann, had been recruited into intelligence work by a German agent aboard ship as he was on his way to Europe to visit his grandmother. Herrmann first served in Scotland as an observer of British naval ship movements at Scapa Flow but was discovered and deported. Two directors of Section 3B, Captains Rudolf Nadolny and Hans Marguerre, now discussed with the visitors the progress of the sabotage campaign in America and persuaded young Herrmann to go back to the United States with Dilger. This meeting among Nadolny, Marguerre, Hilken, Herrmann and Dilger also would take on much greater significance in the case against German sabotage after the war, when Berlin insisted steadfastly that any sabotage plans discussed were meant to be carried out only if and when the United States became a belligerent.

Herrmann was a daring and adventurous fellow who fancied himself a soldier of fortune. He bragged later about performing surgery with a penknife on a fellow spy and saboteur who suffered acute appendicitis while they were fleeing from the enemy across a barren desert in Mexico. A proclivity for such stories did not earn him the best reputation for truthfulness, but he was a dependable operative.

The directors of Section 3B wanted Herrmann to smuggle into the United States a new device that would soon greatly simplify and facilitate the sabotage campaign in America. It was a very thin glass tube divided into two chambers. One was filled with sulphuric acid and the other with chlorate of potash and sugar.

One of the Section 3B officers took an ordinary lead pencil and, by soaking it in water and splitting it in half lengthwise, easily drew out the long, narrow piece of lead and replaced it with the glass tube. Then he simply snapped the pencil in two as a schoolboy might do in a moment of frustration at a difficult mathematics problem. The action caused the two components to mix and immediately a brilliant, hot flame shot out—an ideal, harmless-looking and easily concealed incendiary device for German agents in America. Some were made small enough, Edwin Herrmann, Fred Herrmann's brother, testified later, "for a man to carry into a factory concealed under his tongue and even to swallow if necessary."

Hilken, Dilger and Herrmann all were duly impressed by this new weapon and Herrmann readily agreed to take the first batch with him. Hilken completed his arrangements for receiving the *Deutschland* in Baltimore and buying cargo for it, and all three men returned to the United States. Dilger went back to his germ-manufacturing lab; Hilken established a new firm, the Eastern Forwarding Company, to handle the commercial U-boat's business and to acquire its outgoing cargo of nickel, rubber and tin.

Captain Hinsch, needing a better cover for his various sabotage activities, was assigned to act as a sort of port manager and overseer of the submarine when it came to Baltimore. When Herrmann and Hilken got back there, Hilken introduced Herrmann to Hinsch and Herrmann then went on to Washington, where he helped Dilger make the incendiary "pencils"—also called "glasses" or "tubes." These new devices proved to be much more practical for the work assigned than the old lumpy bombs that were variously called "eggs," "coal," or "dumplings."

Much later, after the war, Herrmann confessed that he and Hinsch drew up a long list of preferential targets for their work and then divided them up. On his own list, he said, was a very large shell assembly plant at Kingsland, New Jersey, about ten miles from the piers along New York Harbor. On Hinsch's list, Herrmann said, was the major storage and loading terminal for Europe-bound munitions in the country, a promontory in the harbor known as Black Tom Island.

As the new recruits and new sabotage devices from Section 3B were pressed into service to undercut American munitions traffic to the Allies, Wilson blissfully continued to pursue the will-o'-the-wisp of peace as if the latest disclosures of German complicity had not occurred.

Right after the first of the year, he sent Colonel House on yet another of his exploratory trips to London, Paris and Berlin. House had come up with a new approach: Wilson would call a peace conference and if either side refused to participate, the United States would enter the war in support of the other. The scheme was clearly designed to force Germany to the conference table, because early conversations with the British and French indicated they would attend. The idea, in fact, eventually became the subject of a celebrated memorandum between House and Sir Edward Grey, the British foreign secretary.

Meanwhile, Lansing proposed to Wilson a modus vivendi he hoped might produce a solution to Germany's submarine warfare against armed merchant ships that threatened American travelers and hence American neutrality. Lansing suggested that Berlin be asked to agree that its U-boats would not torpedo merchant ships without warning, on the condition that the Allies agreed to disarm such ships. Wilson embraced the idea quickly.

At the same time, the president could not still the growing demand in the country for preparedness. He could not seriously refute the allegations that the United States was ill-prepared for war if it did come. But he acquiesced to a military buildup essentially on grounds of the need to protect American commercial rights, especially on the seas. He told the opening of the new session of Congress:

> The urgent question of our mercantile and passenger shipping is closely connected with the problem of national supply. The full development of our national industries, which is of such vital importance to the nation, pressingly calls for a large commercial fleet. It is high time to make good our deficiencies . . . and to restore the independence of our commerce on the high seas.

Wilson also called for an increase in the army and the navy, insisting as he did that the purpose was defensive only. In late January, he undertook a swing from New York to Pittsburgh, Des Moines, Milwaukee and Kansas City delivering a series of preparedness speeches. The country needed to be ready, he said in Pittsburgh, "not for war, not for anything that smacks in the least of aggression, but for adequate national defense." He professed to be amazed and chagrined that anyone would think he had anything but the restoration of world peace on his mind and his agenda. In Des Moines, he said:

> There are actually men in America who are preaching war, who are preaching the duty of the United States to do what it would never do before: seek the entanglement in the controversies which have arisen on the other side of the water, abandon its habitual and traditional policy and deliberately engage in the conflict that is now engulfing the rest of the world.
>
> I do not know what the standards of citizenship of these gentlemen may be. I know only that I for one cannot subscribe to those standards. I believe that I more truly speak the spirit of America when I say that that is a spirit of peace. Why, no voice has ever come to any public man more audibly, more unmistakably, than the voice of this great people has come to me, bearing this impressive lesson, "We are counting upon you to keep this country out of war."

In Milwaukee, Wilson pointedly reminded his audience that "so far I have done so, and I pledge you my word that, God helping me, I will if it is possible." Those words would in a short time become the theme of Wilson's 1916 campaign for reelection—and soon thereafter a haunting reminder of his failure. But public agitation for war, and incidents of German interference with American shipments of munitions to the Allies, clearly were not at this juncture going to shake his resolve to keep America neutral.

In that effort, Wilson continued to work and hope for an amicable resolution of the *Lusitania* matter. Von Bernstorff, wearing his diplomatic hat, which seemed none the worse for wear after the recall of his military attachés, was summoned again by Lansing and told that the president was not going to let the case die. The secretary of state on Wilson's behalf—but with more force and less flexibility than his superior preferred—pressed von Bernstorff to extract a note from

Berlin acknowledging the illegality of the attack and agreeing to indemnification.

But the German government, again embroiled in internal debate over lifting all restraints on submarine warfare, was not disposed to label illegal a policy it might soon embrace unrestrictedly. For a time it appeared that a diplomatic breach was at hand. In fact, Lansing so warned von Bernstorff explicitly, pointedly threatening an American declaration of war. As Lansing later wrote in his memoirs:

> The Ambassador seemed greatly perturbed and sat for several moments considering the situation. He finally said: "And what would be your course in case my government will not accede to these terms, which seem harsh?" I replied: "I see no other course, Mr. Ambassador, except to break off diplomatic relations." The Ambassador said: "I do not see how the matter could stop with the breaking off of diplomatic relations. It would go further than that." I replied: "Doubtless you are correct in this view."

Von Bernstorff agreed to forward to Berlin stiff proposed language recognizing illegality, admitting liability for it and agreeing to pay "a suitable indemnity." But Berlin would have none of it. Lansing was prepared to press on, but House from Europe counseled Wilson not to break relations and go to war over diplomatic language. If the country was to enter the conflict, he argued, better that the catalyst be an immediate incident engaging the public's passions than "over a nine-months-old issue and largely upon the wording of a suitable apology."

Wilson, repeatedly telling the American public on his speaking tour on preparedness that he was determined to stay out of the war, was in a receptive mood for House's counsel toward moderation and restraint. He ordered Lansing to seek agreement on softer language. In the end, von Bernstorff offered amendments in which Berlin, without acknowledging illegality in the sinking of a passenger liner, agreed that retaliation for the British blockade "must not aim at other than enemy subjects." "Assuming liability" in the *Lusitania* sinking, the Foreign Office stated, Germany would be willing to make reparations.

After more negotiations, Lansing finally called the Berlin note "acceptable but not satisfactory." At long last the *Lusitania* issue as a magnet for American entry into the war was desensitized—and Wilson remained steadfastly on the peace road. He could now, in fact, turn his attention to the British, whose blockade in Wilson's view also constituted an abridgement of American rights on the high seas. Protests in that direction from Washington would serve to underscore the president's evenhandedness.

But the peace road was becoming rockier for Wilson with every passing day. Colonel House's peace-conference-or-else scheme was getting nowhere; for one thing, some in London wanted to wait until after the coming spring military actions to see if the Allies could strengthen their bargaining position. As for the Lansing-drafted modus vivendi—no German torpedoing of British merchant ships if they were not armed—the British dismissed it as nothing less than a shooting license for German U-boats.

To make matters worse, the German military was slowly gaining the upper hand in the internal government debate about submarine warfare limits. For months the army chief, General von Falkenhayn, had sided with Chancellor von Bethmann-Hollweg; he had his hands full in the Balkans and he shared the fear that unrestricted U-boat activity would bring America into the war.

By this time, however, Serbia was no longer a military factor and Bulgaria had joined the Central Powers. Von Falkenhayn became more receptive to the navy staff's argument that unshackling the ever-growing U-boat force could end the war before the United States could be a decisive factor.

Von Bethmann-Hollweg, trying to keep the door from opening all the way to the navy position, counseled the kaiser that if unarmed passenger liners and all neutral shipping were exempted, America might yet be persuaded to stay out of the war. The kaiser nevertheless finally decided to permit German submarines to attack all armed merchant ships without warning. But he delayed the starting date until February 29, 1916, to give his chancellor time to find some way to have the policy initiated without bringing America into the war.

Admiral von Tirpitz, taking the decision as a rebuke, resigned, thus enhancing von Bethmann-Hollweg's chances to further delay the unleashing of the U-boat war. Meanwhile, submarine commanders were instructed to be sure merchant ships really were armed. The Allies at once insisted that their merchant ships were armed for defensive purposes only, and would continue to be.

Wilson took the position that as long as Americans traveled on merchant ships defensively armed only, they had every right to do so. In

Congress, however, those who felt strongly that the United States ought not to risk war to protect a few privileged Americans' rights to court peril took matters into their own hands.

Representative Jeff McLemore drafted a resolution in the House calling on the president to warn all Americans not to travel on armed merchant vessels. Senator Thomas Gore authored an even stronger one that would withhold passports from Americans planning to travel on contraband-carrying ships.

Wilson saw the moves as direct, serious challenges to his conduct of foreign policy, and he came down hard on them—harder, some thought, than he did in his dealings with the belligerent nations. Referring to Berlin's latest position on U-boat warfare, the president observed in an open letter to Senator William Stone, chairman of the Senate Foreign Relations Committee and a prominent pacifist, that it "seems at the moment to raise insuperable difficulties. But its contents are at first sight so difficult to reconcile with the specific assurances which the Central Powers have recently given us as to the treatment of merchant shipping on the high seas, that I think that explanations will shortly be forthcoming which will throw a different light on the matter."

Wilson then added—remarkably under the circumstances of recent events: "We have in the past had no reason to doubt their good faith, or the sincerity of their promises, and I, for my part, am confident that we shall have none in the future."

However, the president continued:

> In any event our duty is clear. No nation, no group of nations, has the right, while war is in progress, to alter or disregard the principles which all nations have agreed upon in mitigation of the horrors and sufferings of war; and if the clear rights of American citizens should ever unhappily be abridged or denied by any such action, we should, it seems to me, have in honor no choice as to what our own course should be. For my own part, I cannot consent to any abridgment of the rights of American citizens in any respect. The honor and self-respect of the nation is involved. We covet peace, and shall preserve it at any cost but the loss of honor.
>
> To forbid our people to exercise their rights for fear we might be called upon to vindicate them would be a deep humiliation

indeed. It would be an implicit, all but an explicit, acquiescence in the violation of the rights of mankind everywhere, and of whatever nation or allegiance. It would be a deliberate abdication of our hitherto proud position as a spokesman, even amidst the turmoil of war, for the law and the right. It would make everything this government has attempted, and everything that it has achieved during this terrible struggle of nations, meaningless and futile. It is important to reflect that if in this instance we allowed expediency to take the place of principle, the door would inevitably be opened to still further concessions. Once accept a single abatement of right, and many other humiliations would certainly follow, and the whole fine fabric of international law might crumble under our hands, piece by piece.

The president's firm position forced his congressional critics to back off. Von Bernstorff, however, sought to keep the controversy alive. He reported that Berlin was willing to discuss the distinction between armed ships for offensive and defensive purpose—thus encouraging pacifist congressmen to persevere in seeking the travel warning resolution. But Wilson, sensing his new strength, decided to press for a vote in both houses and won easily.

Opponents, however, insisted that the votes did not indicate agreement with Wilson, but only acceptance of his power to shape foreign policy when he forced a showdown. Bryan, still a strong voice in the pacifist camp, wrote in *The Commoner* that "the real object had been accomplished by the discussion. The people of the United States are not willing to go to war to vindicate the right of Americans to take these risks; neither is Congress. The president knows it and we can now return to our work and await the results, confident that the jingoes cannot drive us into war."

Von Bernstorff as well professed to see the silver lining in the cloud of congressional defeat.

"We have gained the following remarkable advantage as the result of the past weeks," he informed his superior in Berlin, "that the American people have expressed themselves through their chosen representatives against a war with Germany. Your Excellency is well aware that I have always prophesied that this would be the feeling of Congress, although Mr. Lansing, in his talks with me in the course of the negotiations concerning the *Lusitania*, always asserted the contrary."

By this time, too, the subject of the House-Grey Memorandum —the notion that the United States would come into the war on the Allies' side if the Central Powers refused to talk peace at a Wilson-led conference—had been put to rest.

Neither side appeared to take the proposal seriously; Berlin saw it as a trap and London dismissed it for lack of confidence. If Wilson could not be drawn into the war by the killing of so many Americans on the *Lusitania*, who would believe that he would take that step on grounds that one side refused to settle? Germany was still occupying Belgium and northern portions of France, and so von Bernstorff had reason to be content, too, about the demise of this Washington-hatched scheme.

Finally, there was another matter of a distracting nature that occupied Wilson and hence made direct American involvement in the Great War a matter particularly to be avoided at all costs: there was trouble with Mexico again.

In September of 1915, the forces of Venustiano Carranza had finally defeated Pancho Villa and Wilson had accorded de facto recognition to the victor's government. But Villa was persevering as head of a bandit army of harassment. On January 16, some of his troops stopped a train in northwest Mexico, and robbed and then killed sixteen Americans. Amid an outcry at home, Wilson pressed Carranza to bring Villa to justice, to no avail.

Two months later, on March 9, Villa attacked a border town in New Mexico, a little place called Columbus. In the ensuing battle, about twenty Americans and seventy Mexicans were injured or killed. Over Carranza's strenuous objections, Wilson ordered a punitive expedition of about 7,000 men into Mexico to track Villa down, while assuring Carranza he had no territorial designs on Mexico.

As this unsettling affair was being played out south of the border, Wilson's attention once more was jerked back to the Great War and American rights as a neutral. On March 24, an unarmed English Channel steamer, the *Sussex*, was torpedoed without warning, with twenty-five Americans aboard. No one perished, but eighty passengers were injured including four Americans.

Lansing immediately pressed Wilson to break off diplomatic relations with Berlin, or at least insist on an admission that the attack by submarine on what obviously was an unarmed passenger ship was illegal. But again Wilson procrastinated. House rushed to Washington to give his friend some backbone, without success.

"He evidently does not wish to back up his former notes to Germany," House wrote at the time. "He does not seem to realize that one of the main points of criticism against him is that he talks boldly, but acts weakly."

Berlin at first tried to dodge responsibility, saying there was no U-boat patrolling the area where the *Sussex* was hit. A ship had been sunk, Berlin then admitted, but according to the submarine commander it appeared to have been a British minelayer. Those alibis were undone, however, by the discovery of a piece of a German torpedo in the hull of the *Sussex*.

Still hoping desperately to stay out of the war, Wilson finally sent House to warn von Bernstorff that he would break off relations unless Berlin changed its submarine warfare policy. In a note that both Lansing and House deemed woefully weak, Wilson threatened a diplomatic break unless Berlin agreed to "abandon its present policies of submarine warfare and return to a scrupulous observance of the practices clearly prescribed by the law of nations."

In other words, Wilson was demanding only that Germany adhere to the so-called cruiser rules. In the end, Berlin agreed in a note on May 4, on the condition that Wilson press the British to drop its blockade, and said it would pay an indemnity for the *Sussex* episode.

This "solution" was hardly what Wilson had indicated earlier he required—termination of German submarine warfare. In his note of reply he used a favorite gambit to put the German position in the most acceptable light. He assumed the best—that Berlin didn't really mean the condition attached.

"The Government of the United States feels it necessary to state," the official note said,

> that it takes for granted that the Imperial German Government does not intend to imply that the maintenance of its newly announced policy is in any way contingent upon the course or result of diplomatic negotiations between the Government of the United States and any other belligerent Government, notwithstanding the fact that certain passages in the Imperial Government's note of the fourth instant might appear to be susceptible of that construction. . . . Responsibility in such matters is single, not joint; absolute, not relative.

The British, to no one's surprise, did not lift their blockade, but that fact did not obviate settlement of the *Sussex* incident. Berlin decided to curtail submarine construction in light of the expected lessening of sinkable targets, and ordered a respite in unrestricted U-boat warfare. Once again, Wilson had seemed to approach the edge of war without going over it.

At the same time, however, the troubles in Mexico continued to undercut the president's ability to present himself on the world scene in the altruistic role of peacemaker. The punitive expedition against Villa dragged on without success, and with an ever-heightening tension between Washington and Mexico City. In mid-June, as the expedition under General John "Black Jack" Pershing drove deep into Mexico, a pitched battle against Mexican troops at Carrizal resulted in the taking of twenty-five American prisoners. Under intense public pressure, Wilson demanded their release, and not expecting that Carranza would yield, he prepared to ask Congress for a declaration of war.

On the eve of its delivery, Mexico released the American prisoners. Amid a sea of telegrams urging him to hold his hand, Wilson's pacifist instincts prevailed. "Do you think," he rhetorically asked Congress, "the glory of America would be enhanced by a war of conquest in Mexico? Do you think that any act of violence by a powerful nation like this against a weak and distracted neighbor would reflect distinction upon the annals of the United States?"

Still, with the punitive expedition bogged down for additional months, the Mexican troubles continued—a circumstance that was to have a profound effect later in the United States' eventual entry into the Great War.

Von Bernstorff, too, had his distractions in this period of intense diplomatic labors over the *Sussex* incident. In April, von Papen's deputy and successor as a sabotage supervisor, Wolf von Igel, was arrested as an accomplice in the failed Welland Canal bomb plot, and more incriminating documents were seized in his New York office.

Some in Berlin wanted to throw von Igel to the wolves. But von Bernstorff insisted that he be protected by the cloak of diplomatic status so that the principle involved—which also protected himself and all other embassy personnel—would not be jeopardized.

The State Department offered to return the seized documents if von Bernstorff would claim them as official embassy papers; he declined, seeing entrapment in the offer. The Justice Department pushed for a trial against von Igel but eventually he was released without one.

With the furor over German submarine policy cooled somewhat, Wilson turned his attention to British inhibitions of American neutrality rights—the more to emphasize his evenhandedness. He continued to press London on the starvation blockade, while insisting his pressure was not in the context of Berlin's condition to the *Sussex* settlement.

The creation of a Ministry of Blockade in the British cabinet, the censoring of American mail and the blacklisting of American firms alleged to have traded with the enemy infuriated Wilson, and American business especially.

Also, American-British relations were further complicated by the Easter Rising in Ireland—the revolt of the Sinn Fein in Dublin against the British. The Irish revolt set loose a wave of sentiment in favor of the insurgents, especially when a number of them were captured and summarily executed.

Their leader, Sir Roger Casement, also was captured and held for public trial, precipitating a great outpouring of American protest that eventually culminated in a Senate resolution urging clemency. Wilson sent it to London but Casement was hanged anyway.

Evidence of Wilson's determination to walk a line between the Germans and British regarding American neutrality rights was set forth succinctly in a message asking House to impress on the British foreign secretary that British transgressions must cease.

"The at least temporary removal of the acute German question," Wilson said,

has concentrated attention here on the altogether indefensible course Great Britain is pursuing with regard to the trade to and from neutral ports, and her quite intolerable interception of mails on the high seas carried by neutral ships. Recently there has been added the great shock opinion in this country has received from the course of the British government toward some of the Irish rebels.

He told House to make the American case on neutral rights to the British "with the same plain speaking and firmness" used in dealing with the Germans.

House had resumed pushing his notion of a peace conference with Wilson as the chief mediator. If the British weren't interested in that initiative, the president told House to inform Sir Edward Grey, they would have to expect that the United States would demand proper conduct on their part regarding neutrals' rights.

An official note on May 16 informed Grey that "America has reached the crossroads, and if we cannot soon inaugurate some sort of peace discussion there will come a demand from our people, in which all neutrals will probably join, that we assert our undeniable rights against the Allies with the same insistence we have used towards the Central Powers."

Wilson was scheduled to make a major speech in New York to the League to Enforce Peace, and he had hoped to have both British and French acquiescence in a call for a peace conference by the time he was to speak. But the Allies held off, and so Wilson decided to use the speech to introduce his developing dream—an association of nations after the war to keep the peace.

The president expressed American readiness to take part in such an association, but the momentous declaration was somewhat over-shadowed by some unfortunate wording in the speech suggesting to the Allies that Wilson failed to see any difference between the warring factions in the European combat.

He characterized the war as "the present quarrel"—an expression that seemed to trivialize it—and he followed the phrase with an observation that seemed callous: "With its causes and objects we are not concerned. The obscure fountains from which its stupendous flood has burst forth we are not interested to search for or explore."

The British and French did not like what they heard. As a result, they were all the more resistant to a peace conference with Wilson as mediator. The Germans didn't want it either, but took pains not to dismiss Wilson's initiative out of hand, so as not to appear to be responsible for scuttling his proposed conference and perhaps jostle him from his determination to remain neutral.

It was now June, time for the two major American political parties to select their presidential nominees. On June 10, the Republicans gathering in Chicago turned their backs on Theodore Roosevelt and on the candidate of the Old Guard, former Secretary of State Elihu Root, and chose Supreme Court Justice Charles Evans Hughes.

Four days later, the Democrats met in St. Louis and, amid a flood of oratory about Wilson's success in keeping America out of the war in Europe, the president was renominated. Wilson himself oversaw the writing of the party platform, but delegates added a sentence from which the ringing slogan of the 1916 presidential campaign came.

"In particular," it said, "we commend to the American people the splendid diplomatic victories of our great President, who has preserved our government and its citizens, and kept us out of war."

Thus was the stage set for a referendum on Woodrow Wilson's stewardship of the country, and on his tenacious pursuit of peace, even to the point that many supporters of the Allies saw him as indecisive and weak. In July, as the war in Europe ground on, the country as a whole clearly hoped he would be able to keep the war away from America's shores, though its manifestations continued to be seen and felt.

In Baltimore in early July for example, the German merchant submarine *Deutschland* at last made its appearance and was given a friendly welcome. As von Bernstorff wrote later in his memoirs:

> The arrival of the submarine *Deutschland* at Baltimore and Captain Koenig's first visit to the town resembled a triumphal procession. I had intended to go there at once to welcome the hero of the day and his bold seamen, but thought it better to wait and see what would be the American attitude towards the protests of the English and French ambassadors, who had both claimed that the *Deutschland*, as a submarine, should be regarded without hesitation as a ship of war.
>
> On the thirteenth of July a most minute inspection of the *Deutschland* was made by an American government commission consisting of three naval officers, and she was recognized as a genuine merchant vessel. In consequence the *Deutschland* had a right to lie at Baltimore as long as was necessary to take a cargo on board for the return journey.
>
> It was now possible for me to pay an official visit to Baltimore and view the *Deutschland*. The mayor of the town accompanied me and went down with me, in spite of the terrific heat of about forty degrees centigrade, into the lowest parts of the submarine, which cost the stoutly built gentleman considerable effort and a good deal of perspiration. In the evening, the mayor gave a banquet which passed off as in the good days before the war. The rooms were decorated with German and American flags,

the band played the "Wacht am Rhein," and many speeches were made on the good relations between the two countries.

Such demonstrations did not mean that federal authorities were entirely unmindful of suspicious German conduct in the important ports like Baltimore along the East Coast. Congress in this same month authorized the creation of a special Bureau of Investigation within the Department of Justice to handle the growing number of mysterious explosions and bombings, and to tail suspicious characters. These included members of the German embassy, especially after the case of Dr. Albert, "the minister without portfolio."

Participants in the expanding German sabotage network had to be increasingly careful as they planned and executed their activities. In New York, there was no meeting place more favored than the house at 123 West Fifteenth Street. To that address, German diplomats, sea captains and other assorted mystery figures flocked on these hot summer nights to eat, drink, plot and, often, celebrate successes at the table of their always accommodating hostess, Martha Held.

It was on one such night in late July, 1916, that the audacious plan was laid out in detail to pull off the greatest act of sabotage ever seen on the American mainland—the blowing up of the huge munitions terminal in New York Harbor known as Black Tom Island.

II. The Night of Black Tom

For more than a year, the masterminds of the German sabotage ring had had their eyes on Black Tom. As the single most important assembly and shipping center in America for munitions and gunpowder being sent to the Allies, it probably housed the most extensive arsenal anywhere outside the war zone itself. Destroying this huge terminal of death-dealing explosives would be the equivalent of winning a major battle on the western or eastern front of Europe, or of delivering a lethal blow to the reigning British fleet in the Atlantic.

Von Rintelen, never one to minimize his own imagination or importance, claimed later that blowing up Black Tom was his idea. Recalling in his wartime memoirs his role in mid-1915 in the manufacture and disposition of Dr. Scheele's "cigar" bombs, von Rintelen wrote:

> My occasional sojourns on board the *Friedrich der Grosse* meant hours of rest and peace of mind. The ship was an oasis in the desert of my hallucinations—hallucinations that every knock at the door, during the day or during the night, was an invasion of the bomb squad of the New York Police. . . .
>
> One night, as I was leaning over the rail of the *Friedrich der Grosse*, gazing at the peaceful scene bathed in brilliant moonlight, all of a sudden the thought struck me: Why not go to the root of things? Why not go after the piers themselves, the piers at which the munitions carriers were tied up? Gradually, this thought became a desire, the desire a resolution, and the resolution an instruction.

Von Rintelen recounted how he and his associates had actually reconnoitered Black Tom—and dealt with the watchmen at this extremely sensitive facility:

> At the appointed time, as dusk was falling, a powerful six-cylinder car stood at the appointed place on the coast of New Jersey. A ferry-boat had brought it over from New York. I jumped in! Through streets and lanes, across lines of railway track and

ugly-looking spots, littered with rags and rubbish from the last loading or unloading of some tramp, occasionally crossing fields, meadows, marshes and morasses, we finally landed before the gate of a shed, through the bars of whose doors a few inadequate lamps could be made out, indicating just how far the pier stretched out into the Hudson River. One pier after another was inspected, and wherever a night watchman passed by, or took the liberty of objecting, a few dollar bills gently slipped into his hand by Max Weiser [von Rintelen's partner in E. V. Gibbons, Inc.] rendered him as silent as the grave. Measurements were taken; distances were paced out; the possibilities were studied as to whether and where motor-launches could be comfortably fastened—and, if need be, quickly disappear and go into hiding.

Two or three evenings were taken up by these minute inspections, and our plans rapidly matured; here we were, at the root of the evil, and the evil had to be destroyed—no matter what happened—"apres nous le deluge!"—come what might! The War had to be won, and there was no room for other considerations. Our trips along the New Jersey piers, made in a guarded and roundabout way, soon proved just where the most vulnerable, i.e. from my point of view, the most "valuable" spots might be. My general and especially my military knowledge showed me soon what could be achieved here, where trainload after trainload of munitions was discharged into the holds of the munitions carriers.

One of our visits took us to "Black Tom," a rather curious name for a terminal station. It remains clearly in my recollection because of its quaint conformation, jutting out as it did like a monster's neck and head. I suppose that it was for this reason that it had derived the name of "Black Tom." To judge from the numerous railway tracks converging here, it appeared to be one of the chief points for the Allies' export of munitions. I could not help urging myself the advisability of giving Black Tom a sound knock on the head—its mere name sounded so good to me: we could run little risk from paying Black Tom a compliment of this kind. Some peaceful summer evening—all arrangements properly made—a powerful speedboat at hand for us to disappear into the vastness of the Hudson River—it was all so remote from observation, from possible harm that might be done to human life!

Von Rintelen as the original mastermind of the Black Tom destruction was probably more another figment of his fertile imagination than a reality, because he was now imprisoned at Donington Hall in England and his name was not mentioned by other Germans thereafter in connection with the episode. It took no great military knowledge to appreciate the importance of Black Tom to the Allied war effort. And as von Rintelen correctly observed, the installation was sitting there waiting to be hit, an obvious and vulnerable target.

Nor was von Rintelen the only one to come upon the obvious way to deal with the watchmen—employees of a private detective agency hired to provide security. About a month in advance of July 29–30, according to later testimony by Jesse E. Burns, captain of a four-man watch team in the yard, a man approached him at the Jersey Central Railroad station at Communipaw Avenue, Jersey City, as Burns was going to work. The man asked Burns whether he guarded the piers at the end of Black Tom. Burns acknowledged that he did, whereupon the man slipped him some money on the understanding, Burns told Lehigh Valley Railroad lawyers later, that he would not be too careful in watching what might go on.

"I didn't see no particular harm in taking some money that was being handed about," the lawyers quoted Burns as saying, "and I think that I would have been a fool if I hadn't. It wasn't much of anything, only small pieces of change from time to time."

Burns told the lawyers that the man continued to give him small amounts of money, and that he spent much of it on liquor. Another watchman working with Burns, Barton Scott, called "Bert," told the same lawyers that Burns frequently gave him money and sent him to the Whitehouse Saloon on Communipaw Avenue to buy whiskey. Later, when Paul Koenig's notebook listing thirty-four agents involving "D-Cases" (sabotage) was checked, the names of Burns and Scott were found listed in succession, arousing suspicion that the alleged bribery was more than casual.

Well before their recall in December of 1915, von Papen and Boy-Ed, during dinner parties at Martha Held's Manhattan safe house, had often discussed Black Tom as a critically important sabotage target. Much later, one of the frequent guests at the house, the young photographer's model Mena Edwards, already introduced in this narrative, came forward with a detailed account of what went on there, specifically von Papen's and Boy-Ed's involvement.

At the outbreak of the Great War, the young woman was a minor celebrity, known as "The Eastman Girl" because she posed often for magazine advertisements for the Eastman Kodak Company. She came from Wallington, New York, a small town outside of Rochester, where the company was based. She spent a great deal of time, however, in New York City, where she lived in small West Side hotels frequented by women of suspicious employment who described themselves as actresses.

Her introduction to the German diplomatic and military clique, she said, came through a young French woman she knew only as "Vera." The woman spoke fluent German and had made repeated Atlantic crossings on German ships before the war as the guest, Mena Edwards said, "of the captains or other officials of the boats. I think from what she told me that she was an agent of the German government."

"Vera" introduced Mena to a very successful German cotton broker, Eugene Schwerdt, who wined and dined her and eventually introduced her to von Papen at dinner at the Plaza Hotel sometime in late 1914 or early 1915. They became a frequent foursome, sharing late suppers at such fashionable spots as the Plaza, the Ritz, the Majestic, Delmonico's and other expensive places on Park Avenue, and horseback riding in Central Park.

Soon Boy-Ed joined the company, and one night he and von Papen took Mena to the safe house on Fifteenth Street to meet Martha Held, who was then using the name Martha Gordon. The former opera singer, Mena recalled, "had a beautiful voice and there were numerous pictures of her in costumes apparently worn in German opera companies which I saw from time to time on the walls of her home."

In a lengthy affidavit given nearly seven years after the war's end when she was married and living in Washington as Mena Edwards Reiss, "The Eastman Girl" offered this picture of "Martha Gordon's" German hideaway:

> There was a large room in the front part of the basement floor and a kitchen in the rear, and a long hall that extended from the front of the basement to the rear. On one side of this hall was a

toilet room and then a room beyond that where she kept her wine. Mrs. Gordon occupied the entire house. . . . She had two servants, a Hungarian girl whom she called Janushka and a colored maid whom she called Rose.

Apparently Martha Held had no American friends, and she took a shine to Mena, who became a constant companion, accompanying the German "hostess" on shopping trips and helping her select the latest fashions.

Ship captains, Mena testified later, usually went to Frau Held's house "immediately upon arrival, and gave the latest news of submarine activities, et cetera. There were also from time to time a number of curious-looking characters who came to the house dressed in all sorts of garb who I understood were engaged in carrying on different work for the German Government in the United States."

Among those she met there, Mena said, were Horst von der Goltz and Hans Tauscher, who openly discussed their plans to blow up the Welland Canal, a mysterious "Mr. Koch" who handled legal matters for von Papen, and a man who was known as "Mox." (He was later identified as Max Schaal, a Jamaica, Long Island, printer by day who spent his nights obtaining and transporting explosives for sabotage work.)

Also, on two evenings, Mena said, Frau Held's house was honored by a visit from Ambassador von Bernstorff himself. "I remember how all of the Germans present bowed and scraped when Count von Bernstorff came in," she recalled.

"On several occasions," she said,

men would come in to Mrs. Gordon's house from the vessels dressed as stokers who would later prove to be important German officials. Captain Boy-Ed told us that he had made one or two trips back and forth as a stoker. He said that although he could obtain passage through diplomatic channels he made some trips he did not want the United States to know about, and that he also preferred to do it for the excitement. I remember on a number of occasions the men coming in in their overalls and old clothes.

One of them, she recalled, was "a man named Chris, or Christie, from Hoboken. Chris was a very seedy-looking man with red hair and a reddish-brown moustache and a red face." This "Christie" in all probability was Michael Kristoff, a man soon to enter our narrative as a critically central figure in the Black Tom affair.

"The subject of destroying munitions and factories and other supplies which were being used for the Allied Governments," Mena testified,

> was a constant topic of conversation in the dinners and conferences . . . which I overheard. They appeared to have entire confidence in me. I didn't speak German fluently but I could understand it quite well and as a great deal of wine was consumed, the men frequently became very talkative. . . .
>
> When they talked to those queer-looking characters they spoke German but much of the time they spoke English. I remember overhearing Captain von Papen, Captain Boy-Ed, von der Goltz and others discussing various sabotage activities that they were planning from time to time. They usually had some special name to designate a particular plant or point that was to be destroyed. For example they used the term "Jersey" with regard to Black Tom.

Mena Edwards Reiss recounted as well how the Germans brought bombs, apparently the early "dumpling" variety, to Martha Held's house for safekeeping:

> I remember vividly seeing them handed around among the men. They were about the size of a large orange. They were wrapped in a black paper like tissue paper and there were woolen cloths around them that looked like grey underwear. They would bring these there in bags and Martha Gordon would store them in her house.
>
> Other persons would call from time to time at the house and procure these bombs and take them out with them. I know that the man named Mox . . . was one of the men who carried some of the explosives over to New Jersey for the destruction of the Black Tom terminal. . . .
>
> When these bombs were brought there they would take them out of the bags in which they brought them and put them in suitcases and Martha Gordon carried them upstairs. She told me she took them up there to store them in a closet. She said,

"I have to keep these things locked up and I keep the key on my person." My recollection is that in addition to being wrapped in the tissue paper and in the woolen cloths, each one was also enclosed in a tin box. Mrs. Gordon told me that it was necessary to keep them separated and to avoid vibration.

After the recall of von Papen and Boy-Ed, Mena said, she met von Papen's deputy and successor in the sabotage operation, von Igel, and, on an earlier occasion, von Rintelen. Whether it was von Rintelen who introduced the discussions of Black Tom at these dinner parties, as he clearly wanted the world to believe later, or whether he heard them there and made the most of it in his self-aggrandizing memoirs, no one has ever satisfactorily clarified.

Martha Held's guests mixed revelry over successes with serious planning. "The men who came to these conferences and dinners," Mena Reiss said,

> very often had a great many papers and blueprints and pictures with them. . . . There were bars in front of the windows of the front room in the basement, and they would always draw the shades carefully before they got out the blueprints and plans. I naturally did not appear too interested in the papers which they were handling, but I am sure from the conversations which I overheard that these had to do with places that they were planning to blow up in different parts of the country.

When any of the saboteurs left the safe house to do a job, Mena recalled, "they would sing songs together of the kind that they were accustomed to sing in Germany going into battle, and toast the Fatherland . . . 'Deutschland Uber Alles,' 'Die Wacht am Rhein' and other German songs."

The subject of Black Tom had been discussed frequently over many months simply as "Jersey," she said. "Their line of talk made it perfectly clear to me what it was. They talked about wanting to destroy Black Tom particularly because it was the great point of shipment for so much munitions to the Allies." Mena said the Germans had

> inside men . . . actually planted in the employ of the Lehigh Valley Railroad Company or at least who had easy access to the premises, because they would frequently discuss the reports that they had from these men about the layout of the property

and the movement of munitions. In the immediate few weeks before the explosion I overheard conversations which told me exactly what night it was proposed to blow up the Black Tom terminal. They had selected Saturday night and early Sunday morning because they thought there would be fewer people around at that time.

On one particular night, she recalled, two chemists, J. von Bruck and Ludwig Meyer,

had some explosives at the house and were talking to some men and giving them instructions as to how to handle them. I remember their saying words something like this—"These are good for so long," or "These will run for so long," referring probably to the fuses, and mentioning a certain time where I have used the words "so long.". . . There were to be three explosions planned in different places, one on the cars, and the others in sheds, or barges or enclosures. I remember something being said about boats being loaded to go to some place. . . .

This man "Mox" whom I have mentioned before who was a printer in the daytime was selected as one of the men to carry over the explosives to Jersey. He was a very small man with a wrinkled face and wore glasses. They were not horn glasses but ordinary gold-rimmed spectacles. He also had a moustache and wore a cap. Mox was one of the men who was present on the night that I recall von Bruck and Meyer giving instructions about using the bombs. I also recall conversations to the effect that none of these men were to come near the house again until the following Tuesday.

Frightened by what she had seen and heard, Mena made it her business to get out of town over that weekend. She took a train down the Jersey coast to a seaside cottage where a widowed friend was vacationing. She was lying awake in nervous anticipation when the plans she had heard and seen in the making at Frau Held's house came to thunderous fruition.

Two men not mentioned by name in Mena Edwards Reiss' long narrative about sabotage and Black Tom, but who may have been known to her under other names, were Lothar Witzke and Kurt Jahnke—the master team of saboteurs in San Francisco under the direction of the German consul there, Franz von Bopp. Witzke and Jahnke were in San Francisco as late as May of 1916, but they made a trip together to New York shortly afterward and in due course became, along with Michael Kristoff, the major suspects in the destruction of Black Tom.

Why Mena Edwards did not come forward at the time as a loyal American and report what went on at Martha Held's house was not hard to fathom. The house was generally thought to be, and probably was, a brothel, and it required a considerable stretch of imagination to believe that all of the women there, including Mena, were "models" and "actresses."

Indeed, later on the Germans sought to discredit her as a witness on grounds she was a prostitute. The American prosecutors in the sabotage cases did not refute the allegation. Instead, they made the argument that the Germans had chosen their companions and it was not up to the prosecutors to pass moral judgment on them, but only to take and present their testimony.

That Saturday night, with the workmen off for the weekend since 5:00 P.M., Black Tom was what is known in railroading as a dead yard. All locomotives had been withdrawn and all that sat there were loaded freight cars and assorted barges and small boats tied up to the piers. Safety rules explicitedly required that loaded cars were not to remain overnight at the terminal. But the workload was so backed up that many were obliged to wait days and even a week to have their cargoes transferred to barges for movement to ships waiting offshore in the harbor.

There were two separate security forces on duty—one working directly for the Lehigh Valley Railroad and headed by Cornelius Leyden, the other for the Dougherty Detective Agency, hired by the British, and headed by Burns. Still, the yard could easily be infiltrated. There was no gate separating the Black Tom promontory from the mainland and the area was unlighted. Men who manned the barges tied up at the pier came and went unhampered by the lackadaisical guards, and were often unheeded by them.

As far as the water side was concerned, there was no patrol at all of the Hudson River, Upper New York Bay and the harbor, beyond an occasional Coast Guard or New York City police boat that could do little to secure the waters shrouded in the midnight darkness.

In all the years of investigation by New York and New Jersey police and by federal agents that were to follow this eventful night, no one ever firmly established the exact details of how the massive conflagration started, and specifically by whom. The accumulated evidence and testimony nearly a quarter of a century after the fact did establish, however, that German saboteurs certainly did perpetrate the deed, and that the actual culprits probably were the West Coast professionals Witzke and Jahnke and an illiterate and mentally deficient amateur, Kristoff, functioning as their minion.

The most credible hypothesis is the following: Witzke and Jahnke came in to the Black Tom terminal over water around midnight in a small boat laden with explosives, time fuses and incendiary devices. Kristoff meanwhile infiltrated the depot from the land side. They then set small fires in one or more of the boxcars containing TNT and gunpowder, and placed explosives with time fuses there. They also planted time bombs and incendiary devices on a barge—the *Johnson 17*—that was loaded with more explosives and tied up to a pier at another point off the yard. Then Witzke and Jahnke retreated onto the darkened river to await the outcome of their work and Kristoff fled by land. Watchmen sighted the first fires at about 12:12 A.M.; the first explosion occurred in one of the boxcars at 2:08, and the second aboard the barge at 2:40.

Shortly after midnight, a watchman working for one of the barge companies later recalled, he saw a small rowboat bearing two men moving slowly from the farthest Black Tom pier toward Bedloe's Island. Soon afterward, he said, he saw a small fire in one of the boxcars, and unable to locate a Lehigh Valley watchman, he put the fire out and went off duty.

The sighting of the rowboat squared with an eventual confession by Witzke, recanted when he was brought to trial. While drinking with an American intelligence agent he believed to be a fellow German saboteur in Mexico eighteen months later, Witzke told the agent:

> I also did work in New Jersey with Yenky [Jahnke], when the munitions barges were blown up and the piers wrecked. We were out in a small boat and the waves nearly swamped us and we came near drowning. The hardships of the work were many but it was all for the fatherland. The German ambassador and Yenky think very highly of my work and I am proud to have done it. I am a man they know they can depend upon.

After the Black Tom disaster, Witzke and Jahnke vanished, leaving Michael Kristoff, a twenty-three-year-old immigrant from what was then Hungary, as the prime suspect. Until the previous February, Kristoff had worked for the Tidewater Oil Company in Bayonne, not far from Black Tom. At that time he suddenly left the job and did not resume it until June. A month later he quit again, and a few weeks before the explosions he took work at the Eagle Oil Works, which was close to Black Tom.

For four consecutive nights before the Black Tom destruction Kristoff was absent from his job. Then, hours after the disaster, at four o'clock in the morning, he came reeling into the home of his cousin, Mrs. Anna Rushnak, at 76 East Twenty-fifth Street, Bayonne, where he was boarding. Hearing him pacing the floor in his room, she went up to see what was wrong.

"He was in a very excited condition," she told police shortly afterward, "and he told me at the time that he helped to blow up Black Tom." As she pressed him for details all he could say, over and over in accented and anguished English, was: "What I do? What I do?"

Finally, she said, he told her that he had accompanied two other men to Black Tom, where they placed dynamite "on a big steamboat" and that he had received five hundred dollars for his participation. He did it, he said, because he thought it was "the best thing to do to stop the war."

The Black Tom explosions physically shook the New York area and psychologically rocked a nation believing itself to be far removed from the terrors of the Great War. While authorities at first called the event an accident and explicitly ruled out sabotage, the catastrophe forced Americans as never before to face the unpleasant reality: their country was already deeply involved in the war—and in the killing—by virtue of its role as the principal arms merchant. Stories of the sensational disaster consumed the front pages of the New York newspapers for days thereafter and as far away as the British Isles accounts were read with awe and, in some cases, satisfaction.

Von Rintelen, imprisoned at Donington Hall, wrote later that he was thrilled to read in the *Times* of London, "Explosion of Chief Pier of Allied Shipping 'Black Tom' Blown Up by Enemy Agents," and he commented: "I had my own opinion as to how it had come about, and who were the men behind the scenes!"

This recollection, however, clearly was more of von Rintelen's shameless fabricating. Officials and the press at the time of the Black Tom destruction were attributing it to carelessness, not sabotage. The story in the *Times* of London the following day, a brief five-paragraph item buried on page six, actually bore the headline "Great Explosion at New York; Ammunition Stores Blown Up" and included not a single word even hinting at sabotage.

At Martha Held's house on West Fifteenth Street, the rejoicing was unbounded. Mena Reiss recounted how she returned from the New Jersey shore on the Monday morning after the explosions and the very next day received a phone call from "Mrs. Gordon" inviting her to the house for "a large party" that night:

> I went down there, arriving at about seven o'clock. There were already some of the crowd there and several more came in later. They were all members of the crowd that I had met there from time to time before. . . . Among the others there were several German reservists from South America who had come up from Venezuela and other places who had been recalled and were trying to get back to Germany. . . .
>
> They were all talking about the success of the Black Tom explosion and a dinner party followed in honor of that success. There was a great deal of champagne and wine and I remember particularly that some wonderful old vintage wines were brought out for the occasion. There was a great deal of drinking and hilarity, and a great deal of singing and toasts to the Kaiser and the fatherland and also a good deal of hand-shaking.
>
> I particularly remember that when the man named Mox came in—he came in late—he was greeted as a great hero because he had carried some of the explosives over to New Jersey. Von Bruck was also treated as quite a hero because of his leading part in organizing the affair. There were some captains present also from the interned German vessels. I remember a number of questions being asked as to whether anyone knew if any people were killed in the explosion. They seemed to be concerned about that and apparently hoped that they had not killed many people. . . .
>
> Quite late in the evening, about one o'clock I should say, Martin Lange, the owner of the Bismarck Cafe who was in the party, invited those who were still there to go to the Cafe. . . . There

were probably eighteen or twenty of us still there. I remember that we went up in several taxi cabs but we took them at different places and did not all leave the house together.

When we got to the Bismarck Cafe, Mr. Lange opened a great deal more wine. This cafe had been used for some time as a rendezvous for Germans and I had been there several times before. There were some other Germans there when we arrived whom we knew and we drank further toasts and sang German songs there.

Shortly after this party, Mena Reiss said, "I began to get more frightened about the activities of the group, and at about this time I learned from one of the employees of the Eastman Kodak Company that they were becoming very suspicious of me and were thinking that I was perhaps a German agent.

"I was in Rochester a few days later and someone around the Powers Hotel, where I lived when I was in Rochester, told me that there had been a write-up in one of the Rochester papers about me accusing me of being a German sympathizer. This frightened me very much." So she went out to her mother's home in Wallington and stayed there, she said, "for several months without returning to New York City."

Mena Edwards Reiss' detailed inside account of what went on at 123 West Fifteenth Street would eventually become a very significant document in the case against the German saboteurs. At the time of the Black Tom destruction, however, she was saying nothing—and keeping out of sight, and out of further involvement with her German playmates in New York.

Paul Hilken, the Baltimore overseer of the sabotage operations after von Rintelen's departure, told later of two other reactions to the Black Tom success:

I remember that on the morning of Saturday, August 5, Hinsch, Herrmann, Hoppenberg [Paul Hoppenberg, another shipping official] and I were in the office of the Eastern Forwarding Company [set up to handle the *Deutschland* traffic] in the Whitehall Building in New York City, and at that time Hoppenberg facetiously remarked, pointing to the broken windows: "Why, you fellows have broken my windows." Two of the three windows were cracked by the Black Tom

SOMETHING TO GO ON WITH.

PRESIDENT WILSON (*to German Eagle*). "POOR OLD BIRD! DID IT SAY IT WAS BEING STARVED? WELL, HERE'S A NICE SQUARE MEAL FOR IT."

"MISGUIDED LADY" PUTTING UP POSTER.

"FOR WAYS THAT ARE DARK."

EVOLUTION OF A FOX

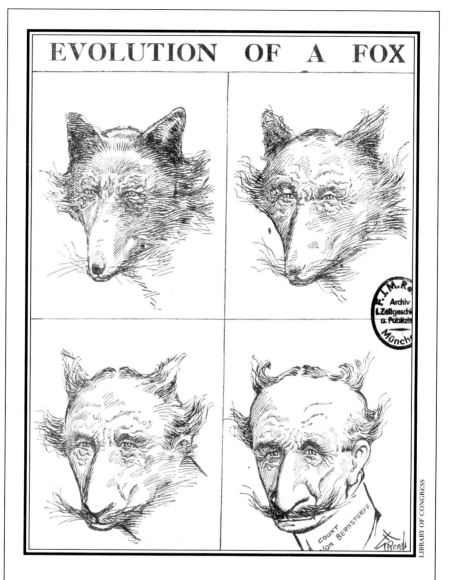

COUNT VON BERNSTORFF

WHERE THEY BREED

GATHERING
BAVARIAN
HOPS

HOCH
DER
KAISER

HOBOKEN

GERMAN
FIRE BUG

Kaiser: "If I can't rule her, no one shall."

"GOTT IN HIMMEL!"

PLEASE OBSERVE, COUNT VON B., THAT YOU ARE PRETTY CLOSE TO THE EDGE YOURSELF.

explosion, which had occurred about six days before.

That is the occasion when Herrmann retorted to Hoppenberg by singing a little song of the War of 1870, "Lieber Moltke, sie nicht dumm, mach mal wider, bumm, bumm, bumm." [Beloved Moltke, not so dumb; he keeps on making bumm, bumm, bumm.] I also remember that when we looked from our office window over at the destruction at Black Tom, that I turned to Hinsch and asked him if he had been instrumental in the destruction of Black Tom, and it was on that occasion that Hinsch said to me, "It is much better if you don't know anything about the details."

Hilken's recounting of Herrmann singing the German ditty to Hoppenberg would resurface much later as an important proof of German complicity in Black Tom.

Hilken's other recollection was of an occasion three days later:

Sir John Hamer [a shipping business associate], Fred Herrmann and I were sitting in the lobby of the Astor Hotel in New York when Hinsch came in with a girl and registered. I called him up later, after he had gotten to his room, represented myself as the hotel clerk, and asked him what he was doing having a girl up in his room, that that was against the rules of the hotel. Hinsch was furious over the whole affair and stated that if we played a joke of that nature on him, he was not going to stop there anymore.

The search to find Black Tom's perpetrators focused at the outset, however, on Kristoff. Mrs. Rushnak, upset over what he had said and how he had behaved on the early morning of the explosions, confided in her daughter, Anna Chapman, who lived in Bayonne and formerly also had Kristoff as a boarder. Mrs. Chapman in turn informed an old friend on the Bayonne police force, Captain John J. Rigney, adding some information of her own.

While Kristoff was staying with her, she told Rigney, he "was in the habit of going away from time to time and that everywhere he went there was an explosion." Whenever he returned from one of these trips, she said, he always seemed to have lots of money.

For about three weeks, Rigney had Kristoff shadowed. Finally Bayonne police arrested him in Jersey City on August 31 and turned him over to the Jersey City Police Department. Kristoff insisted he was visiting a friend in Yonkers on the night of the explosion, and he provided the address—433 Neperhan Avenue. A check produced testimony, however, that Kristoff hadn't been there that night. Pressed about his whereabouts in the first half of 1916, when he was away from his job at Tidewater Oil, Kristoff told police this story:

On January 3, 1916, while he was sitting in the waiting room at Pennsylvania Station in midtown Manhattan, a man came up to him, asked him the time and where he was going. Kristoff said he was on his way to visit his sister in Cambridge, Ohio. The man identified himself as Francis Graentnor or Grantnor; Kristoff wasn't sure of the spelling or pronunciation.

The man offered him a factory job for twenty dollars a week but said he had to do some traveling first and needed Kristoff to carry some suitcases for him. Kristoff readily agreed, and in the next months he traveled with this mysterious stranger—to Bridgeport, Philadelphia, Akron, Cleveland, Columbus, Chicago, Kansas City and St. Louis, all places where important munitions and military supply manufacture was being carried on.

The suitcases, Kristoff said, contained lots of books, money, and blueprints of bridges and factories. He professed not to know what they were for, or whom his boss was seeing in these cities. But he speculated to police that the blueprints were "to show people how to build bridges and houses and factories."

One day in St. Louis at the end of the tour, he said, the man "gave me a dollar to go to the theater, and when I returned, he was gone." Kristoff went back to New York and ran into "Graentnor" three weeks before the Black Tom explosions. Kristoff asked him: What about my job? The man told him to meet him later at the Hotel McAlpin, but when Kristoff went there the man never showed up and he never saw him again.

The story sounded so incredible, particularly Kristoff's interpretation of what the man probably was up to, that the police suspected that Kristoff was mentally deranged. They summoned an alienist—a specialist in conditions of the mind—to interview and examine him. He concluded that Kristoff was mentally deficient, though not dangerously or criminally so.

Mrs. Chapman said later, however, that shortly before the explosions she was cleaning Kristoff's room when she found a letter, not yet mailed, addressed to a Mr. Graentnor or some similar spelling demanding a considerable amount of money. So the story could not be dismissed out of hand.

Because the case against Kristoff was too weak, he was released when one David Grossman, who said he worked with Kristoff, arrived to put up bail. Grossman said he did not really know Kristoff but that other coworkers vouched for him and he was acting at their request. Later it turned out that bail had not been required after all, but Grossman's appearance became a piece of evidence in the effort to tie Kristoff to the German sabotage operation.

Although the police deemed the case against Kristoff as insufficient to hold him any longer, he did have a police record—an arrest in Rye, New York, the previous September for carrying a concealed revolver, for which he served thirty days in jail. So the Lehigh Valley Railroad hired a man named Alexander Kassman from the William J. Burns Detective Agency to shadow him.

Kassman got a job at a chocolate factory where Kristoff now worked and soon was having lunch with him regularly. Kristoff was attending meetings of a German anarchist group and Kassman, himself posing as an Austrian anarchist, often accompanied him, methodically gaining his confidence.

As Burns Operative Z-60, Kassman submitted reports alleging that Kristoff in time acknowledged his central role in the Black Tom explosions. After one late afternoon anarchists' meeting, Kassman, in poor English, wrote this report:

> We then went to lunch. After the lunch I went back with him to Jersey City. On the way to Jersey City, I said to Michael Krestoff [sic] that America is taking part in this War, because they are sending ammunition to Europe and will not stop. Michael then told me he is glad when a ship with ammunition on it that is going from America to Europe is exploded. I then said to him, I think that all the explosions on the ships that is loaded with ammunition and also ammunition places are being made by the Anarchists. Michael Krestoff told me that he knows of a German group who is against America for sending over ammunition to Europe.
>
> The Explosion in Black Tom, Michael Krestoff said, was made by a German group. I said to make an explosion like the one

that was in Black Tom was a very hard job. He told me to find out the plans and to make an explosion in Black Tom was very hard. I then asked him, "How do you know everything?" Michael Krestoff then told me that he belongs to a German group and he was working for the explosion in Black Tom with two other men, and he is very glad that so much ammunition was lost at Black Tom.

The next night after work at the chocolate factory, Kassman wrote, he met Kristoff at a lunch room on West End Avenue:

After lunch I walked with Michael, and I being very anxious to find out some information, asked him, "Say, Michael, how were you working for the explosion in Black Tom? This must be a hard job." He then told me that in the middle of the night with two men he came over to Black Tom. One man told Michael Krestoff to watch the place all around and he, Michael Krestoff, with another man went to a big steam boat with ammunition aboard.

[Kristoff said:] "On the ship where I was there were small cases of powder. I put between the cases two pieces of dynamite, and lit it. The explosion should be about half an hour later. Around the ship where I put the dynamite were steam boats and on the boats were cars of ammunition. My friend also put one on one boat between the cars and half an hour later there was an explosion. The powder that was on the ship and in the cars after the first explosion blew up all the ammunition that was around in Black Tom."

I then said to Michael Krestoff, "The two men who were working with you are Anarchists." Michael Krestoff told me that the two men belonged to a German group. I then asked him, "Where is the place of the German Group?" He told me that he knows only two of the men. Then I asked him, "How do you know this man and where did you meet this man the first time?" Michael Krestoff said, "I will tell you some other time."

Within two weeks' time, Kristoff was asking Kassman "if I would work for good money in an ammunitions factory." Kassman told him he was eager to do so and meanwhile pressed for more information about Kristoff's Black Tom accomplices. "I asked him where were the two men who he was working with in Black Tom," Kassman reported. "I would like to know them because I am against the war and I will be glad at any time to blow up any ammunition place."

Kristoff told him that rich friends against the war had collected three thousand dollars to get him out of jail and that the other two men gave the money to David Grossman for his bail. Then they gave Kristoff himself five hundred dollars "for my work, and together with this the two men told me that the best thing for me to do now is to be careful for the police, and I should never again do the same work like I did in Black Tom because the police will watch you now." They told him, Kristoff said, "that nobody should know that you saw us and worked with us," and he did not see them again after that.

In early December, Kristoff, now thoroughly convinced that Kassman was trustworthy, took him to Grossman's home in Bayonne. Grossman was furious, especially when Kassman informed him that Kristoff had told him all about Black Tom.

"After this," Kassman reported, "David Grossman said to Michael Krestoff, 'If you delight in talking about this explosion in Black Tom, then you must remember you will again soon be in prison.'"

Five months later, after Kristoff had vanished, Kassman went back to see Grossman and, still feigning allegiance to Germany, asked him what really happened at Black Tom. Grossman told him:

> In the Black Tom job Michael Krestoff was working with two men. One of the men watched the place carefully that was near Michael Krestoff and the other man put on a big steamboat, between a number of cases of powder, two pieces of dynamite, and then made a light on both strings, calculating the explosion would occur in half an hour. The other man put dynamite in a boat between cars which were filled with ammunition, and within half an hour there was an explosion. The powder and ammunition that was in the ships and in the cars after the first explosion blew up the place and vicinity in Black Tom.

Grossman himself, however, was not about to testify. So linking Kristoff with the crime and with the German saboteurs in a manner that would hold up in court was no simple matter. Detectives found that Kristoff shortly after his disappearance had given a sister in Byesville, Ohio, five hundred dollars to hold for him, but such evidence was purely circumstantial.

In due course, damage suits were filed against the Lehigh Valley Railroad Company—by Russia, which held contracts for most of the destroyed munitions, and by property owners in the neighborhood of Black Tom. At first, the railroad fell back on the contention that the explosions were the result of spontaneous combustion.

The plaintiffs charged the railroad with negligence in guarding the terminal, particularly in light of the fact that mysterious fires and explosions were occurring with increasing regularity. The railroad's defense in time would come back to haunt it; the German government after the war would itself rely on spontaneous combustion as the cause, in attempting to deflect charges of sabotage.

For all the immediate furor stirred up by the fiery destruction of Black Tom, the American people continued to cling to their desire to stay out of the Great War in Europe—a sentiment on which President Wilson's chances for reelection now rested. And Wilson himself focused at this juncture more on the British and their blacklist against American firms suspected of trading with the Germans than on a regrettable incident at a private railroad terminal off New York Harbor; it was, after all, an incident that investigators had already concluded "cannot be charged to the account of alien plotters against the neutrality of the United States."

Front page of *New York Times*, Sunday, July 30, 1916

Front page of *New York Times*, Monday, July 31, 1916

12. "He Kept Us Out of War"

It was obvious why the British, not the Germans, were the targets of American presidential ire at the time of the Black Tom disaster. Beyond the fact that German complicity in the explosions was neither detected nor alleged, the British were aggressively impeding America's rights as a neutral—at least as President Wilson and Secretary of State Lansing saw those rights.

On June 29, 1916, the British reinstated a blockade-enforced prohibition against the export of American tobacco to Germany through neutral countries. The action enraged planters in the Southern states who, in response to an earlier decision permitting such export, had planted unusually large crops. Although tobacco was not ordinarily considered contraband, the British argued that smoking sustained the endurance of German soldiers at the front. American apples, too, were barred, although Britain did not hinder the export of oranges from its ally, Italy, whose economy relied on that crop.

The arrival of the *Deutschland* in Baltimore as a "merchant submarine" on July 9 was, as we have seen, greeted warmly by the residents of that port city. The welcome provided another indication of a neutral American attitude toward the Germans, or at least a reaffirmation of American evenhandedness.

Just nine days later, the British issued their enlarged blacklist of suspect American firms to be boycotted by British traders. An accompanying declaration that "His Majesty's Government are unable to contemplate the possibility of such advice being disregarded by any British firm" made it a virtual order, infuriating American traders. And an equally stiff reply to an American protest of mail censorship by the British, blasted by the State Department in unusually blunt language as "insolent and imprudent," further irritated United States–British relations.

Wilson on July 23 wrote to Colonel House: "I am, I must admit, about at the end of my patience with Great Britain and the Allies. This blacklist business is the last straw. . . . I am seriously considering asking Congress to authorize me to prohibit loans and restrict exportations to the Allies." He was preparing a note, the president said, and "I may feel obliged to make it as sharp and final as the one to Germany on the submarines."

On July 29, only hours before Black Tom was blown up, the Senate passed its resolution urging the British to grant clemency to Sir Roger Casement, the leader of the Easter Rising in Ireland. The plea was ignored and he was hanged five days later—causing von Bernstorff to write Berlin that "the Irish have come over into our camp like one man." That no doubt was a gross overstatement, but it was true that Irish-Americans and many others here deplored Casement's execution. At the very least, the British shared Washington's doghouse with the Germans at the time of Black Tom.

To put muscle behind his words, Wilson asked and won approval from Congress for strong retaliatory measures against the British blockade and blacklist. They included the prohibition or restriction, at the discretion of the president, of goods into the United States from any country that barred or limited the export of American goods into any other country. And on September 8, Congress approved a huge appropriation for enlarging the American navy to a size second only to the British.

House suggested to Wilson that this move might unduly unsettle Britain, to which the president replied: "Let us build a navy bigger than hers and do what we please." But as always Wilson talked a tougher game than he played, especially when the price for harsher action might put his role as peacemaker in jeopardy, and the British knew it.

Talking tough to the British, to be sure, had its political purpose at this juncture. The 1916 presidential campaign had shifted into high gear and demonstrable evenhandedness toward all European belligerents helped underscore the slogan "He Kept Us Out of War," on which Wilson's reelection chances depended to such a considerable degree.

In mid-September, the British ambassador in Washington, Sir Cecil Spring Rice, wrote Prime Minister Sir Robert Borden of Canada: "The situation here is that the President is losing ground and may very probably be beaten. His advisers may tell him that the only thing which can save him is an appeal to American patriotism against the British."

At the same time, Lansing warned Wilson directly of the political price he might well pay for perceived softness toward Germany. If he failed to protest explicitly and sharply the German invasion of Belgium, which since its occurrence in 1914 Wilson had declined to do, and if he did not finally obtain satisfaction from Berlin regarding the *Lusitania* sinking, Lansing warned the president, he would be punished at the polls for his negligence.

Wilson, however, liked to think that he was above politics. When another Lansing memo also urged him to turn up the heat on the British, the president wrote back at once: "I think it would be quite unjustifiable to do anything for the sake of public opinion which might change the whole face of our foreign relations."

Lansing thought Wilson's single-minded focus on the preservation of American neutrality flew in the face of the true issues posed by the war. In one of many memos the secretary of state wrote for the files that served to present him as more independent than his public posture suggested, Lansing wrote of the president:

> He does not seem to grasp the full significance of this war or the principles at issue. I have talked it over with him, but the violations of American rights by both sides seem to interest him more than the vital interests as I see them. That German imperialistic ambitions threaten free institutions everywhere apparently has not sunk very deeply into his mind. For six months I have talked about the struggle between Autocracy and Democracy, but I do not see that I have made any great impression. However, I shall keep on talking.

In all probability, however, it was not so much that Wilson did not see the basic differences between the two major combatants in the war. Rather, he was determined almost to the point of paranoia not to let such differences deter him from what he saw as his greater mission of bringing peace to the world. Repeatedly during the election campaign, the president seemed to go out of his way in his speeches to trivialize the two sides' reasons for fighting the war.

On August 30 he called the war "just a fight . . . to see who is strong enough to prevent the other from fighting better." On October 5 in Omaha he referred to "obscure European roots which we do not know how to trace." And on October 26 in Cincinnati: "Have you ever heard what started the present war? If you have, I wish you would publish it, because nobody else has, so far as I can gather. Nothing in particular started it, but everything in general."

There was no way, however, that the war would be kept out of the election campaign as a prime issue. In the East, dominated at the time by the opposition Republican party, sentiment favoring the Allies was close to overwhelming; the Midwest had a large German-American vote that usually went Republican; the West had conflicting allegiances and was strongly against intervention on either side.

In 1912 Wilson had benefited from a split in the Republican vote when the GOP nominated William Howard Taft over Theodore Roosevelt and Roosevelt broke away, forming the Progressive party. In 1916, however, Roosevelt came home to the Republicans and campaigned vigorously for their nominee, Charles Evans Hughes, and against Wilson. Roosevelt, as ever a cyclone on the stump, brutalized Wilson as a weak-willed wimp who was forever turning the other cheek, who was "too proud to fight."

Speaking near the end of the campaign of Wilson staying at Shadow Lawn, his New Jersey shore retreat at Long Branch, Roosevelt intoned: "There should be shadows enough at Shadow Lawn; the shadows of men, women and children who have risen from the ooze of the ocean bottom and from graves in foreign lands . . . the shadows of deeds that were never done; the shadows of lofty words that were followed by no action; the shadows of the tortured dead."

Such sentiments doubtless solidified opposition to the incumbent in the Republican East, but fell on deaf ears in the noninterventionist Midwest and West.

These geographical attitudes played significantly in the Wilson strategy to break the Republican national majority for a second time. Even von Bernstorff, as a student of American politics, recognized their importance, and the prospective backlash of the Roosevelt rhetoric. "If Hughes is defeated," he wrote to Berlin during the campaign, "he can thank Roosevelt. The average American is and remains a pacifist."

The Wilson political managers made a decision to downplay the East and to concentrate on the rest of the country. They made a particular effort to woo away progressives who had supported Roosevelt in 1912 but were disenchanted by his return to the Republican fold and, in the Midwest, by his jingoism. Also, all through 1916, Wilson had pushed a progressive domestic agenda in Congress and had obtained important parts of it.

The president in fact shied away from the peace theme at first.

Accepting his party's nomination in early September from the front porch of his rambling house in Long Branch, Wilson provided only a very low-key review of his neutrality policy. And in his first speech on the stump three weeks later he discussed only domestic issues. He did the same in another speech to the Young Men's Democratic League a week later. But at its end he made some extemporary remarks about foreign policy and its effect on American youth that drew him inexorably into the overriding campaign theme—and encouraged supporters to run unshackled with it.

If the Republicans were put in power, he said, the country would be drawn, in one way or another, into the war—a matter that ought to be of special concern to his young male audience.

House at once publicly interpreted Wilson's remarks as a warning that Hughes' election would mean war, and he privately urged a seemingly reluctant Wilson to say more of the same. A week later, the president allowed himself to observe that a Republican reversal of his foreign policies would produce a reversal from peace to war. The Wilson publicists seized the theme with a vengeance. In New York alone, they mailed five million copies of a convention speech by former Governor Martin H. Glynn glorifying Wilson's refusal to be drawn into the European fight.

Soon other issues were being cast in war-and-peace terms; a pamphlet aimed at social reform-minded women boasted that Wilson had kept their underage children out of sweatshops, mills and mines in the same way that he had kept their sons and husbands off the Western Front. In the final days of the campaign, the Wilson managers ran a newspaper advertisement that blatantly blared: "If you want war, vote for Hughes! If you want peace with honor, vote for Wilson!"

Wilson himself preferred loftier rationales for his reelection, foremost among them the pursuit of his dream of a postwar world alliance against war.

"It is our duty," he said in one campaign speech, "to lend the full force of this nation, moral and physical, to a league of nations which shall see to it that nobody disturbs the peace of the world without submitting his case first to the opinion of mankind." But such high-blown sentiments took a back seat to the "Hughes means war" pitch trumpeted by the Wilson camp generally.

On election day, the strategy of writing off the pro-Allied East worked, though barely. The major Eastern states of New York, New

Jersey and Connecticut that usually went Republican did so again, as did Illinois and Indiana in the crucial Midwest. The *New York Times* and even the strongly Democratic *New York World* conceded the election to Hughes; Wilson, playing Twenty Questions with his family at Shadow Lawn, received the news quietly, drank a glass of milk and retired for the night.

He had already decided at House's suggestion that, because of the tense international situation, if defeated he would not cling to the presidency until the end of his term in March. Instead he would set in motion actions that would bring Hughes swiftly into the White House. The lame-duck president would appoint Hughes secretary of state and then have Vice President Thomas R. Marshall resign, leaving Hughes as next in line for succession as the law then specified.

Not until two days later, when North Dakota, New Mexico and finally California all came in for Wilson, did he know he would not have to put that plan into effect. His margin of victory was only slightly more than six percent over Hughes in the popular vote, and twenty-three electoral votes. But in the end he had the mandate he sought —not simply to continue to keep America out of the war but to work toward his vision of a world united against future wars.

Although the election campaign of 1916 dominated the news in the United States in the three months after the Black Tom explosions, activities continued in both of Ambassador von Bernstorff's realms of responsibility: the subversive and the diplomatic.

Weeks after Black Tom, bomb-maker Robert Fay escaped from the federal penitentiary in Atlanta and made his way to Mexico with the assistance of German consuls in key American cities who reported to von Bernstorff. Also in August, two attempts were made to blow up piers of the Pacific Coast Steamship Company at West Coast ports. And in October, mysterious fires broke out on the S.S. *Philadelphia*, the S.S. *Antilla* and the S.S. *Chicago*, all ships in the Atlantic trade route to the Allies.

Diplomatically and militarily, critical developments were unfolding in Europe that engaged von Bernstorff's attention. The failure of the German high command under General von Falkenhayn to score a decisive breakthrough at Verdun brought the general into eclipse. It triggered a shakeup that imperiled von Bethmann-Hollweg's continuing efforts to hold off the resumption of unrestricted submarine warfare. This objective von Bernstorff passionately shared, in his firm conviction that such a decision would bring America into the war on the Allied side.

On August 27, 1916, Romania finally decided to throw in with the Allies and to declare war on the Central Powers, a decision that caught the German high command—and the kaiser—unaware. Two days later Wilhelm II gave von Falkenhayn his walking papers in part for not having warned him of this impending development. The general was shipped forthwith to the new Romanian front.

The kaiser then elevated to commander-in-chief of the high command the hero of the 1914 victory at the Battle of Tannenberg, General Paul von Hindenburg. Von Bethmann-Hollweg welcomed the appointment in the belief that von Hindenburg would be an ally against unleashing the U-boats. But with von Hindenburg, to von Bethmann-Hollweg's eventual mortification, came his brilliant and ruthless chief of staff, Major General Erich Ludendorff, who had other ideas.

Von Hindenburg was now seventy years old and more figurehead than commander. The real power—dictator, many said, considering the pliability of the inept kaiser—was Ludendorff, and he had no patience for the striped-pants wafflers of the Foreign Office who sought to tie one of the fatherland's strong military hands behind its back. Together von Hindenburg and Ludendorff threw their weight behind the position of the military clique advocating all-out submarine warfare to bring the conflict to a do-or-die confrontation.

Von Bethmann-Hollweg, believing the aging von Hindenburg would be easily handled, was rudely jolted by his unexpected support, doubtless prodded by Ludendorff, for resumption of an unrestricted U-boat campaign. The new commander-in-chief urged only that it be delayed briefly until he could see how the Romanian front developed.

Von Bethmann-Hollweg concluded that his only hope to head off the ruinous new submarine policy was to engage Wilson as a vehicle for initiating peace talks with the Allies. At the least, he reasoned, the gesture, even if it failed, might demonstrate German good faith and stem a precipitous decision by Wilson to break off diplomatic relations.

On August 18 the chancellor had already instructed von Bernstorff to sound out Wilson on mediating peace negotiations with the Allies. When he learned of von Hindenburg's position, von Bethmann-Hollweg cabled von Bernstorff on September 2 to pursue the matter with the greatest urgency, even raising the possibility of a German guarantee for the restoration of Belgium:

Confidential. Our west front stands firm. East front naturally threatened somewhat by Romania's declaration of war. Rolling up of front or collapse of Austria, however, not to be feared. Turkey and Bulgaria to be relied on. Greece uncertain. Hopes of peace before winter, as result of Russian or French war-weariness, diminished by this development. Apparently, if no great catastrophe occurs in East, Wilson's mediation possible and successful if we guarantee required restoration of Belgium. Otherwise, unrestricted submarine warfare would have to be seriously considered. Request you give purely personal opinion without inquiry in any quarter.

On September 3, von Bernstorff and his wife went to Colonel House's summer place in New Hampshire for lunch and discussion. House told the ambassador that there could be no mediation role by Wilson until after the election; the president was firm on that position. Von Bernstorff cabled Berlin:

Wilson's mediation postponed until further notice because for the moment out of the question owing to Romania's entry into war and consequent renewed prospect of victory for our enemies. Wilson thinks he cannot now mediate before the election, because England might pay little attention to him until after the election, and if he were not elected would have nothing further to do with him.

But von Bethmann-Hollweg was insistent. With the kaiser's approval, and with language inserted by the dominant Ludendorff making clear that Germany still held the strong upper hand militarily, the chancellor sent new instructions to von Bernstorff on September 26. He told him to inform Wilson that mediation by him could forestall unrestricted submarine warfare, but added:

Should Mr. Wilson insist on waiting until immediately before or after the election, he would lose the opportunity for such a step. . . . A further prolongation would be unfavorable to Germany's military situation, and would result in further preparations being made by the Powers for the continuance of the war into next year, so that there would be no further prospect of peace within a reasonable time.

Von Bernstorff was instructed further to "discuss the position cautiously with Colonel House and find out the intentions of Mr. Wilson. A peace movement on the part of the President which bore the outward appearance of spontaneity would be seriously considered by us, and this would also mean success for Mr. Wilson's election campaign."

Already, however, the German navy had stepped up its application of the cruiser rules and had markedly increased its tonnage of Allied shipping sunk. A military version of the *Deutschland*, the *U53*, surfaced in Newport with a letter for von Bernstorff, submerged, and went outside American territorial waters and sank nine ships, all within bounds of the *Sussex* pledge.

There was no slackening off of the war's effect on American trade. But again Wilson held firm to his insistence that he could not act during the campaign. He seemed immobilized by a fear that any mediation effort on his part then would be seen as politicizing foreign policy for his own narrow gain. Thus the argument that von Bethmann-Hollweg put forward—that moving now would help Wilson get reelected—cut no ice with the proper academic from Princeton.

With von Bethman-Hollweg still pressing him, von Bernstorff on October 9 went to Shadow Lawn for a private interview with the president, but could not budge him from his position. Part of the hitch was also that the kaiser wanted the initiative for talks to come publicly from Wilson, so as not to appear that he was begging for peace. Wilson for his part left the impression with von Bernstorff that he wanted to be asked openly to play the mediator, which would have made a pre-election move more palatable politically at home.

In any event, the whole effort collapsed when the Reichstag, whose support von Bethmann-Hollweg needed to hold the line against the U-boat war, passed a resolution undercutting him. It seemed now only a matter of time before the unshackled submarine terror would begin again, with the dire consequences for continued American neutrality that von Bernstorff as well as von Bethmann-Hollweg so wholeheartedly feared.

Furthermore, the German navy was well on the way to establishing a runaway submarine policy on its own. On October 28, an armed British merchantman, the *Marina*, was torpedoed with heavy loss of life, including six Americans in the crew. But when Lansing pushed the president to demand that Berlin adhere to the *Sussex* pledge,

Wilson waved him off. He told House, his friend reported later, that he didn't believe "the American people would wish to go to war no matter how many Americans were lost at sea."

On election day itself, an armed British liner with Americans aboard, the *Arabia*, was torpedoed in the Mediterranean with the loss of fifty-seven lives. No Americans died, however, and no American protest was made until twelve days later. Then Washington merely asked Berlin for an investigation because the action did not seem to square with the *Sussex* pledge.

During the election campaign, in fact, Wilson continued to concern himself as much with the British threats to American neutrality as he did with the German. He warned the British of the impending retaliatory legislation from Congress, a warning that sunk in with officials in London concerned with the flow of foodstuffs and other supplies to the island empire. One British planner predicted in late October that the interference from submarines and other sources could, by the next June, force the British to sue for peace. Prime Minister Asquith received but rejected subordinates' suggestions that Britain frankly lay out her terms for a settlement as a way of possibly breaking the impasse. Speaking to the House of Commons, he declared firmly, with a wry poke at Washington:

> The strain which the war imposes upon ourselves and our Allies, the hardships which we freely admit it involves on some of those who are not directly concerned in the struggle, the upheaval of trade, the devastation of territory, the loss of irreplaceable lives—this long and somber procession of cruelty and suffering, lighted up as it is by deathless examples of heroism and chivalry, cannot be allowed to end in some patched up, precarious, dishonoring compromise, masquerading under the name of Peace.

Meanwhile, with von Bernstorff's full knowledge, Germany's undeclared war against American munitions-making went on. A grim reminder came in late October when the body of the captain of the barge *Johnson 17*, which had blown up in the destruction of Black Tom, washed ashore in New York Harbor.

Although Woodrow Wilson had, indeed, kept his country out of war and was reelected largely because of that fact, keeping America neutral in his second term clearly would be a greater challenge. How much longer would Wilson in his own mind be able to balance off German submarine and other outrages with the irritations to American trade of the British blockade? While he struggled to treat both offenses with equal dismay, the Germans were smuggling new saboteurs onto American soil—seeking out, and finding, new targets for their special line of work.

13. New Recruits and the Kingsland Fire

With the Black Tom "victory" fresh in the minds of Section 3B's directors, they smuggled onto American shores more men practiced in the arts of destruction who were eager and determined to duplicate that feat. Among them was one Charles Wunnenberg, self-styled "The Dynamiter," a German who was a naturalized American citizen.

Wunnenberg, despite his gaudy nickname, was as much a propagandist, recruiter and all-around hustler as he was a functioning saboteur. In 1915 he persuaded a string of American newspapermen of German sympathies in England to spy for the fatherland. Later, at the German naval laboratories at Wilhelmshaven, he learned how to use high explosives and bombs and was sent to the United States. There he began recruiting and directing German saboteurs, among them Kurt Jahnke of von Bopp's San Francisco operation, linked later to Black Tom as Lothar Witzke's sidekick.

One of Wunnenberg's less appealing habits was getting German women to go to America with him posing as his wife, to provide cover. The Justice Department learned in October, 1916, that one of his traveling companions, Freda Prestine, the wife of a German soldier at the front, had come to the United States with Wunnenberg the previous August on a phony marriage certificate. She confided to a friend, who later informed federal agents, that aboard ship he performed an abortion on her himself, apparently out of concern that her pregnancy might complicate his safe passage.

The informant, Mrs. Robert Davis, wife of a man Wunnenberg tried to recruit to place bombs on munitions-bearing ships, told the Justice Department that Wunnenberg had been staying with her and her husband in New York but returned to Germany "to get married." When he came back, she said,

> He had a marriage certificate and plenty of money. I said to Charlie, "Are you married?" And he said, "No, the government fixed this for me and got me a wife." Then he went back with a passport to bring on a wife and he brought Freda . . . to

my house and introduced her as his wife. . . .

Then when Charlie went out and stayed all night, this girl came to my room and told me she was not his wife; [she] showed me the picture taken of her husband while at the front. When she started she was going to have a child, and coming over on the *Oscar II* this year Charlie had bought an instrument in Kirkwell which he used to cause a miscarriage. . . . Charlie had used her as a wife all the way over; they had the same stateroom and everything. . . . She opened her trunk and showed what had happened on the trip. Some things I burned and the rest I sent to the laundry. . . . The instrument that was used in the operation was shown me by Freda, and it was in a filthy condition, having never been cleaned since the operation. . . .

The girl cried every night about her being here with Charlie, and her husband at the front. The report got out that Charlie was a white slaver and he came to the house and told me that I had better get out of that house because if he was caught it would look bad on me. Freda was never as a wife to him in my house for she slept right with me every night.

Mrs. Davis said she found "explosives and clocks" packed in cotton in Wunnenberg's bedroom dresser, and when she asked him what they were for, "he said the clocks he made, and would pay men to install in outgoing ships. He offered Mr. Davis in my presence one thousand dollars for every one he would install in outgoing ships loaded with supplies for the Allies." Davis refused, she said. Wunnenberg also offered her a thousand dollars, she said, to go to Germany and back with him posing as his wife. "I told him nothing doing," Mrs. Davis said.

As for the man's sabotage activities, she said, "I cannot say to my knowledge that Wunnenberg had anything to do with the Black Tom Island explosion or not. . . . In speaking of this disaster, Wunnenberg said those barges were loaded for the Allies but that is some of the stuff 'the God Damn Lime Juice Sons of Bitches will never get.'"

Another new recruit was Willie Woehst, a young German sent originally to Baltimore to help direct sabotage when the workload got too heavy for Hilken. In a letter to the chief German agent in South America shortly after Woehst's arrival and produced by federal authorities later, Hilken wrote:

Our principals abroad, realizing that my other interests require too much of my time and make it impossible for me to devote my time to their interests, have sent a young man who arrived a month ago, and whom I have since initiated into our American trade. He brought with him several new samples which may also find a market in the Argentine.

The "American trade" to which Hilken referred was, obviously, sabotage, and the "new samples," he testified later, were "pencils —incendiary devices of some sort," to be used in the United States and in Argentina, where German agents were also operating. These obviously were the new devices Hilken first encountered at Section 3B headquarters in February, 1916.

Woehst, working with Frederick Hinsch, overseer of the loading and unloading of the *Deutschland* in Baltimore and secret director of all the sabotage forces under Hilken, soon became a central operative. So did Fred Herrmann, the young Brooklynite who had brought the first batch of incendiary "pencils" or "glasses" into the United States earlier in the year. Woehst and Herrmann became roommates in New York, and fast friends.

Sometime shortly after Wilson's reelection, Hinsch began to discuss with Woehst and Herrmann another special target not quite as large as Black Tom but formidable nonetheless. It was one of the most important on the list assigned earlier by Hinsch to Herrmann: the new Canadian Car and Foundry Company plant in Kingsland, New Jersey, about eight miles northwest of Black Tom.

When the war broke out, the Montreal-based company quickly obtained large contracts from Britain and Russia for the manufacture of artillery shells. Its Montreal plant was soon working at capacity, and early in 1915 it obtained a whopping $83 million contract from the Russians for five million more shells. To fulfill the contract, the company built a new plant at Kingsland to assemble and ship the shells.

Together with other contracts, Kingsland by late 1916 had 1,400 workers turning out three million shells a month as casings, shrapnel and powder flowed into the plant from subcontractors everywhere. As a target for Hinsch and his subordinates, the Kingsland factory was indeed a worthy successor to the scarred ruins of nearby Black Tom.

In light of the recent Black Tom experience, Canadian Car and Foundry constructed a strong six-foot fence around the entire plant. The firm assigned security guards around the clock to patrol it, and to screen each of the workers as he or she entered the plant daily. If Hinsch's men were to pull off the destruction of Kingsland, they would need help from the inside.

Hinsch, with the assistance of Herrmann and Woehst, therefore set about establishing that critical contact. According to testimony after the war from Herrmann and other principals, Hinsch selected a Baltimore neighbor, a German native who was born Curt Thummel but used the name Charles Thorne, who was working for Hinsch as an undercover transatlantic courier.

The son of a onetime German soldier, Thorne's sympathies were heavily with his old country, although at the time he met Hinsch at a bar in Baltimore in 1914 he was serving in the United States Coast Guard. Thorne was a frequent visitor aboard Hinsch's interned ship, the *Neckar*, and when his Coast Guard tour was up in the spring of 1916, Hinsch recruited him for the courier work.

One of Thorne's jobs was to bring incendiary "pencils" into the United States from Germany. Edwin Herrmann, brother of Fred, testified later that Thorne on one occasion "was carried off a steamer . . . on a stretcher feigning illness and was met by a private ambulance, the purpose of the plan being to take off the boat a supply of tubes or other materials that were being used."

Thorne soon balked at this assignment, fearing the British were on to him. In September, 1916, he went to New London, Connecticut, to request another job from Hinsch, who was there along with Hilken awaiting Germany's second commercial submarine, the *Bremen*. The sub was mysteriously lost at sea, but as the Baltimore operatives waited for it, Thorne arrived. After meeting Hilken, he agreed to take a position at Kingsland arranged through a New York contact. The job, as an assistant employment manager, became the key to infiltration of the saboteurs' target. In the next weeks, Hinsch sent several men to Thorne, who hired them for routine jobs within the sprawling plant.

The most important of those hired was a man actually sent to Kingsland, most probably at Hinsch's suggestion, by the Russian vice consul in New York, Dimitri Florinsky, who later was fired by his own government for suspected pro-German activities.

Because Kingsland was now almost exclusively working on Russian contracts, it was easy for Florinsky to get employment at the plant for the man, Theodore Wozniak (originally Fiodore Vozniak), a Pole from what then was Austrian Galicia. Wozniak had been in contact with Florinsky for several months earlier, as established by a permit issued to Wozniak by the vice consul in April of 1916 permitting him to return to Galicia for a visit. It noted that the man was "personally known" to the Russian consulate general.

Wozniak was given a job in Building 30 of the Kingsland plant. There, workers stood along benches and cleaned out shells with a dust brush, removed the protective grease with which the shells were coated for shipment with a cloth soaked with gasoline, and then dried them with another cloth. A shell was fitted onto a rotating machine that turned it slowly as the worker performed the cleaning operation. Smoking was forbidden in this area and, indeed, in any area of the entire plant, for obvious reasons.

Herrmann, who had drawn Kingsland as one of his assignments in originally going over Hinsch's list of potential targets, was frustrated at the outset by the plant's heavy security. In December of 1916, he called Hinsch at the Hotel McAlpin in New York. Hinsch told him he had already solved the problem and had the right man for the job in place. Hinsch introduced Herrmann to Wozniak at the McAlpin, and Herrmann, although he immediately took a dislike to the man, agreed to work with him. Herrmann, in a deposition long afterward, described his early dealings with Wozniak:

> I asked him if he was working with the Canadian Car and Foundry plant at Kingsland. To this question he answered yes, and that he had some friends there. If I remember correctly he mentioned a man in charge of employing men there. The situation was explained to him which he fully realized, also if possible to get another man to work there, which he thought he could do.
>
> I gave him forty dollars and told him he could meet me three days later in the Barclay Street Ferryhouse on West Street around five o'clock and report. . . . Several days later I met Wozniak at the above mentioned place and he told me that everything was okay. At this time I did not like him as I thought he was slightly out of his mind.

The man Wozniak arranged to be hired through Thorne was a Puerto Rican known to the Germans only as "Rodriguez." Another Hinsch recruit, he reported to Herrmann at the ferryhouse, where Herrmann in turn introduced him to Wozniak. Rodriguez was given a job at the work bench in Building 30 next to Wozniak's. A week later, by prearrangement the two men rendezvoused with Herrmann at the same place.

"Wozniak and Rodriguez told me they were working," Herrmann testified later. "I then gave each one of them several pencils and a small package of white powder, with full instructions how to use it."

Before putting the "pencils" to work, however, Wozniak embarked on the construction of a cover for himself. First, claiming he was really a Russian, he applied to the Russian embassy in Washington for citizenship. Next, he wrote a letter to a General Khrabroff, president of the artillery commission of the Russian supply committee, alerting him about considerable carelessness in the making of the shells at Kingsland. Finally, on January 10, 1917, Khrabroff received a postcard from Wozniak, in Russian, that warned: "Things are getting worse and worse with us. There will be a catastrophe."

These moves were familiar gambits with the German saboteurs. Witzke similarly had applied for American citizenship and Jahnke had once warned American officials in San Francisco in advance of an explosion at the navy yard where he was then working.

Interestingly, the British secret service had an explicit warning about Wozniak from an agent, known only as "Operative No. 45" at the time, but ignored it. An informant reliable in the past warned that "Wozniak is in the pay of the Austrian or German secret service and is acting under orders to make friendly contacts with Russians in New York, especially among members of the Russian Commission, with a view to finding out about munitions plants."

The report went on to say, "Wozniak has succeeded in obtaining employment in the Kingsland, New Jersey, plant of the Agency of Canadian Car and Foundry where ammunition for Russian Government is being made and stored." It specifically said Wozniak got the job "through the Russian Vice Consul" and that "as a blind, Wozniak has written two letters to the President of the Russian Supply Committee in New York about so-called irregularities at the plant."

Unsurprisingly in retrospect, Wozniak's warnings were prophetic. At 3:40 P.M. on January 11, five and a half months after New York City had been rocked by ear-splitting explosions at Black Tom, the thunderous bombardment was heard again. For more than four hours it lasted, and was detected as far north as Westchester, New York, as far east as Long Island, and all across northern New Jersey. An estimated half-million, three-inch high explosive shells burst into the air as fire swiftly raced through the Kingsland plant and engulfed it.

The charges to project the shells were ignited but, fortunately for people in the area of the plant, the shells were not yet equipped with detonators. So, when they crashed to earth they did not explode. Still, the towns of Kingsland and neighboring Rutherford were thrown into a panic, and many homes were riddled with gaping holes in roofs and walls from the falling shells. Hundreds fled, particularly from a shantytown of Italian workers' families inelegantly known as Guinea Hill overlooking the plant site in the New Jersey meadows.

In contrast to the actual explosion of lethal charges as at Black Tom, the Kingsland spectacle was all smoke and flames, and a continuing rumbling as the shells shot hundreds of feet into the air.

"Those who knew the sound of a cannonade," the *New York Times* reported the next day, "were at first inclined to think that some of the harbor forts were testing their guns; but the sound was too loud and too continuous for that." As night fell, this account went on, mobs of New Yorkers once again flocked to the Hudson River waterfront, and

> the flash of bursting shells was compared by observers to the repeated opening of a furnace door in a darkened cellar, and the rumble of the explosions gave to thousands a pleasurable and entirely safe feeling of being under fire. This sense of life in the war zone was increased by the numbers of returning travelers from Jersey who crossed the ferries in the evening, bringing with them unexploded shells as souvenirs. Attempts on the part of the ferry officials and the Hoboken police to stop this practice met with little success, and a great deal of trinitrotoluol (TNT) was brought back into New York City.

The fire started in Building 30 at Wozniak's bench, by his own later admission and the eyewitness reports of several other workmen. Just what started it, however, was in dispute, although as in the Black Tom disaster there was at first little official speculation about sabotage. "No Hint of a Plot," observed a subheadline on the *Times'* story. "Somehow, from somewhere," the paper's report said, "a spark fell into a tub of the alcohol [used to clean shells] and set it ablaze. One theory was that an electric droplight, hung above the tub, had become short circuited" and threw the spark. Other eyewitnesses, however, said they saw no such spark.

As the 1,400 workers—including Wozniak and the man working next to him listed in official records as "M. Rodriguez"—streamed out of the inferno, it rapidly spread to all the other thirty-seven frame buildings with corrugated iron roofs in the Kingsland complex. The more than two hundred security guards on duty tried to direct the fleeing workmen through the plant's outer gates, with little success, as the plant's hired firemen made a half-hearted effort to combat the flames.

The *Times*, reflecting the dominant racial attitudes of the time, reported the scene this way:

> The negroes in the fire-fighting force, stiffened by a few Italians, had been wavering in the face of the blaze before this, but when the fire reached the stores of loaded shells, they could be held in check no longer. They broke and fled in all directions, and the plant was abandoned to the fire.
>
> Meanwhile, other workmen, dropping their tools and swarming toward the exits at the sound of the fire whistle, had made their way to the six-foot iron fence, topped with barbed wire, which surrounded the grounds. Here the armed guards of the plant were on guard, and their commander, Harvey D. Hatch, was trying to herd the frightened workmen out by the regular gates through which they come to and leave the plant every day. But not [a] man of them would wait for the gates. They poured in a pushing, frantic throng to the nearest part of the fence and literally rolled over it, barbed wire and all, by the dozens as fire alarms clanged their warnings."

Once past the gates, the workmen escaped over the frozen marshes of the Jersey meadowlands, which in summer would have formed an arresting moat that might have trapped them all and sentenced them to a fiery death.

On Guinea Hill, the *Times* reported,

> Children who had been playing in the streets and had run toward the blaze in eager excitement at first were now running away from it as hard as they could. Older children who had been in their classes in the schools were dismissed just about the time

that the rumble of low explosions and the thud of falling shells were awakening Kingsland to the realization of the disaster. Most of these children lived on Guinea Hill and their natural impulse was to rush home in time of trouble. But as they ran homeward they met their mothers and the smaller children running away. The streets were jammed for a time, families were broken up and separated, women in terror and alarm who didn't know where to go outside their own district ran this way and that, and the cries of lost children were heard on all sides.

Miraculously, no one was killed or even seriously injured as a direct result of the fire. One man died, however, in a freak accident caused indirectly by it. A laborer who lived on Guinea Hill but worked at another nearby plant received a phone call at work from his panicked wife, fleeing their besieged community. Fearing from her description that the whole area would be engulfed, he ran to the nearest railroad station and tried to board a passing train. In his lunging attempt, he slipped, fell onto the tracks and was killed.

Other workmen frantically attempting to get home to their families on Guinea Hill were caught in huge traffic jams. The police chiefs of Kingsland and neighboring Rutherford reported that as they were driving through the streets of the shantytown a three-inch shell fell into their car, wrecking it, but they were unhurt.

Guinea Hill itself was peppered by falling shells. "Scarcely a house in the one hundred city blocks on the hill above the plant escaped being hit by projectiles," the *Times* said. "Some of the buildings resembled collanders, so perforated were their walls. . . . Five houses were burned to the ground from flames started by the shells, and fire in four or more others partly destroyed them." Not all the residents of Guinea Hill fled; firemen working through the night found scores of women and children huddled in their basements, as well as an eighty-year-old man "almost dead from fright and exposure," the *Times* reported.

In another community overlooking the Kingsland plant—a county government complex including a prison, poorhouse and insane asylum known as Snake Hill—the inmates, residents and patients were petrified. At the asylum, the *Times* said, the superintendent, Dr. George W. King, reported that many of the nine hundred patients thought the world was coming to an end and were in a perfect frenzy. Dr. James T. Meehan, chairman of the Hospital Committee, learned of Dr. King's plight with his charges and hurried to the hospital with supplies of ice cream, fruit and candies. He assembled the inmates in the lecture hall and gave them a party, first allaying their fears by telling them that the European war was at an end and the explosions were the detonations of guns in celebration of the event.

The Kingsland plant itself was completely destroyed, with estimated damages of seventeen million dollars. A later inventory indicated that 275,000 loaded shells and more than a million unloaded shells, nearly half a million time fuses, 300,000 cartridge cases and 100,000 detonators, plus huge amounts of TNT, were destroyed in the fire. The big losers, in addition to Canadian Car and Foundry and their insurers, were the Russian government and its eastern front against the Germans.

An investigation launched by the company quickly pointed to Wozniak. A workman three benches away from him, Thomas Steele, told company officials:

> I was working in No. 30, No. 2265. The fire broke out in the liquid pan of an Austrian workman just after three o'clock. This Austrian had been there working for at least three weeks. I saw the fire burning up in his pan about four or five inches high. The Austrian said nothing but ran for his coat and, taking it, ran through the freight car opening out into the back yard. I was the third man from the Austrian.

A foreman, Morris Musson, corroborated the story and provided even more incriminating testimony:

> I noticed that this man Wozniak had quite a large collection of rags and that the blaze started in these rags. I also noticed that he had spilled his pan of alcohol all over the table just preceding that time. The fire immediately spread very rapidly in the alcohol-saturated table.
>
> I also noticed that someone threw a pail of liquid on the rags or the table almost immediately in the confusion. I am not able to state whether this was water or one of the pails of refuse alcohol under the tables. My recollection, however, is that there

were no pails of water in the building, the fire buckets being filled with sand. Whatever the liquid was, it caused the fire to spread very rapidly and the flames dropped down on the floor and in a few minutes the entire place was in a blaze.

A third witness, Domenick Lascola, told of seeing another employee in Building 30, according to the *Times*, "using a pocketknife to remove a bit of brass that made the inside surface of one of the shell cases uneven. A moment later . . . he saw the floor of the shop aflame. . . . When he saw the flame he attempted to smother it with his coat, but fled with the other men in the shop when it was evident that the fire could not be controlled."

Wozniak himself, located and summoned by the authorities later, told them: "The only theories which I can advance as to the cause of the flame bursting out in the shell are: Someone may have put something in the shell while it was on the table before I took it. Or someone may have put something in the rag which I used to clean it."

Both Wozniak and the man listed in company personnel records as Rodriguez were called in by the company. C. H. Cahan, a director who interviewed both of them, reported that Wozniak acknowledged that the fire had started at his bench but insisted it had been through no fault of his. As Cahan testified later:

> I told him that most of his fellow workmen agreed that the flames had first been seen at or near his table. He admitted to me that the flames had originated there and he said that they had started in some cloths which he was using to clean one of the shells. Wozniak told me that several days before the fire occurred he had found matches deposited in one of the shells, among the cloths, "rags" he called them, which he used for cleaning shells. He seemed to lay singular stress on the fact, which at the time created suspicion in my mind that he was developing a story to throw suspicion on one of his fellow workers. . . . He said that he was taking the third step in the process of cleaning a shell, that is, drying the inside with a clean cloth, when a flame burst from the opening of the shell.

Cahan said he questioned Wozniak about the man at the bench next to him, "and he said that the man working next to him on the day of the fire was a new man who came on that bench that day for the first time. . . . He said that he did not know his name."

Cahan had Rodriguez brought into the office, who "declared that he had been absent from the works on the day of the fire and that he had been home all day with his family. . . . There was some family fete on that day and he had stayed home with some relatives and others." The man said he was from Puerto Rico, Cahan said, and "had the appearance of the Spanish Creole type—smooth face, dark."

It was a description that would not square at all with later eyewitness accounts of what the "Rodriguez" of the day of the Kingsland fire looked like. Adding to the suspicion that this Rodriguez had been replaced by another man for the day of the fire, and for the specific purpose of aiding in its start, was the fact no one ever came to the plant to pick up the pay due for work performed at the bench next to Wozniak's.

As for Wozniak himself, Cahan said, "I had the impression from his nervous behavior, from his demeanor when led into apparent contradictions, and from other incidents in our interviews which were significant to me but difficult to describe, that he knew that the fire was no accident and that he personally was implicated in its origins."

Company officials told Wozniak that he was to stay in New York to testify as the investigation proceeded, and that he would be kept on the payroll during that time. He went to live at the Russian Immigrant Home on Third Street in Manhattan. Although private detectives were hired to tail him, he eluded them in a matter of weeks and disappeared.

By this time, the authorities were not so willing to dismiss the possibility of "alien plotters against the neutrality of the United States," as they had after the Black Tom disaster. A company statement allowed that its preliminary examination "has created the impression that it is possible, if not probable, that the fire was of incendiary origin." Also, since the Black Tom catastrophe, two more major plants had been destroyed, five more ships carrying munitions had been sunk or severely damaged by "mysterious" fires and twenty bombs had been found on the American merchant ship, S.S. *Sarnia*, as it approached France, causing it to be beached and flooded off Cherbourg.

The *New York Times* on the last day of 1916—eleven days before the Kingsland fire—estimated that "incendiary loss in 1916 was easily $25 million, or $15 million above normal," and Kingsland alone now threatened to approach that figure. The Russian government had contracted for $83 million in shells and had already taken delivery of a considerable number, but lack of shipping had led to the stacking of much of the purchase at the plant. Ultimately, the Russian government—the Soviet Union after the war—would sue Germany for more than $6 million for the Kingsland fire alone.

The night after the fire, a Mr. and Mrs. Wightman dined at Healey's Restaurant, a favorite German hangout on Forty-second Street opposite the Hotel Manhattan. At an adjoining table, a German man with glossy black hair and moustache, wearing gold pince-nez, was heard to say to the large buxom blonde woman across the table from him:

> Paul pulled off a good job in New Jersey last night. The Kaiser has the Allies beaten now, but they will be beaten worse than ever now. He damaged them ten million dollars last night. If he can pull this other stunt, and do as good a job as he did last night, then the Allies will be beaten sure enough.

The Wightmans immediately reported the conversation to the New York police. But all it was, as far as anyone could prove, was talk. Later, there was conjecture that "Paul" must have been Paul Koenig or Paul Hilken, but only conjecture.

At any rate, one might have thought that the accumulated calamities would have been more than enough finally to jar President Wilson out of his lofty reveries about playing peacemaker between two belligerents whose "present quarrel" was none of his, nor America's, concern.

Wilson's reveries, however, continued, although they were about to encounter a much more devastating shock. The jolt would soon be delivered by Count von Bernstorff, not in his capacity as saboteur-overseer but rather in his role as diplomat—a diplomat who was finally playing his last card to sustain American neutrality, and was seeing it trumped.

14. Von Bernstorff Plays for Time

Von Bethmann-Hollweg and von Bernstorff, unable to budge President Wilson on mediating peace negotiations in advance of his re-election, took him at his word that he would plunge into peacemaking immediately afterward. They resumed pressure on him, with encouragement from Colonel House.

On November 16, 1916, nine days after the American election, German Foreign Minister Gottlieb von Jagow cabled von Bernstorff: "Desirable to know whether President willing to take steps toward mediation, and if so, which and when? Question important for decision of possible steps in same direction elsewhere." And six days later, von Jagow wired: "For Your Excellency's strictly personal information. So far as favorable military position permits we intend, in conjunction with our allies, immediately to announce our readiness to enter into peace negotiations."

Wilson, however, had his own ideas about bringing peace. He was determined to present a personal peace message, not simply to the warring governments but to their people, that would be so persuasive, so just, that it could not be turned away. He told House that unless he straightforwardly demanded that the belligerents end the fighting the United States would certainly be drawn into the war over the submarine issue. House, obviously considering this approach naive, attempted to dissuade the president, but to no avail.

On November 21, von Bernstorff cabled Berlin that House said Wilson wanted him to know "that he is anxious to take steps toward mediation as soon as possible, probably between now and the New Year." But Wilson insisted, House added, that as little as possible be said publicly about mediation, because American public opinion was aroused against Germany as a result of the deportation of Belgians to Germany as laborers. House also warned that there could be no more controversies over submarine practices; they served only to counter American negative feelings toward the British as a result of their blacklist and mail censorship policies.

Another reason Wilson wanted no publicity about mediation, obviously, is that he hoped to hold off any German initiative that might complicate his own plans for his personal appeal for peace, which he saw in historic terms. He intended to make the speech, he confided to House, "the strongest and most convincing thing I have ever penned."

As Wilson thus labored over this latest exercise in peacemaking, important political changes were occurring in London and, more significantly, in Berlin. They would have more to do with war and peace than any rhetoric from Wilson, no matter how carefully crafted. David Lloyd George replaced H. H. Asquith as British prime minister and Ludendorff, moving to assert German civilian as well as military dominance, pressured a weakened von Bethmann-Hollweg into dismissing von Jagow and elevating Arthur Zimmermann to foreign minister.

Lloyd George talked resolutely of delivering a "knockout blow" to the Central Powers, while Ludendorff and von Hindenburg were wearing down von Bethmann-Hollweg's resistance to unleashing the U-boat fleet. The atmosphere for peace, and the time frame in which negotiations toward it might yet be possible, seemed to offer Wilson little grounds for his tenacious optimism about bringing the belligerents to their senses.

Ludendorff particularly cast a long shadow over Wilson's ambitions. Convinced that the only reason Germany had not won victory in the field was that it had not yet devoted its full resources to the effort, he was instrumental in the policy of deporting Belgian manpower for the German war effort that so aroused negative public opinion in America. And as part of the same conviction that a Germany unleashed would certainly be a Germany victorious, Ludendorff backed the navy in its eagerness to return to unrestricted submarine warfare with the aim of bringing the Allies to their knees by the next summer.

Wilson had Lansing send off a confidential protest to Berlin on the matter of the Belgian deportees, always being careful not to sink into belligerent tones unbecoming a peacemaker. He told Lansing to make the protest "in a friendly spirit but most solemnly." At the same time, as if to notify the British he was still being evenhanded, he asked House to write to Grey "in the strongest terms" that the American people "were growing more and more impatient with the intolerable conditions of neutrality, their feeling as hot against Great Britain as it was at first against Germany."

Meanwhile, Wilson labored over his peace draft that he told Mrs. Wilson "may prove the greatest piece of work of my life." The draft he read to House made the usual arguments about how the war was casting a pall on belligerents and neutrals alike and how nobody would win if both sides persevered to exhaustion. Again, too, he had words certain to enrage the British, suggesting there was no great moral issue at stake. "The reasons for this upheaval of the world," he wrote, "remain obscure." All he was proposing, the draft said, was that the belligerents get together to define their terms and decide what they were fighting about.

In the meantime, Bucharest had fallen to the Germans on December 6 and Berlin decided that this event made it possible to call for peace talks without looking weak—always a German concern. The Foreign Office cabled von Bernstorff that the peace offer would be made at this time because "we do not at the present moment run any risk of damaging our prestige or showing signs of weakness. Should the enemy reject the offer the odium of continuing the war will fall on them." Von Bernstorff replied at once that "the Belgian question stands very definitely in the way." But there was nothing von Bethmann-Hollweg could do about it with Ludendorff now so firmly in the saddle.

When the German note arrived in Washington, merely offering to negotiate but with no terms mentioned, Wilson decided to have it passed on to the Allied powers as received, deferring the sending of his own note in order that they would not be linked. But the contents of the German note had already reached the Allied capitals and had been rejected. One reason was an arrogant speech given by the kaiser to German troops. He had proposed negotiations, he told them, "in the conviction that we are the absolute conquerors" and thus the Allies might be ready to sue for peace.

Lloyd George, addressing the House of Commons for the first time as prime minister, observed:

> To enter on the invitation of Germany, proclaiming herself victorious, without any knowledge of the proposals she proposes to make, into a conference, is to put our heads into a noose with the rope end in the hands of Germany. . . . The mere word that led Belgium to her destruction will not satisfy Europe anymore. . . . We shall put our trust in an unbroken army rather than a broken faith.

Wilson then released his own peace note. He had deleted the phrase that House said would offend the Allies. But he had substituted another just as offensive: "The objects which the statesmen of the belligerents on both sides have in mind in this war are virtually the same, as stated in general terms to their own people and to the world."

The implication, whether Wilson intended to leave it or not, was insulting: that the belligerents were killing each other en masse mindlessly, simply for the killing's sake. It may have seemed that way to Wilson, and to a goodly number of other Americans, but the contention hardly was likely to woo the enemies to the negotiating table.

Lansing then made matters even worse. Wilson's note, coming as quickly as it did on the heels of American circulation of the German note, had left an impression that Wilson supported the German proposal. In a press conference, the secretary of state denied it; the fact was, he said, the United States was interested only in seeing the war end. Then he added:

> I mean that we are on the verge of war ourselves, and therefore we are entitled to know exactly what each belligerent seeks, in order that we may regulate our conduct in the future. . . . The sending of this note will indicate the possibility of our being forced into the war. That possibility ought to serve as a restraining and sobering force, safeguarding American rights. It may also serve to force an earlier conclusion of the war. Neither the President nor myself regard this note as a peace note. It is merely an effort to get the belligerents to define the end for which they are fighting.

In the context of the latest submarine controversies and Wilson's protests, however, many reporters present seized on Lansing's stark observation that "we are on the verge of war" as a suggestion that if there were no peace talks now, the United States would enter the war on the Allied side. The "verge of war" remark grabbed the next day's headlines, rocked the stock market and outraged Wilson. So did Lansing's disclaimer that the message over which Wilson had sweated for so long was a peace note. The president instructed Lansing to put out a clarifying statement saying America's neutrality policy had not changed. He did so, but the clarification did little to quiet apprehensions raised by his original remarks.

The Allies were chagrined at Wilson's note, which again failed to recognize the justice of their cause. For financial reasons, however, they were obliged to be restrained in their response. The Federal Reserve Board in the United States had already tightened its policy toward loans to France and Britain, and British estimates warned that the country's financial ability to pursue the war would evaporate by spring without American monetary aid. So the British stalled, and in the meantime the Germans on December 26 responded to Wilson's call for a definition of objectives by declining to provide one. The note von Bernstorff handed to Lansing again called for direct talks between the belligerents, with no terms laid out in advance.

The terse German answer gave the Allies a chance to gain some credits with the Americans, if nothing else. The Allies quickly rejected the German note out of hand as mere gamesmanship, but carefully prepared a substantive response to Wilson. The terms it set were the restoration of Belgium and Serbia, with indemnities; evacuation by German troops of invaded portions of France, Russia and Romania, with "just reparation"; restitution of other land taken in the past; the liberation from foreign domination of Italians, Slavs, Czechs and Romanians; expulsion of Turkey from Europe; and independence for Poland as promised by the czar.

Lansing appealed to von Bernstorff for an explanation of why Germany would not specify her terms. Von Bernstorff, sharing von Bethmann-Hollweg's desire to involve Wilson in negotiations, urged Berlin to meet Wilson's request to provide the terms secretly only to him. Von Bethmann-Hollweg drafted specifics but apparently he was unable to win Ludendorff's approval. And so, on January 7, von Bernstorff received a cable instructing him merely to hold off for a while.

Two days later, the die was cast. The kaiser at last bowed to the German navy demand for unrestricted submarine warfare, to begin on February 1. When the terms the Allies sought were published the next day, they merely reinforced the German military view that Germany could win its objectives only on the battlefield, and with her U-boat fleet unfettered under the sea.

For the rest of January, von Bethmann-Hollweg and von Bernstorff labored desperately to bring Wilson into negotiations in some way. On January 15, not yet knowing of the fateful decision of January 9 to unleash the U-boats, von Bernstorff called on House. Armed only with the cable from Berlin telling him to stall, he took it upon himself to make tempting offers to the American government for which he had no authorization.

He said Germany was willing to sign a nonaggression pact with the United States of the sort Bryan as secretary of state had made with numerous other countries; he said Germany was ready to start talks at once on a postwar conference to establish Wilson's much-sought-after peace league; he pledged that Germany would not annex Belgium, would restore Serbia and would assure the independence of Poland and Lithuania.

The proposal not surprisingly bowled over House, who promptly wrote to Wilson: "This is the most important communication we have had since the war began and gives us a real basis for negotiations and for peace. . . . They consent to almost everything that liberal opinion in democratic countries has demanded. . . . If a false step is not taken, the end seems in sight."

But while Wilson considered his next move, von Bernstorff got the word on the U-boat decision. Frantically, he cabled back to Berlin:

> War inevitable in view of the proposed action. Danger of rupture could be mitigated by the fixing of a definite interval of time, say one month, so that neutral vessels and passengers may be spared, as any preliminary and timely warning seems impossible if present program is carried out. I shall have to give the password for unnavigable German steamers [that is, destroy their engines] on February 1st, as effect of carrying out of my instructions here will be like declaration of war, and strict guard will be kept.
>
> In any case, an incident like that of the *Lusitania* may be expected soon. If military reasons are not absolutely imperative . . . postponement most urgently desirable. Wilson believes he can obtain peace on the basis of our proposed equal rights of all nations. House told me again yesterday that Wilson proposed to take action very shortly, for in view of our declaration regarding future peace league, etc., he regards prospects of a peace conference as favorable.

But von Bernstorff was now trying to roll back the ocean's tide. On January 20 he was obliged to write to House: "I am afraid that it will be very difficult to get any more peace terms from Berlin at this time." Under strict orders not to reveal the decision to resume unrestricted sub warfare, von Bernstorff lamely explained that "the exorbitant demands of our enemies, and the insolent language of their note to the President, seem to have infuriated public opinion in Germany to such an extent that the result may be anything but favorable to our peace plans."

Von Bernstorff did hint, however, of what was to come: "In Berlin they seem to believe that the answer of our enemies to the President has finished the peace movement for a whole long time to come and I am therefore afraid that my Government may be forced to act accordingly in a very short time. . . . Every question leads us to the same problem, viz., which methods my Government will be obliged by public opinion to use against the English starvation."

Wilson remained determined, however, to save the world from further bloodshed. On January 22, he addressed the Senate with his painstakingly crafted appeal to common sense, selflessness and justice —known thereafter as his "peace without victory" speech. Peace would have to come sooner or later, he said, and because to be lasting it would require the support of America, he felt justified in speaking out.

Any peace, he said, "must be a peace without victory. . . . Victory would mean peace forced upon the loser, a victor's terms imposed upon the vanquished. It would be accepted in humiliation, under duress, at an intolerable sacrifice, and would leave a sting, a resentment, a bitter memory upon which terms of peace would rest, not permanently, but only as upon quicksand. Only a peace between equals can last."

Of equal importance, Wilson said, was the postwar creation of a worldwide mechanism to insure the keeping of the peace—the long-range aspect of his dream, with an explicit call for the mechanism to be backed up by collective military strength.

"Mere agreements may not make peace secure," he said.

It will be absolutely necessary that a force be created as a guarantor of the permanency of the settlement so much greater than the force of any nation now engaged or any alliance hitherto formed or projected that no nation, no probable combination of nations, could face or withstand it. If the peace presently to be made is to endure, it must be a peace made secure by the organized major force of mankind. . . . Only a tranquil Europe can be a stable Europe. There must be, not a balance of power, but a community of power; not organized rivalries, but an organized common peace.

The Senate received Wilson's speech enthusiastically, but both the Central Powers and the Allies were turned off by it. For one thing, Wilson observed at one point that "no peace can last, or ought to last, which does not recognize and accept the principle that governments derive all their just powers from the consent of the governed, and that no right anywhere exists to hand peoples about from sovereignty to sovereignty as if they were property." That observation, seemingly so reasonable when expressed to the people of his own functioning democracy, was certain to be seen as a direct threat to the functioning true monarchies reigning in Berlin and Vienna.

As for the Allies, they objected to another Wilson plea for freedom of the seas, which the British particularly viewed as a challenge to their survival. They received the speech as a whole as more pie in the sky that failed to recognize once again that the war was, as they saw it, a clash of good and evil. A British Conservative leader, Andrew Bonar Law, observed bitingly: "What Mr. Wilson is longing for, we are fighting for."*

The president, however, seemingly inspired by his own words and not knowing that Germany had already crossed the Rubicon on unleashing her U-boat fleet, asked House to make one more approach to von Bernstorff. "Tell him that this is the time to accomplish something," Wilson said,

> if they really and truly want peace . . . otherwise with the preparations they are apparently making with regard to unrestrained attacks on merchantmen on the plea that they are armed for offense, there is a terrible likelihood that relations between the United States and Germany may come to a breaking point. . . . Feelings, exasperations are neither here nor there. Do they in

---

*On the same day that Wilson made his "peace without victory" speech, von Bernstorff cabled Berlin for "authority to pay up to fifty thousand dollars in order, as on former occasions, to influence Congress through the organization you know of, which perhaps can prevent war. I am beginning in the meantime to act accordingly." The organization to which he referred apparently was the National German-American Alliance, which lobbied Congress heavily. The cable fell into American hands and was made public, creating an uproar over the "bribing" of Congress. Lansing diplomatically observed that "I do not see how the Bernstorff message in any way reflects upon Congress or any member," and a congressional investigation was averted.

fact want me to help? I am entitled to know because I genuinely want to help and have now put myself in a position to help without favor to either side.

House conveyed the plea to von Bernstorff. The ambassador told him there was little hope, what with Ludendorff and the high command now in full control in his country, but that he was still trying.

Immediately after Wilson's speech, von Bernstorff had cabled Berlin on January 23:

> As a result of proposed unrestricted U-boat war, peace movement will presumably come to an end. Nevertheless it is possible on the other hand that Wilson will make redoubled efforts for peace, if a time limit be allowed. I should like to leave no stone unturned in order to avert war with United States. Would it perhaps be possible, before opening the unrestricted U-boat war, to state the peace terms which we should have submitted at the Peace Conference we proposed, and to add that in view of our enemies' insolent rejection of our scheme, we could no longer abide by these moderate terms? And then we might hint that, as victors, we should demand an independent Ireland. A declaration of this sort would win over public opinion on this side, as far as this is possible, and might perhaps also satisfy public opinion in Germany.

Without waiting for a reply to this cable, after his meeting with House von Bernstorff sent off another to Berlin relaying Wilson's almost pleading offer of mediation:

> House revealed to me following thoughts of the President. Our enemies had openly expressed their impossible peace terms. Thereupon the President had, as a direct contrast to these, developed his program. Now we are also morally bound to make our peace terms known, because our desire for peace would otherwise appear insincere. . . .
> Wilson hopes that we shall communicate our peace terms to him, which might be published both in Germany and over here, so that they could become known immediately all over the world. If only we had confidence in him, President was convinced that he would be able to bring about both Peace Conferences [including the one for the League of Nations]. . . . President is

of opinion that note sent to him by the Entente was a piece of bluff which need not be taken seriously. He hopes definitely to bring about Peace Conferences, and quickly too, so that the unnecessary bloodshed of the Spring Offensive may be averted.

Von Bernstorff again inserted his own warning:

> If the U-boat campaign is opened now without any further ado, the President will regard this as a smack in the face and war with the United States will be inevitable. The war party here will gain the upper hand and the end of the war will be quite out of sight as, whatever people may say to the contrary, the resources of the United States are enormous.
>
> On the other hand, if we acquiesce in Wilson's proposal, but the scheme nevertheless comes to grief owing to the stubbornness of our enemies, it would be very hard for the President to come into the war against us, even if by that time we began our unrestricted U-boat war. At present therefore it is only a matter of postponing the declaration for a little while so that we may improve our diplomatic position. For my own part, I confess that I am of opinion that we shall obtain a better peace now by means of conferences than we should if the United States joined the ranks of our enemies.

But it was much too late now. The U-boat fleet had sailed with its new orders. On January 29, von Bethmann-Hollweg urged the kaiser and von Hindenburg to disclose the German war aims to Wilson personally, if only as a means of delaying American entry into the war. They agreed, while insisting that the military plans would go forward. The chancellor cabled von Bernstorff with the best he could do under the circumstances—a private communication only of German peace terms, but coupled with reaffirmation of the start of the all-out submarine war:

> Please thank the President on behalf of the Imperial Government for his communication. We trust him completely, and beg him to trust us likewise. Germany is ready to accept his secret offer of mediation. . . . We wish our acceptance of offer, as well as the offer itself, to be treated as quite secret. A public announcement of our peace terms is at present impossible, now that Entente has published their peace terms which aim at the

degradation and annihilation of Germany and her Allies, and have been characterized by President himself as impossible. We cannot regard them as bluff, as they entirely agree with professed opinions of enemy Powers expressed not only before, but afterwards. . . .

Von Bethmann-Hollweg then conveyed privately only what Germany's terms would have been had the Entente accepted Berlin's earlier proposal for a conference without public terms. They included: restitution to France "of that part of Upper Alsace occupied by her"; "acquisition of a strategical and economic safety-frontier zone separating Germany and Poland from Russia"; restitution of colonies "which would secure Germany colonial possessions compatible with the size of her population and the importance of her economic interests"; restoration of part of France occupied by Germany on the condition "that certain strategic and economic modifications of the frontier be allowed," plus financial compensation; "restitution of Belgium under definite guarantees for the safety of Germany," after negotiations with Belgium.

But von Bethmann-Hollweg specifically instructed von Bernstorff to "give President these details at the same time as you hand him note relating unrestricted U-boat war," and to inform him that "if this offer had only reached us a few days earlier, we should have been able to postpone opening of the new U-boat war. Now, however, in spite of best will in the world it is, owing to technical reasons, unfortunately too late, as far-reaching military preparations have already been made which cannot be undone, and U-boats have already sailed with new instructions."

The chancellor also told von Bernstorff to assure Wilson that concerning the U-boat decision "we are prepared at any moment to make every possible allowance for America's needs," to urge him to continue his peace efforts, while the German leaders "declare ourselves ready to discontinue the unrestricted U-boat war the moment we are completely assured that the President's efforts will lead to a peace that would be acceptable to us."

Von Bernstorff well knew that he had reached the end of the line. On the morning of January 31, the day he was to convey the bad news to the American government, he began to act on the decision. He ordered, he wrote in his memoirs, "that the engines of all ships lying in American harbors were to be destroyed. . . . It was dangerous to allow of any delay, for on the evening of January 31st our ships were already seized by the American police. As far as I know, however, all of them without exception were made unfit for use before this occurred."

Then, in the late afternoon, after sending the confidential letter of the German terms to House for conveyance personally to Wilson, the ambassador went to the State Department and handed to Lansing the note announcing unrestricted submarine warfare. The secretary of state read it somberly without comment and said he would pass it on to the president.

After von Bernstorff had left, Lansing called the White House but was told that Wilson was out—a falsehood, presumably because the president had already heard the news from House and wanted time to think alone, without the expected pressure from Lansing to break off diplomatic relations at once. Lansing sent the note over and after dinner met with Wilson, at which time the secretary of state did indeed urge speedy and decisive action. But the president held him off.

Wilson, incredibly to Lansing and others of like mind, continued to hold out the hope that there still might be some way to let the cup of severed diplomatic relations, and certain war, pass. He repeated to Lansing his conviction that America's proper role was as peacemaker, and he even raised again his complaints against British infringements on American rights as a neutral. By conversation's end, he agreed only that Lansing would draft a note breaking off diplomatic relations with Berlin, and that they would talk again.

House, at the State Department's request, rushed to Washington and conferred with the president the next morning, presenting him the letter including the terms Germany would have sought at Wilson's peace conference. It was clear they went far beyond what Wilson had hoped Berlin would demand. The president also met with his cabinet, but no conclusion was expressed by him.

The next day, February 2, Lansing came in with the draft and the cabinet met again, this time openly invited by Wilson to discuss the course he should take. But first he again recited his yearnings for peace. The cabinet nevertheless was overwhelmingly in favor of a break, and at last Wilson reluctantly agreed.

On February 4 the president addressed Congress, conveying his decision to a wildly applauding audience that obviously equated the action with war. The Senate passed a supporting resolution by 78 to 5, and both the war and peace advocates shared the impression that a declaration of war against the Central Powers would soon follow.

Theodore Roosevelt commended the Democratic president he had so castigated in the 1916 campaign and asked the War Department for authority to recruit and lead an infantry division; William Jennings Bryan at the same time pleaded with the American people not "to march under the banner of any European monarch or die on European soil."

But Wilson was far from ready to see his dreams crumble. In breaking off relations, he pointedly told Congress:

> I refuse to believe that it is the intention of the German authorities to do in fact what they have warned us they will feel at liberty to do. . . . Only actual overt acts on their part can make me believe it even now. . . . We shall not believe that they are hostile to us unless and until we are obliged to believe it; and we purpose nothing more than the reasonable defense of the undoubted rights of our people. . . . God grant that we may not be challenged to defend them by acts of willful injustice on the part of the Government of Germany.

As Wilson spoke, the State Department officially notified von Bernstorff of the break in relations, obliging him to prepare his own departure as required by diplomatic protocol. Even now, however, he tried to stem the inevitable. Working through the Swiss minister, he informed the State Department that Germany was willing to negotiate with Wilson while the unrestricted U-boat war proceeded—a notion that the president for once rejected out of hand.

On February 14, after safe conduct for the German embassy personnel and families had been obtained by the Swiss legation, Count Johann von Bernstorff finally departed the United States aboard the Danish liner *Friedrich VIII*.

The ambassador—and secret overseer of the German sabotage network in all of the Western Hemisphere—left amid considerable praise for his efforts to achieve peace. He later proudly quoted a farewell letter from Colonel House: "It is too sad that your government should have declared the unrestricted U-boat war at a moment when we were so near to peace. The day will come when people in Germany will see how much you have done for your country in America." Those words, to be sure, would take on an ironic twist later, when the full scope of von Bernstorff's activities became known.

Lansing, too, wrote that "I shall bear in mind all your earnest efforts in the cause of peace. . . . I am not unmindful of the efforts which you have made to prevent the breach which has occurred in the diplomatic relations of this country with Germany." And the *New York Tribune*, a leading anti-German paper of the time, said:

> The sailing of *Friedrich VIII* invites the cordial obituary style, though diplomatic deaths are supposed to warrant no sadness. And yet, curiously enough, Count Bernstorff probably finds himself leaving when more people are personally for him and fewer against him than at any time in the last two years. A less distinguished diplomat would not have had the art to stay so long. . . . At his departure many persons, close friends of the last eight years and newspaper correspondents, are going to miss his amazing charm and the easy candor of his talk. He has had an intimate directness in his dealings with all sorts and conditions of people, that only a personage of magnetic personality can adopt.

Although von Bernstorff now headed back to Germany, his role in the tug-of-war over American involvement in the war was not yet over. Soon to be disclosed was one final, routine von Bernstorff act that would contribute greatly to the demise of the American neutrality he had so earnestly sought to preserve, and precipitate America's entry into the war against Germany. In the meantime, however, the sabotage operation that had flourished under his direction for more than two years continued, even as some of its leading players fled to Mexico and South America in anticipation of America's belligerent status.

On February 17, three days after von Bernstorff's ship left New York, American agents in Jersey City arrested three Germans and charged them with attempting to blow up Black Tom Island, now back in operation as a munitions terminal, for a second time. The three, Fritz Kolb, Hans Schwartz and Jean Humbert, were frustrated by bad weather and their own ineptness. In Kolb's Hoboken apartment, police found enough incriminating evidence to put them out of business.

Such incidents, however, were now eclipsed by the widespread public anticipation that outright war was not far off for the United States—an anticipation tempered only by the president's continued agonizing and soul-searching for a way out.

On February 7, Wilson seized on a feeler from Vienna that Austria might want to negotiate a separate peace under his terms, provided he could guarantee that the Entente's plans to dismember the Austro-Hungarian Empire could be derailed. Wilson at once contacted Lloyd George, who sidestepped the matter, denying any plan of dismemberment. But he observed critically that a separate peace with the failing Austria would remove an increasing burden on the German war effort.

Wilson listened attentively to appeals that he adopt a policy of "armed neutrality" that would leave the United States short of open belligerency. American shipowners, temporarily cowed by the new German U-boat policy into keeping their ships in port, appealed to the State Department for advice. Suggestions that the American navy provide convoy protection were summarily rejected. At first the president agreed only that American merchant shippers could arm their vessels on their own if they chose, with very restrictive defensive uses of the guns specified. But there was no practical way for the ship owners to buy the necessary weapons on the public market and to man them.

As American shippers, faced with economic ruin if they remained paralyzed, warily ventured to sea in mid-February, Wilson finally asked Congress for authority to arm merchant ships with defensive weapons. Meanwhile he continued to wait for an "overt act" that would prove beyond any doubt that Berlin really meant to sink American ships, or ships carrying Americans, without warning.

Surprisingly, considerable opposition surfaced in the Senate to the armed ships bill. It was rescued only by a bizarre development that in a short time proved to have an infinitely more far-reaching impact on Wilson's diminishing hopes to keep the country out of the war. It was the development alluded to earlier as von Bernstorff's last, routine role in the dashing of those hopes.

The straw that would finally break neutrality's back was the discovery that Berlin, using von Bernstorff as the conduit, was enticing Mexico to attack the United States on the promise of regaining her "lost territory"—the states of Texas, New Mexico and Arizona! The evidence was the now-famous Zimmermann telegram.

III: AMERICA AT WAR, 1917-1918

I5. The Zimmermann Telegram—and War

For a considerable time, Berlin had been interested in exacerbating the trouble between the United States and Mexico. Doing so could divert Wilson's attentions and energies from the European conflict and, in the process, make it less likely that he would enter the war. If Wilson had his hands full with the punitive expedition, which was still thrashing around south of his own borders, the Germans reasoned, he would not want to take on serious military obligations elsewhere.

At the same time, Berlin knew of, and hoped to fan, continuing tensions between the United States and Japan that stemmed from repeated rumors that the Japanese sought a foothold on the North American continent in defiance of the Monroe Doctrine. Not only would such tensions further occupy Wilson; they might also lead to a break by Japan with the Allies and a new partnership with the Central Powers—an objective Germany would greatly welcome.

A full six years before the outbreak of the Great War, the kaiser had given a sensational interview in which he predicted war between the United States and Japan. The prediction came on the heels of reports of a secret treaty between Mexico and Japan providing for a Japanese naval base at Magdalena Bay, on Mexico's Pacific coast. At the time, President William Howard Taft dispatched 20,000 American troops to the southern borders and sent large segments of the fleet into the Gulf of Mexico, allegedly on maneuvers, further feeding the rumors. In fact, the American show of force related to the troubling internal situation in Mexico that later produced such headaches for Wilson.

The notion of somehow pitting both Mexico and Japan against the United States continued to intrigue the kaiser through the first years of the Great War. The idea grew in his mind particularly as the battlefield stalemate dragged on and America's role as the arms supplier to the Allies became ever more critical.

In April, 1915, a Japanese battle cruiser, the *Asama*, was reported sighted in Turtle Bay off Mexico's Baja California, the long, narrow peninsula jutting down from California. Rumors flew again, along

with unproved reports of Japanese clandestinely infiltrating peninsula ports. Nothing came of the reports, but they did serve to establish a climate in which suspicions of intrigue—by the Mexicans, by
the Japanese, and by the Germans encouraging both—henceforth
flourished.

At this juncture, Captain Franz von Rintelen, "The Dark Invader,"
was dispatched to New York. Along with his prime assignment of
fomenting bomb plots and other assorted mischief on the piers of the
American East Coast, he undertook to help the now-deposed Huerta,
now also in New York, regain power in Mexico.

Von Rintelen had spent a year in Mexico six years earlier and knew
the Mexican despot, who the Germans felt could be helpful in distracting Wilson. But in spite of discussions between Huerta and von
Rintelen, nothing serious came of them, and Huerta died shortly
afterward back in Mexico without having regained power.

The idea of inducing Mexico and, if at all possible, Japan to engage
the United States continued to feed the kaiser's fertile imagination.
On November 16, 1916, a hint of what was brewing came in a brief,
seemingly innocuous question concluding a five-line cable from von
Jagow in Berlin to von Bernstorff, primarily addressed to Wilson's
willingness to mediate peace talks.

"How does Mexican question stand?" the soon-to-be deposed foreign minister asked his ambassador in Washington. Von Bernstorff
replied a few days later: "The Mexican question is still in a state of
stagnation as a result of diplomatic negotiations." Von Bernstorff
referred, accurately, to bogged-down talks between Washington and
Mexico City over the withdrawal of the punitive expedition that had
been sent into Mexico to deal with the rambunctious Villa.

Hoping to prey on this continuing impasse for Wilson, Berlin
instructed its minister in Mexico, Heinrich von Eckhardt, to inform
President Carranza of the imminent policy of unrestricted submarine
warfare, and of Germany's consequent need of Western Hemisphere
bases. What would Mexico want in return for granting Germany har-
boring rights?

While Carranza meditated on the proposal, and the kaiser on January 9 finally signed off on unleashing the U-boats, Berlin cooked up a
concrete offer. By now, Zimmermann had replaced von Jagow, and he
conveyed the offer in a signed telegram attached to the one on January 16 that informed von Bernstorff of the final U-boat decision.

Because the message was so sensitive, originally it was to be taken by hand to von Bernstorff aboard the *Deutschland*, scheduled to leave for Baltimore on January 15. But the departure of the merchant submarine was postponed and Zimmermann decided to send the telegram two ways—by a roundabout route through neutral Sweden and directly to von Bernstorff over the State Department cable.

The latter route had been made available to Berlin by Wilson to be used in cipher for conveying urgent messages pertaining to the peace negotiations the president so earnestly desired to launch. The Foreign Office instructed von Bernstorff to relay the proposal to Mexico to von Eckhardt, taking the usual precautions.

The failure of the *Deutschland* to sail on schedule proved to be one of those fateful events on which history often turns. The consequent decision to use the State Department facilities unwittingly channeled the explosive message into the hands of British naval intelligence, which had obtained early in the war a critical German code book and keys to solving the German cipher used on the most sensitive messages.

On the morning of January 17, the intercepted message came into Room 40 O.B. (for Old Building) of the British admiralty. In these small, innocuous quarters two expert cryptographers, a middle-aged Presbyterian minister named William Montgomery and a young London publishing house employee named Nigel De Grey, labored daily and routinely over an endless stream of mysterious numbers in code and cipher. Code was the basic obfuscation of the message through use of fixed number, letter or symbol substitutions recorded in a code book; cipher was a more complex use of numbers in certain sequences, the key to which was not written down and was changed frequently. In this case, cipher was imposed on top of the code, causing Montgomery and De Grey to work hours cracking the message. Even then they were able at first to solve only part of it.

What they unscrambled, however, was enough to electrify the head of British naval intelligence, Admiral Hall. When they finally cracked all of it about a month later, Hall knew he had a development on his hands that could achieve the one objective now sought by the Allies more than any other—the entry of the United States into the war on their side.

As conveyed through von Bernstorff to von Eckhardt in Mexico City, the message, roughly translated, was:

Strictly secret, yourself to decipher. We intend from the first February unrestricted U-boat war to begin. It will be attempted to keep United States neutral nevertheless. In the event that it should not succeed, we offer Mexico alliance on following terms. Together make war. Together make peace. Generous financial support and understanding our part that Mexico conquer back former lost territory in Texas, New Mexico, Arizona. Settlement in the details to be left Your Excellency.

You will inform the President [of Mexico] of the foregoing in strictest secrecy as soon as war's outbreak with United States is certain and add suggestion that he immediately join in inviting Japan and at the same time mediate between us and Japan. Please inform the President on this point that ruthless employment of our U-boats now offers prospect England in few months to be compelled to peace. Acknowledge receipt. Zimmermann.

The sheer audacity of the proposal was mind-boggling, although the Germans, and Zimmermann in particular, apparently did not think it so. Appreciating that the decision to resort to unrestricted submarine warfare most likely would bring America into the war as an enemy, Berlin saw itself merely taking the natural step of doing what it could to hamstring the new expected foe, by tying the United States down in its own backyard. In such circumstances, warring nations seeking alliances had always promised the moon to those who would help them; in this case Berlin simply saw the moon as the three American states bordering on Mexico proper. What could have been simpler?

Carranza after all had shown definite signs of friendliness toward Berlin. He was now warning of a possible embargo on the sale and shipment of Mexican goods to all belligerents—an obvious and very serious threat to the British, whose fleet depended mightily on oil from Mexico's resources at Tampico.

In the difficult process of decoding and deciphering the message, the Room 40 experts at first figured out only the general proposal of a Mexican and Japanese alliance against the United States. The middle portion of the message, which bore the most scintillating morsels —the reconquest of Texas, New Mexico and Arizona—was not cracked for about a month. Even without this portion, however, Admiral Hall understood that Germany proposing an alliance with Mexico to make war on the United States would have a tremendously negative effect on American public opinion toward the Germans.

Still, Hall had a major problem in deciding what to do with the information. It had to be conveyed to President Wilson, there was no doubt. Here Wilson was negotiating seriously and conscientiously through von Bernstorff on peace talks, and at the very same time von Bernstorff was acting as the conduit for this nefarious deal with the Mexicans! At last the British seemed to have the vehicle to shake the American president out of his daydreams.

A simple, straightforward release of the Zimmermann telegram, however, would uncover one of the most important military secrets the British had—that they had obtained the German code books and cipher keys and had been routinely cracking the enemy's communications traffic, especially between Berlin and Washington. Hall deliberated long and hard even about informing his own Foreign Office across the way from the admiralty, and in fact did not do so until nearly three weeks after the telegram's receipt. By this time, he had hit upon a way to cover his tracks, and at the same time prove that the telegram was authentic.

Such proof was essential, because pro-Germans and pacifists in America, if not the reluctant dragon Wilson himself, certainly would claim the message to be an outlandish hoax. If it could be established that von Bernstorff had indeed transmitted the telegram from Washington on to Mexico City in substantially but not precisely the form in which Room 40 had intercepted it, its disclosure could be laid to agents in either of those two capitals far from London, and its authenticity established.

In this regard, Hall had one fortuitous ally—the supreme arrogance of the Germans. Hall correctly figured that the Germans were confident that their codes and ciphers were so cleverly conceived that no mere non-German could ever break them. They would immediately conclude on disclosure of the telegram, therefore, that it had been stolen after arrival in Washington or Mexico City, or leaked by a faithless embassy employee. This colossal conceit did in fact govern the Germans' subsequent search for the culprit in the Western Hemisphere who had done them in, enabling Hall to keep his critical secret through the end of the war.

On February 5, the day Hall advised the Foreign Office of the telegram, the British picked up yet another from Zimmermann to von Eckhardt—in the same supposedly undecipherable code—and promptly decoded it. This one went via the Swedish route, since Wilson had by now broken off diplomatic relations with Germany and von Bernstorff had received his walking papers.

This second telegram proved to be equally significant. It instructed von Eckhardt not to wait for America's entry into the war, but to approach Carranza "even now" on the scheme "provided there is no danger of secret being betrayed to United States." Berlin now considered a war declaration from the United States so likely that Zimmermann apparently felt there was no time to lose.

Hall decided there was no need to disclose this second telegram and further jeopardize the secrecy of the Room 40 operation. The second message, however, gave the lie to Zimmermann's later defense that the scheme was a contingency only, with no German intent to press it unless the United States actually did enter the war.

Hall now addressed himself to constructing his own deception about the origin of the first decoded telegram. Five days later, on February 10, a British agent in Mexico forwarded to London a copy from the telegraph office in Mexico City that showed von Bernstorff had transmitted Zimmermann's message in substantially the form in which he received it. He had made just enough changes of his own to identify it as having been sent from Washington. And shortly after that, out of Room 40 came the completed decipher, including the astounding proposed grab of Texas, New Mexico and Arizona. It was time to turn the bombshell loose on the Americans.

Hall himself took the telegram to the American embassy. There, he proposed ways to further obscure the source of its discovery and assure that it would be believed. The American ambassador, Walter Page, agreed to cable the message to the State Department. He would include instructions on how to find it in State's own files—since it had been transmitted over the State wire—or at the Western Union office in Washington, from whence von Bernstorff's copy to von Eckhardt had been dispatched.

Once the State Department had thus obtained the telegram, it was to wire it back to the American embassy in London. An American cryptographer would then be given access to Room 40's German code books so he could verify its authenticity himself: verification by an American on American "soil"—the embassy.

Page also wrote directly to Wilson explaining to him in veiled terms how the telegram had been obtained. He fudged in saying it had been acquired in Mexico, but informed Wilson in the greatest secrecy that the British had the German codes. The president was free, however, to have the telegram itself published as long as there were no British fingerprints on it.

On Saturday evening, February 24, Page's message arrived at the State Department in Washington. Lansing was taking a long weekend in the West Virginia mountains and his deputy, department counselor Frank Polk, perused it and took it at once to the White House. Wilson read it, Polk reported later, with "much indignation," not simply because of the audacity of the proposal to Mexico but because of its timing. The telegram had gone to the Mexicans precisely as von Bernstorff was insisting so urgently that he was laboring relentlessly to have his government accept Wilson's peace mediation efforts.

Wilson apparently never questioned the authenticity of the message himself, but Hall's procedure was carried out, though with some difficulty. The Western Union office in Washington for nearly two days insisted on its own security and privacy as a free entrepreneur in a peacetime democracy, refusing to release its copy of the von Bernstorff-to-von Eckhardt version. Eventually, however, the State Department convinced the telegraph office that the national interest required the release, and the copy was ferreted out and produced.

If there was any question up to this point whether Wilson would make the Zimmermann telegram public, it vanished in short order. For one thing, the president needed it as a prod to Congress. When Wilson went to Capitol Hill on the next Monday, February 26, to appeal for the armed ships legislation, he ran into unexpected opposition from the neutralists. He said he had the power already to arm the merchantmen but wanted congressional backing. He asked not only for the specific authority to arm the ships, but also "to employ any other instrumentalities or methods that may be necessary or adequate to protect our ships and our people in their legitimate and peaceful pursuits on the seas."

It was this broad language to which some senators objected. Also, Wilson's severest critics decided to filibuster the armed ships bill, being considered in the waning hours of the regular session of Congress, as a way to force the president to call a special session. If they could talk the bill to death until the regular adjournment, he would be obliged to call Congress back to a special session—and hence would not be left on his own, with Congress out of town, in this tense period of foreign-policy decisionmaking.

Wilson, in addressing Congress, said passage of the armed ships bill might yet persuade the Germans against committing an "overt act" of unrestricted sub warfare against American interests and citizens. But even as he spoke, word was reaching Washington that the British liner *Laconia* had been sunk the night before, killing several American passengers and crew members. Among the passengers were a mother and daughter who were friends of Mrs. Wilson.

The news no doubt stiffened Wilson's resolve, as did a bit of private information conveyed to him—with some relish, no doubt—by Lansing, who had now returned from his long weekend. The secretary of state had repeatedly objected to the procedure whereby von Bernstorff at House's instruction was permitted to use the State Department wire to communicate with Berlin. Now he made a check and was able to tell Wilson that the Zimmermann telegram had been transmitted through this unusual courtesy. Wilson was outraged all over again.

It was time to make use of the telegram. First, Wilson showed it to Senator Gilbert Hitchcock of Nebraska, a senior member of the Foreign Relations Committee and a prominent pacifist who had voted against the armed ships bill in committee. Hitchcock agreed at once to undertake leadership of the bill for the administration on the Senate floor. Next, the question was how to make the telegram public knowledge.

At Wilson's instruction, Lansing called an Associated Press correspondent, E. M. Hood, to come to his home that evening. Lansing gave Hood a paraphrased version of the telegram and extracted from him a pledge of secrecy concerning where he got it. The bargain was an easy one for the reporter, who suddenly found himself with the biggest journalistic scoop involving the United States since the beginning of the Great War.

The next morning, March 1, the story broke in newspapers across the country. The *Washington Post* bannered the shocking revelation, emphasizing von Bernstorff's role: "German Plot to Conquer United States with Aid of Japan and Mexico Revealed; Details of Machinations, Begun in Berlin January 19, Furthered by Von Bernstorff, in President's Hands." And the *New York World* proclaimed: "Mexico and Japan Asked by Germany to Attack U.S. If It Entered The War . . . Bernstorff, as Chief of Diplomats Concerned, Believed to Have Directed Conspiracy."

Hood's story, bearing no byline, specified that Zimmermann's instructions

> were transmitted to von Eckhardt through Count von Bernstorff, the former German Ambassador here, now on his way home to Germany on a safe conduct obtained from his enemies by the country against which he was plotting war. . . . Count von Bernstorff's connection with the plot, further than serving as the channel of communication, is intensified by the fact that the German Embassy was not merely the medium of delivering the message in this instance, but was really a sort of headquarters for all German missions in Central and South America.

The news stunned the country—and chagrined pro-German and neutralist elements. Publisher William Randolph Hearst ordered his editors to consider the telegram "in all probability a fake and a forgery."

The House, ignoring such observations, quickly passed the armed ships bill by a vote of 403 to 13, but the Senate balked. Senator Henry Cabot Lodge of Massachusetts, a prime ally of Theodore Roosevelt in demanding American entry into the war, pushed through a resolution calling on the president to verify the authenticity of the telegram—a means to get him personally to acknowledge the supreme insult, and hence to force his hand to action against it. The Senate passed the resolution in a somewhat watered-down version, as the State Department pressed the American embassy in London to verify the telegram's authenticity by the procedure suggested by Hall.

That night, with the verification in hand for his own satisfaction only, Wilson issued a statement. It said the administration had in the past week obtained proof of authenticity but could provide no more information. The doubters not surprisingly continued doubting; one senator, Oscar Underwood of Alabama, even defended Zimmermann. The German foreign minister, he said, was only taking a reasonable contingency step against the possibility that the United States might become a combatant in the war against Germany. Wilson for his part could do no more about dispelling the doubts, having agreed to secrecy to protect the existence and effectiveness of Room 40.

Through all this, Berlin said nothing. Von Eckhardt in Mexico City denied having received any such telegram and the Mexicans and Japanese said they knew nothing about it and had not been approached by the Germans. Lansing for his part absolved both Mexico and Japan of any knowledge of or susceptibility to the German scheme.

Room 40, however, knew that at least preliminary overtures had been made. On February 26 von Eckhardt had wired Zimmermann: "Beginning negotiations. . . . Could we provide munitions?" And again on March 2: "[The Mexican Foreign Minister] took the matter into consideration and thereupon had a conversation with the Japanese Minister, the substance of which is unknown to me. He subsequently went away to see the president."

The clear expectation was that Zimmermann would flatly deny the telegram, leaving the matter to one of credibility—his against Wilson's. But then, incredibly, a colossal break came Wilson's—and the Allies'—way.

At a press conference in Berlin the next day, March 3, the American correspondent for Hearst, William Bayard Hale, earlier a biographer of Wilson and later accused of having been a wartime German agent, addressed Zimmermann in a manner seemingly designed to get him off the hook.

"Of course Your Excellency will deny this story," Hale began.

"I cannot deny it," Zimmermann interrupted. "It is true."

The startling admission overjoyed the State Department and the occupants of Room 40, and sent the pro-Germans and neutralists reeling. Why would Zimmermann confess to having sent this very damaging telegram, not intended for public disclosure?

The only explanation that made any sense at all was that if he really believed that there was nothing wrong with making such a contingency proposal in the event America became a fighting enemy, he could believe as well that there was nothing wrong in owning up to it.

Zimmermann indeed argued that the telegram made clear "that Germany expected and wished to remain on terms of friendship with the United States, but that we had prepared measures of defense in case the United States declared war on Germany. I fail to see," he went on, "how such a 'plot' is inspired by unfriendliness on our part. It would mean nothing but that we would use means universally admitted in war in case the United States declared war. . . . The whole 'plot' falls flat to the ground in case the United States does not declare war on us."

There was, however, that later telegram, not disclosed until after the war, in which Zimmermann instructed von Eckhardt not to wait for American entry into the fighting, but to approach Carranza at once "provided there is no danger of secret being betrayed to the United States."

Zimmermann also contended that in the telegram Berlin was suggesting nothing more than what Washington itself had done. Defensively, he accused the United States of trying to organize South American countries into an alliance against Germany—a charge the State Department swiftly dismissed as ridiculous.

Whatever Zimmermann's reason or rationale, his confession was a godsend to the Allied cause. Here was clear-cut evidence that Germany meant to do harm to the United States in a direct and very tangible way. Here was something to fight about that could be understood by the average American not convinced that the rights of wealthier Americans to sail the Atlantic was worth going to war over.

In terms of American foreign-policy priorities, the Zimmermann telegram also helped induce some clear thinking by Wilson in an area where he long had let his emotions hold sway—dealing with Mexico and her assorted tyrants. Lansing had already persuaded the president that actions tying down the United States in Mexico only benefited German objectives. On February 5 the punitive expedition under General Pershing had at last been withdrawn. On March 3, the same day of Zimmermann's "confession," the American ambassador to Mexico presented his credentials to Carranza, thereby according American diplomatic recognition to his government.

What the Zimmermann telegram did not do, however, was persuade a few neutralist and pacifist diehards in the Senate to end their filibuster against the armed ships bill. On March 4 the Sixty-fourth Congress adjourned without passing it. Wilson was furious.

"The Senate of the United States is the only legislative body in the world which cannot act when its majority is ready for action," he charged. "A little group of willful men, representing no opinion but their own, have rendered the great government of the United States helpless and contemptible."

The armed ships rebuke was not, as history later recorded on the much more significant issue of the League of Nations, the last encounter Wilson would have with "a little group of willful men" in the Senate. Shortly afterward, Wilson went ahead and authorized arming American merchantmen anyway, after seventy-five senators signed a statement saying they would have supported the authorization had it

come to a Senate vote. But the president attached stringent regulations to the use of the guns, undercutting the effectiveness of their
installation.

In Berlin, now that Zimmermann had owned up to authoring the
explosive telegram, he pursued the alliance with Carranza, and with
equal zeal sought to find out how the scheme had become known to
Wilson. Von Eckhardt, for his part, had already begun a diligent effort
to shift the blame onto the now-defenseless von Bernstorff, who was
at sea en route home and knew nothing of the furor.

"Treachery or indiscretion here out of the question," von Eckhardt
cabled Zimmermann. "Therefore it apparently happened in U.S.A.
or cipher 13040 [the German diplomatic code] is compromised. . . . I
denied everything here."

Zimmermann wired back—in the same code used in the original
compromised telegram (designated No. 1 by Zimmermann) and in
the second (designated No. 11), ordering von Eckhardt to act "even
now": "In connection with this, emphasize that instructions were to
be carried out only after declaration of war by America. Dispatch
No. 11 is of course being kept strictly secret here also." And later:
"Most secret. Decipher personally. Please cable in same cipher who
deciphered Nos. 1 and 11, how the original and decodes were kept
and in particular whether both dispatches were kept in the same
place."

Von Eckhardt, clearly on the defensive, reported that both telegrams had been deciphered by his personal secretary, a man named
Magnus, and kept "in an absolutely secure steel safe procured especially for the purpose and installed in Magnus' bedroom." Magnus
read them to him "at night, in a low voice," von Eckhardt cabled
Zimmermann, and the originals "were burned by Magnus and the
ashes scattered."

The German minister also conveyed word from an embassy subordinate, who had been transferred from Washington when that embassy
was closed, that under von Bernstorff "even secret telegrams were
known to the whole staff" and copies were made.

Berlin finally let von Eckhardt off the hook. "Hardly conceivable
that betrayal took place in Mexico," the Foreign Office wired. "No
blame rests on either you or Magnus."

The finger of guilt now pointed inevitably at von Bernstorff, and
Admiral Hall helped the process along. When von Bernstorff's ship

arrived at Christiania (Oslo), the German minister to Norway at Berlin's orders rushed aboard to interrogate him. The recalled ambassador said, truthfully, that he had no idea how the Zimmermann telegram, which he had merely passed on to von Eckhardt, was discovered by the Americans.

Soon a story circulated that the British had searched the *Friedrich VIII* when it put in at Halifax, Nova Scotia, and had found a trunk belonging to the officially neutral but transparently pro-German Swedish government. The trunk's diplomatic seals had been broken, the story went, and it was found to have contained among other things Swedish diplomatic documents.

The clear implication was that von Bernstorff had secreted some of his own papers—including a copy of the Zimmermann telegram—in with the Swedish papers before the ship set sail, and the copy had been lifted by a diligent American agent in New York Harbor. The fact is that there was such a trunk. But the only place the seals on it had been broken was in the fertile imagination of Admiral Hall, again bent on protecting the secret of Room 40.

In any event, von Bernstorff was in the doghouse when he finally arrived in Berlin—so much so that the kaiser vetoed a von Bethmann-Hollweg suggestion to send him on a special mission to Stockholm, and refused to see him for nearly two months. Von Bernstorff, writing about the snub in his memoirs, laid it in part to the story of the Swedish trunk, or "diplomatic box," as he called it:

> This box, the very existence of which we knew nothing about, was taken possession of by the British authorities in Halifax, and dispatched to England. The London newspapers then reported that a dispatch box, belonging to Count Bernstorff, and containing documents of the German Embassy, had been opened there. Although the mistake, whether intentional or the reverse, was very soon elucidated, someone had laid the matter before the Kaiser in a distorted light. Apparently the Kaiser was allowed to form the suspicion that the opening of the box had betrayed the secret of the Mexico telegram.

The "someone" very likely was Zimmermann himself. He badly needed a scapegoat in the diplomatic corps, and he had been plagued by von Bernstorff's relentless pressures on him to delay the unleashing of the U-boat fleet. In any event, whoever was determined to keep von Bernstorff out of action succeeded for a full six months. Not until September, 1917, was he at last allowed to depart the diplomatic doghouse. He drew the German embassy in Constantinople, where thirty years earlier he had begun his diplomatic career.

Wilson, meanwhile, on March 5 took the oath for his second term. He delivered his inaugural address on the Capitol steps in a driving rain and wind so severe that two days later he was forced to bed with a debilitating cold. There he stayed with only occasional interludes, considering the narrow options he faced as the nation watched and waited.

In an ironic way, Wilson's extreme reluctance to confront the prospect of going to war—a reluctance that generated the ire of the likes of Roosevelt and even allegations of cowardice—bred a certain public confidence in him. If Woodrow Wilson in the end said that America must take up arms, then surely that step could not be avoided, and was a just action.

The growing drift from neutrality could be perceived on March 8. The Federal Reserve Board announced that far from cutting off British and French loans, as had been threatened and feared by the destitute Allies, it saw nothing wrong with them as "a very important, natural and proper means of settling the balances created in our favor by our large export trade." The Entente breathed easier, while hoping for more definitive action against the Central Powers from Washington.

Then, in the six days between March 12 and 18, came news that left Wilson no choice on what to do. On that first date, a merchant ship, the *Algonquin*, bound for London, became the first American vessel to be sunk since the German declaration of unrestricted sub warfare. But the ship was sunk by shelling, not torpedo, and crew and passengers were permitted to escape in small boats.

On March 16, news came of the czar's abdication and the Kerensky Revolution in Russia, which enabled Wilson to look upon the Entente Powers as now unequivocally democratic. Finally, on March 18 came word that three more American ships had gone down, two by gunfire and with only one crew member wounded, but the third, the *Vigilante*, torpedoed without warning en route to LeHavre, with the loss of fifteen members of the crew.

On March 20, Wilson met with his cabinet, sounding out the sentiment, which was strongly in favor of declaring war, but giving no indication himself of where he stood. However, he asked Lansing to stay behind and inquired of him how long it would take to put war-making legislation before Congress.

The next day the president called on Congress to come back on April 2 "to receive a communication concerning grave matters of national policy which should be taken immediately under consideration." Still, with Wilson's long record of temporizing, the uncertainty continued. Wilson disclosed his intentions to no one until he advised House on the night of March 27 that he had no other course but to ask for a declaration of war.

On the weekend before his appearance before Congress, Wilson composed his message at his own typewriter. On the morning of the appointed day, he played golf with his wife, lunched with House and some relatives, dined early with the family, then motored to the Capitol. An army cavalry unit rode alongside the president's car on the short trip up from the White House, protecting him from a large crowd that had assembled. Inside the House chamber, the galleries were packed, waiting for the historic message.

The president began by reviewing the circumstances that led to this fateful night, and why the most recent step he had taken, authorizing the arming of merchant ships, was not the answer:

> Armed neutrality, it now appears, is impracticable. Because submarines are in effect outlaws when used as the German submarines have been used against merchant shipping, it is impossible to defend ships against their attacks as the law of nations has assumed that merchantmen would defend themselves against privateers or cruisers, visible craft giving chase upon the open sea. It is common prudence in such circumstances, grim necessity indeed, to endeavor to destroy them before they have shown their own intention. They must be dealt with upon sight, if dealt with at all.

Then Wilson said: "There is one choice we cannot make—we are incapable of making; we will not choose the path of submission." The statement produced wild cheering and applause from members of Congress on the House floor and from the galleries. Instead, he said, America would be guided on the battlefield by the high purpose to which he had already assigned her in his own, now failed, efforts to achieve peace. He continued:

Our object now, as then, is to vindicate the principles of peace and justice in the life of the world as against selfish and autocratic power, and to set up amongst the really free and self-governed peoples of the world such a concert of purpose and of action as will henceforth ensure the observance of those principles.

The president made specific reference to the "criminal intrigues" of the "Prussian autocracy" by its spies and saboteurs in the United States. That Berlin "means to stir up enemies against us at our very doors," he said,

the intercepted note to the German Minister at Mexico is eloquent evidence. We accept this challenge of hostile purpose. . . . We are glad, now that we see the facts with no veil of false pretense about them, to fight thus for the ultimate peace of the world and for the liberation of its people, the German peoples included: for the rights of nations great and small and the privilege of men everywhere to choose their way of life and of obedience.

"The world," Wilson said, in what was to become his most famous utterance, "must be made safe for democracy. Its peace must be planted upon the tested foundations of political liberty."

At last, the president of the United States was demonstrating in his words and deeds that he understood and appreciated the differences between the combatants of the Great War who had been putting their treasure in lives and resources on the line for nearly three years.

Now he was asking Congress to join that war that for all that time he had been telling the American people, in effect, was not worth the candle. And so the challenge for Woodrow Wilson was to put aside for a time his cherished role as peacemaker and accept the role he abhorred and sought so singlemindedly to avoid—that of warmaker.

If America was to "make the world safe for democracy," it would require resoluteness—even ruthlessness—in its leadership, not the lofty idealism with which Wilson had sought to lead America and the world to peace until now. He would not, could not, abandon that higher goal—a League of Nations to guarantee the peace after the conclusion of the present war. But he could no longer give it the dominant place in his thoughts, words and deeds. There was now a war to be won, and a people to be inspired to wage and win it, against an enemy now clearly and unmistakably identified.

16. The Herrmann Message

Four days after Wilson's speech, Congress formally took the irreversible step of a declaration of war against the Central Powers. And four days after that, a large munitions plant at Eddystone, Pennsylvania, was blown up, killing 112 workers, most of them women and young girls. The deed was presumed to be the work of German saboteurs. Shortly afterward a German agent, Dr. Louis Kopf, attempted to dynamite the Elephant-Butte Dam on the Rio Grande River, but was thwarted and caught.

Sabotage, now that America was at war, would no longer be punished simply by a prison sentence but by death. Perhaps mainly for this reason, most German saboteurs fled the country, principally to Mexico and South America, and the incidence of suspected bombings tapered off sharply in the United States.

Surprisingly, Martha Held, the operatic hostess of the safe house in Manhattan, continued until June of 1918 to rent the brownstone that had been the scene of so much earlier mischief and revelry. The landlord later testified that

> I received a telephone call stating that the house was vacant and that Martha Held and everybody had disappeared. . . . We sent down there and found that the keys had been left next door, and that no one knew where Martha Held had gone.

Among those who escaped to Mexico was Kurt Jahnke. A month after America's entry into the war, he became the head of German sabotage working out of Mexico City. In a cable to a superior in Antwerp in early 1918, he boasted that "the destruction of war factories and provisions in the U.S.A. is working satisfactorily. Since May 1917 my people report as destroyed the English S.S. *Clark*, Japanese S.S. *Itfh* [*sic*]. I am now occupied in causing strikes and mutinies in the army. . . . Am I to undertake anything against Japanese Colony in California?"

If the saboteurs were operating within the United States on anywhere near the scale they pursued while America was neutral, however, that fact escaped the detection of beefed-up American counter-intelligence and security forces. They did, though, have a fairly early line on Jahnke's Mexican activities, as witnessed by this report by an American agent around the time Jahnke was boasting to his superior:

> Intelligence officers will be interested to know that the present task of promoting a mutiny in the U.S. Army has been entrusted by Berlin to one of their star agents, one K. A. Jahnke of Mexico City. This event is scheduled for the Autumn. Jahnke also has taken under his wing the general supervision of sabotage in the U.S., the Panama Canal and American possessions generally, including especially sabotage of ships transporting War material and material for ship construction.
>
> His program covering the foregoing ambitions has been approved by the German Government, with an available credit of 100,000 marks per month, and an additional large commission on results accomplished. . . . He has already had some experience in the control of German agitators, defeatists and I. W. W. agitators in this country, and is regarded as an ideal man for the job. Jahnke's official appointment seems to be that of sole naval confidential agent in Mexico. . . . Intelligence officers will probably never have the pleasure of meeting Mr. Jahnke personally, but it is not at all unlikely that he will give them something to think about. Hence this note in advance.

The last comment proved to be quite prophetic. Until Wilson asked Congress to declare war, America's defenses against infiltration and sabotage had been practically nonexistent. The army intelligence service had operated in Washington in 1916 on a budget of a mere $11,000. But with the war declaration, a new military intelligence service was created with the advice and counsel of the British secret service.

At the same time, a large volunteer arm called the American Protective League was established under the purview of the Justice Department. A quarter of a million Americans signed on to be on the lookout for spies, saboteurs, labor agitators and draft dodgers. Wilson had requested selective service the day after war was declared.

The president himself had now at last faced the reality of the von Bernstorff two-faced mission. In a Flag Day speech on June 14, he said that mission had given him no alternative but to put the country into the war:

> It is plain enough how we were forced into the war. The extraordinary insults and aggressions of the Imperial German government left us no self-respecting choice but to take up arms in defense of our rights as a free people and of our honor as a sovereign government. The military masters of Germany denied us the right to be neutral. They filled our unsuspecting communities with vicious spies and conspirators and sought to corrupt the opinion of our people in their own behalf. . . .

> Some of these agents were men connected with the official embassy of the German government itself here in our own capital. They sought by violence to destroy our industries and arrest our commerce. They tried to incite Mexico to take up arms against us and to draw Japan into a hostile alliance with her —and that, not by indirection but by direct suggestion of the Foreign Office in Berlin. . . . What great nation in such circumstances would not have taken up arms?

Wilson's call for the draft, and Congress' enactment of it, was a first priority. At the time America became a combatant, she had only about 300,000 enlisted men under arms, including the regular army, the National Guard and reserves, and fewer than ten thousand officers.

The secretary of war, Newton D. Baker, was a pacifist opposed to a draft. Much of the American military was decentralized into state militias, a circumstance that compounded the state of unpreparedness in which the country found itself.

There was no immediate plan to send an expeditionary force to France, and indeed the Allies at first were much more interested in receiving American material and financial assistance. They did, however, urge that for morale purposes a small American force be sent. Under General Pershing, lately relieved of his frustrating responsibilities chasing Villa in Mexico, two thousand American soldiers were dispatched in June and July.

These and subsequent American reinforcements sent to Europe in 1917 were largely armed with rifles and artillery from the Allies. They were now turning out a surplus and preferred to have the American industrial giant concentrate on mobilizing its own capacity for a massive effort in 1918 and beyond. Not until the battle of the Meuse and

Argonne in 1918 were American automatic rifles and heavy machine guns in the hands of American troops in great numbers. Nor was a full squadron of American planes in combat over Europe until August of 1918.

This concentration on American industrial mobilization persuaded Wilson to issue a proclamation seeking to put the worker at home and the soldier and sailor in combat on a par in the great national challenge:

> In the sense in which we have been wont to think of armies, there are no armies in this struggle; there are entire nations armed. Thus, the men who remain to till the soil and man the factories are no less a part of the army that is in France than the men beneath the battle flags. It must be so with us.
>
> It is not an army that we must shape and train for war—it is a Nation. To this end our people must draw close in one compact front against a common foe. But this cannot be if each man pursues a private purpose. All must pursue one purpose. The Nation needs all men, but it needs each man, not in the field that will most pleasure him, but in the endeavor that will best serve the common good. Thus, though a sharpshooter pleases to operate a trip-hammer for the forging of great guns, and an expert machinist desires to march with the flag, the Nation is being served only when the sharpshooter marches and the machinist remains at his levers. The whole Nation must be a team, in which each man shall play the part for which he is best fitted.

At the executive level, a Council of National Defense comprised of six cabinet members was charged with "coordination of industries and resources for the national security and welfare." In July the War Industries Board was established, eventually to be chaired by Bernard Baruch. The shipping of food to the Allies became the responsibility of Herbert Hoover, a California mining engineer who had been in charge of American food relief for Belgium. Liberty bonds and thrift stamps helped finance the war effort at home.

Through all this, while Wilson sought to mobilize the will and spirit of the American people, he never let go of his longer-term objective of a postwar community of nations. In this regard, he took pains to identify the enemy not as the German people, but as their autocratic, deceitful government. "We have no quarrel with the German people," he said. "We have no feeling towards them but one of sympathy and friendship."

That sentiment did not sit well with critics who felt it was no way to generate fervor for victory on the home front and on the battlefield. But he pursued it, and when Pope Benedict XV in August called for peace talks, Wilson observed:

> The object of this war is to deliver the free peoples of the world from the menace and actual power of a vast military establishment controlled by an irresistible government. . . . This power is not the German people. It is the ruthless master of the German people. . . . We cannot take the word of the present rulers of Germany as a guarantee of anything that is to endure, unless explicitly supported by such conclusive evidence of the will and purpose of the German people themselves as the other peoples of the world would be justified in accepting.

On the battlefield, the war slogged on with no appreciable impact from the American entry. The Germans were beaten back on the Somme front in the spring of 1917 but they regrouped and held on, and a French offensive was repulsed. The Russian armies were demoralized and the Italians in collapse.

The Bolshevik revolution indicated Russian withdrawal from the war and a consequent transfer of heavy numbers of German troops to the Western Front. By year's end, American reinforcements were much in demand, by which time the American armed strength had quadrupled, to 1,250,000 enlisted men and 100,000 officers. On December 2, Pershing cabled Washington: "The Allies are very weak and we must come to their relief this year, 1918. The year after may be too late. It is very doubtful if they can hold on until 1919 unless we give them a lot of support this year."

Meanwhile, in Mexico, the German saboteurs who had fled there just before or after the American declaration of war were reorganizing. Von Eckhardt, the German minister in Mexico City, having survived the Zimmermann telegram, was now fulfilling the dual role of diplomat and overseer of anti-American subversion that had been carried out for three years by von Bernstorff before his forced departure from Washington.

Among the first of the saboteurs to arrive from the United States in 1917 were Fred Herrmann, the young American recruit who brought the first supply of incendiary "pencils" or "glasses" to America and who had been involved with Theodore Wozniak in the Kingsland fire, and Raoul Gerdts Pochet, called simply Gerdts, who worked as Herrmann's chauffeur and sidekick.

Herrmann and Gerdts fled by way of Cuba to Vera Cruz. On the boat to Vera Cruz, the Spanish steamer *Monserrat*, they fell in with a German national named Adam Siegel who told them he had escaped from a Russian internment camp. He was broke and was looking for a way to make money and at the same time help Germany.

The three men took a train together to Mexico City and stayed at a cheap hotel, the Juarez. From there, Herrmann and Gerdts went to the German legation to see von Eckhardt. Herrmann told the minister he had been ordered, first by the German General Staff and later by Hilken in Baltimore, to destroy the oil fields at Tampico. He needed money.

Von Eckhardt was suspicious. For clarification, on April 12 he cabled Marguerre and Nadolny, mentioned by Herrmann as his recruiters at Section 3B in Berlin the previous year. In the cable, later uncovered, von Eckhardt wired:

> Where is Lieut. Wohst [Woehst] stationed? Has he sent about $25,000 to Paul Hilken? He or somebody else is to send me money. . . . With reference to the previous paragraph, Herrmann (a smart fair-haired German with an Anglo-Saxon accent) professes to have received from General Staff a year ago, and renewed in January by Hilken, a commission to set fire to the Tampico Oil Field, and proposes now to carry it out. He asks me whether he is to do it. Would it not be well for me to answer that I am not in communication with Berlin? Verdy [apparently a legation aide] believes him and his companion . . . Gerds [*sic*] to be English or American spies. Request immediate answer. Most immediate!

The next day, Section 3B cabled back:

> Herrmann's statements are correct. Nothing is known of Gerds. Wohst has been retired. The firing of Tampico would be valuable from a military point of view, but the General Staff leaves to you to decide. Please do not sanction anything which would endanger our relations with Mexico or, if the question arise, give Herrmann any open support.

Herrmann thus was left hanging. He decided to appeal directly to Hilken, the saboteurs' paymaster in Baltimore, for the money. This seemingly insignificant decision by a relatively secondary figure in a sabotage operation that went all the way up to ranking diplomatic officials in Berlin would prove in time to be catastrophic for Germany.

The result was the single document that two decades later did more than any other one piece of evidence to brand Germany as guilty beyond doubt of sabotage against neutral America. The document did not surface, however, until some thirteen years later. And when it did, the Germans—with notable success for a considerable time —moved heaven and earth to challenge its authenticity.

Herrmann sat down at a table in his room at the Hotel Juarez and composed a long letter in code for Hilken or his New York deputy, Paul Hoppenberg, asking for money for the Tampico operation. At the same time, he conveyed enough information about German sabotage operations to confirm beyond any doubt to the recipients that the message was coming from him.

First Herrmann wrote out the letter as he wanted it, in English. Then he transformed it into the code and gave it to Siegel. Next, he took a copy of a magazine he had bought in Havana for the boat trip to Vera Cruz. It was a popular magazine of feature articles of the day known as the *Blue Book*, dated January, 1917. With Siegel dictating to him, Herrmann turned to a book-length novel called *The Yukon Trail*, by William MacLeod Raine. He held it sideways and proceeded to write the coded message in lemon juice over the printed material, so that the print and Herrmann's message were perpendicular. In a few moments, the lemon juice soaked in and the message disappeared.

Herrmann then took a small pin and jabbed tiny holes in certain pages of the magazine, over particular letters. As later deciphered, numbers in the message referred to specific pages, with the first number discarded and the next three reversed. For example, the first number in the message was 1775, which meant the reader was to turn to page 577. Then he was to hold the page to the light and spell out the word according to the tiny pin holes over certain letters. The technique was one the Allies already knew the Germans employed.

Herrmann then gave the book to Gerdts, telling him to take it to Hilken in New York or Baltimore, or to Hoppenberg in New York. At the same time, Herrmann told Gerdts to instruct Hilken to apply a hot iron to the pages to make the lemon-juice message visible. The message, given here with the code numbers for the persons mentioned and then the decoded names, was:

Have seen 1755 [Eckhardt]. He is suspicious of me. Can't convince him I come from 1915 [Marguerre] and 1794 [Nadolny]. Have told him all reference 2584 [Hinsch] and I, 2384 [*Deutschland*], 7595 [Jersey City Terminal], 3106 [Kingsland], 4526 [Savannah], and 8545 [Tony's lab]. He doubts me on account of my bum 7346 [German]. Confirm to him through your channels all O.K. and my mission here. I have not funds. 1755 [Eckhardt] claims he is short of money. Send [by] bearer U.S. 25000. Have you heard from Willie. Have wired 2336 [Hildegarde] but no answer. Be careful of her and connections. Where are 2584 [Hinsch] and 9107 [Carl Ahrendt]. Tell 2584 [Hinsch] to come here. I expect to go north but he can locate me thru 1755 [Eckhardt]. I don't trust 9107 [Carl Ahrendt], 3994 [Kristoff], 1585 [Wolfgang] and that 4776 [Hoboken] bunch. If cornered they might get us in Dutch with authorities. See that 2584 [Hinsch] brings with him all who might implicate us. Tell him 7386 [Siegel] is with me. Where is 6394 [Carl D.]. He worries me. Remember past experience. Has 2584 [Hinsch] seen 1315 [Wozniak]. Tell him to fix that up. If you have any difficulties see 8165 [Phil Wirth National Arts Club]. Tell 2584 [Hinsch] his plan O.K. Am in close touch with major and influential Mexicans. Can obtain old 3175 [cruiser] for 50000 West Coast. What will you do now with America in the war. Are you coming here or going to South America. Advise you drop everything and leave the states. Regards to 2784 [Hoppenberg]. Sei nicht dum mach doch wieder bumm bumm bumm. Most important send funds. Bearer will relate experiences and details. Greetings.

Beyond the obvious name references, some of the others would be clear to Hilken: "Jersey City Terminal" was obviously Black Tom; "Savannah" apparently referred to the germ inoculations of horses at that port; "Tony's Lab" was Anton Dilger's germ-manufacturing laboratory in Chevy Chase; "Willie" was Willie Woehst, Herrmann's old roommate and close companion in New York at the time of the Kingsland fire; "Hildegarde" was Woehst's cousin, Hildegarde Jacobsen, who had often accompanied Woehst and Herrmann to give them a cloak of respectability.

The specific mention of Kristoff was a clear indication that he along with the others was a German agent. But it must be remembered that this secret message did not come to light until long after the war. So although Kristoff was regarded from the outset as the prime Black Tom suspect, he remained a mystery figure for years after the war's end. "Wolfgang" was a young German who had assisted Herrmann in the United States in the fall of 1916. The reference to obtaining an old cruiser, it was learned much later, related to a Hinsch scheme whereby he hoped to become skipper of a cruiser with which to raid American merchant shipping along the West Coast. And the German words at the end were a reference to the windows in Hoppenberg's New York office being blown out by the Black Tom explosions and the joke made at the time: "Don't be dumb. Make again boom, boom, boom."

Gerdts dutifully made his way back to the United States with the *Blue Book* and its secret message written in lemon juice and tiny pin pricks, with instructions to bring back the $25,000 he would be given. According to Gerdts' own testimony later, he first went to New York, but Hilken was not there and Hoppenberg, it turned out, had died just the day before. So Gerdts went on to Baltimore and gave the *Blue Book* to Hilken there. As Gerdts described the scene after the war:

> He [Hilken] went to the cellar of the house to decipher the order and then told me that he did not have that amount of money, but that I should stay at his home while he went to New York to procure the money. Three days later he returned and told me that he was going to send the money, but that another friend of his who he expected in a few months was going to take the money to Mexico.
>
> Shortly afterwards, a man was introduced to me as Captain Hinsch. He told me that he was a Captain of the North German Lloyd that towed the *Deutschland* to the harbor at Baltimore. He told me to go back to Mexico and gave me a thousand dollars. The balance of $24,000 he told me he was going to take himself. He asked me to tell Herrmann that he [Hinsch] was busily engaged in getting guns of 705 millimeters across the border into Mexico which were to be used to equip a destroyer in Mazatlán, intercepting ships carrying cargoes from San Francisco. . . . This was how I met Captain Hinsch and this was the nature of my relationship with him.

Gerdts said that on returning to Mexico City, "on different occasions Herrmann spoke about the desirability of setting fire to the tanks of petroleum at Tampico. . . . One day Herrmann said he would give me $25,000 to do it. I refused this offer and a few days later he discharged me, telling me that I was not the man they wanted. . . . My relations with Herrmann at the end were very disagreeable. . . . When I did not have enough money to go back to Colombia he answered, 'Go to the devil.'"

Gerdts did go on to Colombia, landing a job as an agent for the Sun Life Insurance Company in Bogotá. Again, it must be remembered that none of these activities linking the German saboteurs in Mexico to Hilken's American operation was known at the time, or until long afterward, when the trail of all these perpetrators was being pursued. In due course, however, we will return to Herrmann, Gerdts, Hilken and the *Blue Book* as vital players in the unraveling of the German conspiracy.

Of more immediate interest to the American intelligence forces now were the activities of other suspected German saboteurs identified by Allied agents who had infiltrated their ranks in Mexico. One of these saboteurs was soon to become the only German spy condemned to death in the United States during the Great War—Lothar Witzke, one of the prime suspects in the Black Tom disaster. How that death-penalty conviction came about was the next piece in the intricate puzzle of German deception American investigators labored diligently to solve.

17. Unquiet on the Mexican Front

Captain Hinsch did indeed go to Mexico later in 1917, evading a presidential warrant issued for his arrest. Until then, Kurt Jahnke assumed control of the sabotage operation there himself, after satisfying the always wary von Eckhardt that he was Berlin's authorized agent.

On November 12, 1917, the German minister cabled Berlin to check out Jahnke's claim that Charles "The Dynamiter" Wunnenberg, code name "Son Charles," had given him the sabotage mandate. The cable, intercepted by the British at the time but not delivered into American hands until after the war, said:

> Kurt Jahnke, who states that he has been appointed by Wunnenberg, alias Son Charles, for secret service in U.S.A., reports as follows from Mexico. Charles and Sanders [another German agent] are in prison in New York. With the remainder of the money Kurt has established S. Service in accordance with instructions which were brought by a drunken Danish Captain from Switzerland. He cannot be responsible for the service in Mexico because he cannot receive money from U.S.A. Kurt asks for further instructions in order to have a basis for Mexico, and asks to be informed in what manner he is to expect his instructions. He proposes that a naval expert should be sent to Mexico, as hitherto nothing has been done there in the naval line.*

Another cable, from Berlin to the German embassy in Madrid dated four weeks later, said:

> If your messenger of December 21st [apparently going to Mexico] is trustworthy please give him the following instructions for Jahnke and the Legation. Jahnke is to get into communication with the military Representative at the Legation in Mexico in

---

*Wunnenberg had been arrested in the United States on February 1, 1917, and convicted of violating neutrality laws. Hence, Jahnke's acknowledgment that he had worked for Wunnenberg confirmed that he was active in the United States before the American entry into the war.

order to operate principally against ships with S. undertakings. He is to try and send an agent from Mexico to U.S.A. . . . As soon as a messenger arrives in Mexico he should discuss the Mexican matter with the M.A. [Military Attaché] there.

As a result of these instructions, Jahnke checked his roster for the right man to go back into the United States to continue, among other tasks, the blowing up of munitions plants and shipments. It so happened that one of those most proficient at these skills was now in Mexico. He was a veteran agent with whom Jahnke had worked in California and New York—his old sidekick in the earlier von Bopp operation in San Francisco, Lothar Witzke.

A second man who had been carrying on anti-American activities in the States, the Irishman Jim Larkin, was also in Mexico City with the German conspirators at this time, but he was experienced chiefly as a labor agitator.

Jahnke chose Witzke for the job and sent him with two other trusted operatives who had become members of his clique in recent months, Dr. Paul Altendorf and William Gleaves. Altendorf, Gleaves, and a third man, William Neunhoffer—each unknown to the other two —were in reality Allied agents who had infiltrated the German operation. Their superiors had guessed correctly that as soon as America entered the war the Germans would set up such an operation in Mexico. Together the three contributed to the only really significant break in the mystery of the Black Tom explosions until well after the war.

Altendorf, the major figure in the episode, was of Polish origin and had been a medical student at the University of Krakow. After extensive travels in South America, he went to Mexico and became a colonel in the Mexican army under the military governor of the state of Sonora, on the border with Arizona. There he was recruited into the U.S. Military Intelligence Division. Proficient as he was in German, Spanish and English, Altendorf was sent to Mexico City, where without difficulty he met Jahnke and joined his operation.

Gleaves, a black Canadian who as a youth had lived in Pennsylvania, was a British intelligence agent in Mexico City who also infiltrated the Jahnke team. Jahnke assigned him to join the IWW to foment disorder among black American soldiers in El Paso. He did so, but reported back to Jahnke that he needed help from someone who was more familiar with the United States than he was.

That request landed him an assignment with Witzke.

Neunhoffer, a Texan of German parentage, was a young lawyer in San Antonio and a member of the mobilized National Guard sent to the Mexican border. His skills in German and Spanish also led to his recruitment by the American Justice Department. He was sent to Mexico City to pose as a draft-dodger. He, like the others, met Jahnke through Otto Paglasch, owner of the Juarez Hotel—where Herrmann penned the critical lemon-juice message to Hilken.

On January 16, 1918, Witzke, accompanied by Altendorf and Gleaves, left Mexico City for the port of Manzanilla. There they were to board a ship to Mazatlán and then a train to Nogales, on the border between Sonora and Arizona. Altendorf's assigned task from Jahnke was to introduce Witzke to his superior in the Mexican army, General Elias Calles, the military governor of Sonora.

The trip was long and tiring, and Witzke, traveling under the alias Pablo Waberski—one of several he affected—began drinking. The more he drank the more he talked—of the mission on which he was now embarking and, of equal interest to Altendorf, his past accomplishments.

Later, according to Altendorf (known to American intelligence as Operative A-1), Witzke confided that he was going to Nogales to kill an American and to

> blow up things in the United States. . . . There is something terrible going to happen on the other side of the border when I get there, and I can't tell you what it is. If I get the job done well, I will have saved Germany, and after I return from the United States you will see it in the papers, but you must never mention it to anyone. You will know that it was my work.

Witzke also told him, Altendorf testified later, that he had blown up a black powder magazine at Mare Island, near San Francisco. It was during this trip that Witzke confided, "I also did the work in New Jersey with Yenky [Jahnke], when the munitions barges were blown up and piers wrecked. We were out in a small boat and the waves nearly swamped us and we came near drowning." Witzke added, Altendorf reported, that "I have many lives on my conscience and I have killed many people, and will now kill more."

Altendorf's testimony regarding what Witzke had said about "the work in New Jersey" was largely overlooked at the time because Witzke was facing court martial regarding only his activities from Mexico after the American entry into the war. But that testimony was to take on major significance later on.

When Witzke, Altendorf and Gleaves arrived at the headquarters of General Calles in the town of Hermosillo, Altendorf introduced Witzke to Calles. It was clear to Altendorf that the general had been expecting the German agent. Witzke asked Calles to assure him safe passage through Sonora and to forward to the German legation in Mexico City any coded messages he might telegraph from the United States. Calles, anti-American and hence pro-German as was most of the Carranza government, agreed. He also gave Witzke a revolver and a permit to carry it in Mexico. At this point, Altendorf's assigned task was over and he left the company of Witzke and Gleaves in Hermosillo.

It was now two weeks since the departure of the three men from Mexico City. Witzke and Gleaves boarded a train for Nogales, Sonora. Later that night, Altendorf on his own hopped a freight and, unbeknownst to either Witzke or Gleaves, got into the same town a night later. Witzke on arrival went to the American consulate to have his passport stamped for entry into the United States. He showed the immigration authorities a Russian passport, issued in Mexico City, giving his name as Paul Waberski. He claimed, however, to have been a resident for the last seventeen of his twenty-two years in New York and San Francisco. The American authorities, tipped off by Altendorf, were watching Witzke from the moment he arrived in Nogales and they gave him enough rope to hang himself.

A special agent of the American Military Intelligence Division at Nogales, Byron Butcher, who had recruited Altendorf, was at the consulate. He cleared Witzke to cross the border.

"He returned to Mexico and made two trips across the border during the day," Butcher reported later. "In view of the fact that he left his baggage on the Mexican side, I did not molest him, awaiting the opportunity to secure his baggage and him together."

When Altendorf arrived, he joined Butcher in Nogales, Arizona, just across the border, briefing him on what Witzke had said and done on the trip from Mexico City. He informed Butcher that "the German always carried his papers on his person."

The next morning, Witzke again crossed over from the Mexican side into Arizona. Butcher and another agent, armed with revolvers, seized and handcuffed him and took him into custody. In searching him they found, in addition to his Russian passport, a Mexican passport giving his name as Pablo Waberski; an American draft card issued in San Francisco; a Mexican permit to carry a pistol; a San Francisco driver's license; and a list of women's names and addresses, some with pictures, that provided a key to his recent travels.

Butcher and another agent went to the seedy hotel on the Sonora side of the border and seized Witzke's baggage, which yielded a letter in code and a cipher table. But the table was of no use in decoding the letter, so it was sent to the U.S. Army's Cryptographic Bureau in Washington.

Gleaves, meanwhile, had lost track of Witzke. His assignment from his British superiors had been to turn over Witzke and Altendorf to the American authorities in Sonora and he feared he had botched the job. He finally went to the American consulate, where he confirmed to Butcher Altendorf's account of their trip from Mexico City. His own mission for the Germans in Nogales, Gleaves reported, was to have been, along with Witzke, to meet delegates of the IWW from California, Arizona and New Mexico and "to carry out a resolution calling for an uprising of the Negroes, strikes, the blowing up of mines, industrial plants, railroads, bridges and telegraph and telephone systems." It was not until now, after Witzke's arrest, that Altendorf and Gleaves each was told that the other was an Allied agent.

Witzke denied that he was a German agent or that he had confessed to Altendorf his complicity in blowing up Black Tom or in any other acts of sabotage. He was taken to Fort Sam Houston in San Antonio and interrogated for months thereafter. By this time, the coded letter found in his baggage had been broken and the translation sent back to San Antonio. Dated January 15, 1918, the day before Witzke, Altendorf and Gleaves departed Mexico City bound for the border, it was a letter of introduction for Witzke to other German diplomatic authorities from von Eckhardt. It read:

> To the Imperial Consular Authorities in the Republic of Mexico. Strictly Secret! The bearer of this is a subject of the Empire who travels as a Russian under the name of Pablo Waberski. He is a German secret agent. Please furnish him on request protection and assistance, also advance him on demand up to one thou-

sand pesos Mexican gold, and send his code telegrams to this Embassy as official Consular dispatches.

The Americans had the goods on Witzke. But they continued to press him for a confession, and for information about other German agents and activities in Mexico directed against the United States. In one conversation with Butcher, during which stenographic notes were made, Witzke acknowledged that he had told Altendorf of some of his own activities. Butcher told him that if he hoped to save himself, he had better come clean.

"As you have already guessed," Butcher said, "we know nearly all about you. We are in war now, and also as you know spies are hung." But Witzke held firm against informing. ""No, I can't do that," he said, according to the stenographic notes. "I am very young to die, twenty-two years. But I have done my duty. If I told you I would be a traitor and that I will never be. . . . I will probably be the first man to die in the United States for my country, won't I?"

Then he added: "You know all the details, all right, and I think it was that Dr. Altendorf who told you, as I told him a lot of things in conversation."

Witzke was not brought to trial until August of 1918, before a military commission at Fort Sam Houston. Under direct examination, Altendorf told about a dinner with "Waberski" (Witzke) in Mexico City at which he "talked about where they were laying mines off an island in New Jersey and how a wave came up and almost washed away Jahnke, and that Waberski helped to save Jahnke. . . . They were also preparing for a big explosion that happened in New Jersey. . . . by direct orders from the German ambassador, von Bernstorff." But again, the focus of the trial was not on Black Tom, and so the testimony stirred little interest at the time.

Witzke offered in his own defense a farfetched story about shipping out on steamers along the West Coast of South America at the age of ten. He said he fell in with some Mexican bandits robbing gold and silver mines, then encountered German agents at the Juarez Hotel in Mexico City and rejected an offer to work against the United States.

Finally, he said, he went to Sonora at the behest of a Mexican to spy on Mexican rebels there. Instead, he contended, he set off to return to San Francisco, where he had registered for the draft, in order to inform the authorities he was a Russian. On the way he met at Mazatlán the beautiful daughter of a mine owner and promised to marry her on his return from San Francisco. At this point, he insisted, he met Altendorf, who was down on his luck, and took him along with him to Sonora.

Witzke's assigned counsel, Colonel W. J. Glasgow, said he was unable to bring any witnesses in his client's behalf in from Mexico, and Witzke was found guilty of being a German secret agent in time of war, operating against the United States from Mexico. The Black Tom disaster was not a specific part of the case against him. He was sentenced to death by hanging and held at Fort Sam Houston.

Twice after Witzke's imprisonment he tried to escape, and once did manage to get out of the prison, but was recaptured the same day. On Witzke's return to his cell, the guard on duty, Private Henry Brackett, noticed that as Witzke entered he glanced up at an overhead corner. Brackett and another guard, Corporal Roy Stephens, searched the area and found wedged into the wall a razor blade and a piece of cigarette paper, Brackett later testified, "on which there was some writing, rolled up in the shape of a ball." The message, in German and in Witzke's handwriting, was translated into English and said:

> My right name is Latar Witzke [cq]. Born in Poznen and for that reason I only understand Polish and not Russian. I was lieutenant on Cruiser *Dresden* that was sunk near Valparaiso, Chile. I lay two months in the hospital, which is the reason I escaped internment. The rest of the crew is interned.

Witzke's admission that he was not a Russian and that he had been in the German navy ruled out any chance of a successful appeal.*

Meanwhile, Jahnke was having trouble from another quarter—the arrival from Baltimore of Captain Hinsch, bringing the money to Mexico City requested by Fred Herrmann in the lemon-juice message. Hinsch, accustomed to running things himself, had no intention of taking orders from Jahnke, his subordinate in the United States. Hinsch had a ready ally in Anton Dilger, the operator of "Tony's Lab" for germ manufacture in Chevy Chase, another fugitive to Mexico after Congress declared war. Dilger now was operating, apparently as

---

*On November 2, 1918, only nine days before the armistice was signed in Europe, his sentence was confirmed by the commander at Fort Sam Houston and he awaited his execution. The end of the war, however, put everything on hold.

the overseer of all German intelligence in Mexico in conjunction with von Eckhardt, under the alias "Dr. Delmar."

On December 27, 1917, only days after Berlin had confirmed to Von Eckhardt that Jahnke was an authorized agent, this radio message came back from Mexico City:

> From a conversation Delmar has received the impression that not alone Jahnke is not self-reliant but that he is not entirely reliable. Therefore . . . I have handed the contents of No. 196 to the messenger for Captain Hinsch especially as he is a German and also because he enjoys the confidence of the Minister. I have also given him the new method of ciphering. A safe opportunity of sending by post to Mexico only occurs once a month by a Spanish steamer, leaving Coruna every 21st either by a special messenger or a man belonging to the crew.*

Berlin agreed to demote Jahnke and to consider elevating Hinsch. The Foreign Office dispatched a telegram to "Delmar" on January 4, 1918—twelve days before Jahnke sent Witzke, Altendorf and Gleaves on what proved to be an ill-fated mission for Witzke.

"The Admiralty has withdrawn the commission to Jahnke for sabotage undertakings," it said, "and contemplates appointing Hinsch instead. As the latter is already in service with you, The Admiralty agree that Hinsch shall remain under your orders and shall be occupied in naval business in January. His activities, however, must be under your control in agreement with the Embassy."

Jahnke responded by leaning on Von Eckhardt all the harder, and with success, as seen by another message sent by an obviously outraged German military attaché in Madrid to Berlin on March 28. Jahnke, it said, had submitted a long report to the admiralty "which represents Delmar and Captain Hinsch as . . . actually criminal and claims for himself sole direction. The dispatch . . . in my opinion is absolutely shameless both in form and matter. The dispatch was accompanied by a telegram for the Minister for Foreign Affairs which the Ambassador [to Spain] will forward and which unfortunately proves

*This and subsequent German cables, radio messages and telegrams quoted here were among a host of intercepted messages uncovered after the war in the files of Admiral Hall, the head of British naval intelligence already mentioned as the key figure in the disclosure of the Zimmermann telegram. Hall, as we shall see, became an important contributor to the postwar effort to prove German responsibility for the Black Tom and Kingsland explosions.

that the Minister [von Eckhardt] who according to Delmar's previous statements is easily swayed is at present entirely under the influence of Jahnke."

That latter judgment seemed to be true. Von Eckhardt's telegram said: "Cooperation between Jahnke and Hinsch is, in consequence of their mutual distrust, impossible. Jahnke's work must not be interrupted and he is therefore receiving financial support through me. In consequence of very grave discoveries I request permission to [dismiss] Delmar, Hinsch . . . approval to be indicated by telegraphing the word 'dismiss.'"

Jahnke several days later also cabled to the head of intelligence activities operating out of Antwerp:

> The instructions given by Lieut. Stephan to Captain Hinsch placing me under his orders was a painful surprise to me. According to my instructions from Son Charles, I was to work independently in the U.S.A. and Mexico. I am accustomed to doing this. My successes justify the confidence which has been placed in me. Dr. Delmar neither knows anything of my activities nor is he in a position to judge. Hinsch has absolutely no organization; it is out of the question placing my services at his disposal; and besides Hinsch has no experience, is incapable and tactless and works with characteristic pettiness and personal spite.

Jahnke then went on to boast about his accomplishments as a sabotage leader since the previous May, as already reported here. Berlin, apparently after checking with other agents, wired back to Madrid a few days later:

> According to Jahnke, detailed accounts of the successes mentioned appear credible. His cooperation for the Admiralty Staff must therefore unquestionably remain. A direct telegram from Jahnke has arrived saying that he cannot work in company but must be independent. . . . Nothing is to be undertaken in Mexico by us until the arrival of further instructions, in order to avoid disturbing political relations. Jahnke should therefore only operate against the U.S.A. and Canada. With reference to his further questions and proposals, a decision will soon follow.

Finally, on April 29, a General Staff wire settled the matter: "Please inform Delmar . . . that Jahnke has been made sole Naval Confidential Agent in Mexico." Jahnke apparently operated in that capacity out of Mexico City until the war's end.

The German saboteurs' best efforts, however, could not seriously impede the impact of growing American manpower and resources going into 1918. On January 8, already assuming ultimate victory, Wilson outlined his historic Fourteen Points for a peace settlement. They were a mixture of his idealistic visions for a world perpetually at peace—including a league of nations, his final point—and hard-nosed territorial and political aims.

The first five called for "open covenants for peace, openly arrived at, after which there shall be no private international understandings of any kind"; assurance of "absolute freedom of navigation upon the seas . . . alike in peace and war"; "the removal, so far as possible, of all economic barriers and the establishment of an equality of trade conditions among all the nations consenting to the peace"; the reduction of armaments "to the lowest point consistent with domestic safety"; an "impartial adjustment of all colonial claims, based upon . . . the interests of the populations concerned"; and "the equitable claims of the government whose title is to be determined."

The other eight points were: evacuation and restoration of all conquered territories in Europe; assuring the sovereignty of Belgium; righting "the wrong done to France by Prussia in 1871 in the matter of Alsace-Lorraine"; readjusting Italy's frontiers "along clearly recognizable lines of nationality"; according the people of Austria-Hungary and Turkey "the freest opportunity for autonomous development"; determining Balkan borders "along historically established lines of allegiance and nationality"; providing permanent access to the Dardanelles by all nations; and establishment of a free Poland to "include the territories inhabited by indisputably Polish populations, which should be assured a free and secure access to the sea."

The terms were designed to be broad and vague enough to satisfy all the Entente Powers and to be acceptable and not humiliating to the Central Powers. If the terms were not accepted, Wilson said, there would be "but one response possible from us: force, force to the utmost, force without stint or limit, the righteous and triumphant force which shall make right the law of the world and cast every selfish dominion down in the dust."

But as always, Wilson emphasized his quest for a just and compassionate peace:

What we demand in this war is nothing peculiar to ourselves. It is that the world be made fit and safe to live in; and particularly that it be made safe for every peace-loving nation which, like our own, wishes to live its own life, determine its own institutions, be assured of justice and fair dealing by the other peoples of the world as against force and selfish aggression. All the peoples of the world are in effect partners in this interest, and for our own part we see very clearly that unless justice is done to others it will not be done to us.

The warning and the appeal were both brushed off at first, as German offensives in March, April and May lifted the hopes and spirits of the Central Powers. But in late May and early June, American forces, coming to the aid of the retreating French, drove the Germans back at Chateau-Thierry on the Marne. In July and into August French, British and American troops on all fronts began at last to turn the tide in a decisive way. Pershing had not yet brought all the American troops together into a separate army, because priorities demanded the shoring up of the Allied forces. But in September, a largely American army overwhelmed the Germans at Saint-Mihiel, and in the next two months the Allies broke the vaunted Hindenburg line—and the Central Powers crumbled.

Weeks before the end, Ludendorff warned the kaiser that there would be a complete military collapse unless an armistice was signed soon. The Reichstag, though with no real power, had already passed a peace resolution via a coalition of the Center, Liberal and Social Democratic parties. At the end of September, the kaiser with great reluctance was forced to sign a decree creating a parliamentary government in the British mode. Prince Max of Baden, a centrist and a realist, became the last chancellor under the kaiser, at the head of a peace cabinet formed by the same elements that had passed the peace resolution.

Soon, however, a group of left-wing Social Democrats, led by Karl Liebknecht, broke away and formed the Spartacus League, forerunner of Germany's own Communist party. Sailors mutinied in Kiel and soon sailors' and soldiers' councils, their members waving red flags and wearing red swatches on their uniforms, menacingly roamed the streets of Hamburg, Cologne, Bremen, Munich and other major cities. Mobs gathered in Berlin.

Von Hindenburg and others counseled the kaiser to abdicate. But, as always isolated from reality, he insisted for days that his reign would survive even defeat in the Great War. Meanwhile, Germany's allies —Austria-Hungary, Turkey and Bulgaria—all sued for peace. On November 6, Prince Max at last asked for an immediate armistice and terms based on Wilson's Fourteen Points.

Wilson, reflecting the effect of his transition from idealistic neutral to belligerent, replied that he for one would not negotiate with "the military masters and the monarchical autocrats of Germany." He insisted that the kaiser had to go. Wilhelm, threatened by incipient revolt into leaving Berlin, moved to the imperial military headquarters at Spa, from whence he finally agreed to seek asylum in Holland. Driven to the Dutch border, in one last humiliation he was obliged to wait all day while the Dutch stubbornly negotiated the terms for his safe conduct. The next day, the German government accepted the Allies' terms, then only a broad outline of what the victors, principally the French, would eventually exact.

By Armistice Day, November 11, 1918, nearly 1,400,000 American troops had joined the fighting in a remarkable mobilization. But some —defenders of Wilson—argued that his unwavering statements all through 1918 about the absolute necessity of compassion along with justice in any peace terms were also critical in the eventual decision of the Central Powers to lay down their arms. In any event, Wilson did not allow the passions of the war itself to smother his postwar dream.

Now that the war was over, Wilson could address himself fully to the pursuit of that dream. When the United States in early 1917 was still a neutral, Wilson's ambitions to play a major role in shaping the postwar peace had been handicapped by the very fact that he was a kibitzer only; he had no legitimate claim on a seat at the peace-conference table. Now that his country was a full-fledged member of the victorious side, he could not be denied that seat—and a powerful voice in the deliberations. There was no doubt whatever that he would press with all his energy for the creation of the League of Nations that he saw as the only guarantee for a postwar world at peace.

Ending also with the cease-fire on the Western Front was the four-year covert German war against the United States that had begun almost with the outbreak of the shooting in Europe and had shifted its base to Mexico after the American declaration of war. Some of this secret war's participants remained where they had been all through it—in New York, in Baltimore, in Mexico City and elsewhere in the Western Hemisphere—and some returned to Germany.

For several of the principal players in the covert war, however, the experience was far from over. Still ahead for them was an unprecedented peacetime manhunt and international legal battle that would go on for twenty-one years.

A cable dispatched to German consulates abroad two months after the armistice, later acquired by the United States, instructed:

> Please carefully and immediately burn without remainder, and destroy the ashes of, all papers connected with the war, the preservation of which is not absolutely necessary. . . . Strictest silence concerning the existence and activity of these representatives [presumably the saboteurs] is to be observed now and for all future time, even after the conclusion of peace, which might be compromising or even unpleasant for us if they came to the knowledge of our enemies.

As Woodrow Wilson launched his campaign to bring a League of Nations into being, this cable underscored the hardships ahead for American authorities who now undertook another challenge: to find the men who had committed sabotage against the United States, and to prove that they had acted under the direct orders of the government of the defeated German nation.

The Herrmann Message: A page from the *Blue Book* magazine, January, 1917, on which Fred Herrmann wrote a secret message in lemon juice to saboteur-paymaster Paul Hilken in Baltimore, requesting funds to destroy the Tampico oil fields. The message later became a central element in the proof of German culpability.

NATIONAL ARCHIVES

254 *America at War 1917–1918*

IV: GERMANY ON TRIAL, 1919-1939

18. Building the Case

From the outset of the postarmistice period, efforts to fix responsibility for the sabotage committed in America were eclipsed by the quest for a peace treaty and lasting security in Europe. The whole thrust of President Wilson's involvement in the treaty negotiations was to avoid rancor toward the defeated German nation and vengeful terms of settlement for its actions on the battlefield. Wilson hoped and fully intended to be the principal architect of a swift and durable peace that would include his dream of a community of nations to guarantee it. Chasing down the saboteurs who had plagued his efforts to keep the United States neutral was none of Wilson's concern; he was determined to be the peacemaker.

The task of going after the saboteurs at first remained with the local police in New York and New Jersey, with some assistance from the Justice Department. They focused for some time on one man: Michael Kristoff, the young Austrian immigrant who two witnesses said had confessed to them his involvement in Black Tom.

Kristoff had enlisted in the army in May, 1917, occasionally writing to his relatives in Jersey City and Bayonne assuring them, as in one letter, that "I am not against America. I am ready to die for this country at any time, and they should not send any detectives after me. I am not a spy." But such assurances did not deter the sleuths. Soon after this letter was written, the army detected tuberculosis in Kristoff and discharged him. When he disappeared, they placed a private detective as a woman boarder in the home of Anna Rushnak, Kristoff's aunt. The aunt had testified how, in the early hours of the night of Black Tom, he had anguished to her over what he had done. She had later recanted, however, obliging the police to release him. Now the detective ingratiated herself to Mrs. Rushnak and culled from her an admission that her original account was correct. "Even though you do swear to something that is not true," Mrs. Rushnak confided, "you are not committing a sin for trying to save a man's life."

This confession helped convince the police that Kristoff was their man. He next turned up in jail in Albany in 1921, convicted of petty larceny and making a fraudulent statement of his army enlistment. He had identified himself as "John Christie"—the same name mentioned by Mena Edwards in identifying callers at Martha Held's retreat for German saboteurs in Manhattan. Into an adjacent cell the police slipped an undercover man who told Kristoff how he had stolen plans for the Germans while he was in the navy and had received a large amount of money. Kristoff peppered him with questions about who had paid him, until word got around the jail that the man was a plant, and Kristoff clammed up.

On his release, he disappeared again, not surfacing this time until 1927, once more in jail on Welfare Island, New York, convicted of larceny. Still he would not talk. Released again, he wound up a year later in a Staten Island hospital, where he died of tuberculosis. He was buried in a local potter's field, and with him the mystery of the "Francis Graentnor" who he said had approached him at Penn Station in New York months before the Black Tom explosion and had taken him around the country as his baggage handler. The identity of this Graentnor remained a pivotal question in the Black Tom case.

The other two prime suspects of the investigators were Lothar Witzke and Kurt Jahnke. The American undercover agent, Paul Altendorf, testified at Witzke's espionage trial that Witzke had boasted about how he and Jahnke blew up Black Tom. But the testimony was not corroborated at the time and Witzke was convicted on other evidence involving his activities in Mexico. After the war, Jahnke dropped completely out of sight, so Witzke, incarcerated at Fort Sam Houston, became the investigators' target. Interrogated in late 1919 by Inspector Tunney of the New York bomb squad, he denied he had told Altendorf that he and Jahnke had almost drowned pulling off the Black Tom job. Witzke was questioned again at Fort Leavenworth in 1923 and again denied it.

In a subsequent letter to the interrogating lawyer, Witzke wrote that compared to Altendorf, "Conan Doyle was a pauper in imagination." If it was really believed that he at the age of twenty had "committed the most clever exploits imaginable and in quantities unsurpassed by anyone throughout the history of the world," Witzke wrote, "why not acclaim me a superman, free me and allow me to employ my talents now, since the war is over, for the benefit of the world at large?"

Congress, too, addressed itself after the armistice to the issue of

German sabotage in the United States. The Senate Judiciary Committee, after hearings in 1919, came up with a ridiculous conclusion. It decided that Captain von Papen "was the responsible and directing head of practically all of the violence work done by the German agents in the United States, and it was through his agents and under his direction that numerous fires and explosions in munitions factories were brought about, and attempts at labor disturbances."

Since both Black Tom and Kingsland, however, occurred after von Papen's recall in December, 1915, this conclusion was clearly erroneous. The real sabotage overseer, von Bernstorff, remained in Washington through both disasters in New Jersey, one in July, 1916, and the other in January, 1917.

But such matters as blame-placing for the Black Tom explosions and the Kingsland fire took a back seat in the United States to Wilson's quest for a new world community to end all future wars. Only when that effort met bitter failure, and ironically as a consequence of that failure, was the international machinery established that led to a marathon pursuit of the saboteurs, and the eventual fixing of responsibility.

Even before the armistice, Wilson's political difficulties at home foretold the disappointments he would encounter in achieving his dream in the international arena. His Democratic party lost both the House and Senate in the congressional elections a week before the armistice. As he prepared to sail for France and the peace talks, Theodore Roosevelt exulted: "Our allies and our enemies and Mr. Wilson himself should all understand that Mr. Wilson has no authority whatever to speak for the American people at this time. His leadership has just been emphatically repudiated by them." Wilson at the same time undercut his own objectives by declining to name any of the Senate's ranking Republicans to the Paris delegation.

Wilson became the first American president to leave the hemisphere while in office when he sailed aboard the *George Washington* on December 4, 1918, amid shrieking sirens in New York harbor and military planes and a dirigible flying overhead. The battleship *Pennsylvania* and a destroyer escort led the presidential vessel out to sea, but the display camouflaged growing dissatisfaction with Wilson at home. Confusion and doubt reigned over what his pet project, the League of Nations, might mean to American security and obligations in Europe.

When his ship arrived at Brest nine days later, it sailed through a veritable armada of Allied warships as guns fired presidential salutes and bands blared a wholehearted welcome. His motorcade through Paris suggested that the French considered him the savior of Europe itself, and subsequent visits to London and Rome were the same. But behind this facade of goodwill and gratitude, Allied coolness to Wilson's talk of "peace without victory" grew. French Premier Georges Clemenceau referred to, and worried over, Wilson's "noble simplicity," fearing it did not give adequate weight to the threat to France of a recovered Germany.

Already, ominous signs were coming from Berlin. When some two million German troops marched home after the armistice, they returned to a defeated homeland wracked not only by starvation but by political turmoil and rebellion as well—and the threat of the "Red Peril."

A People's Naval Division of Communist sailors for a time occupied parts of the imperial palace in Berlin and Spartacus riots swept Munich, Hamburg, Dusseldorf and other major cities. Left-wing radicals seized power in Munich and proclaimed the Bavarian Republic. The Spartacus League declared itself to be the Communist party of Germany and geared up for a putsch against Berlin itself.

It began on January 9, 1919, and at first swept over everything in its way. Lenin sent congratulations from Russia. But a counterattack prevailed and elections a few days later rejected the routed Communists. The Social Democrats captured a plurality of seats in the new National Assembly and a new constitution was drafted in the town of Weimar with a distinctly liberal and democratic framework. The Weimar Republic was born.

Economically, however, the country was stripped bare, and the necessity of suppressing the revolt was a grim, constant reminder of the politicians' dependence on the surviving military leadership. The kaiser was gone, but not his generals. This was the shaky foundation of the new order in Germany that now had to face the demands of the Allies who had defeated her, with Wilson her best hope for a compassionate peace.

A week after the Paris Conference convened on January 18, 1919, Wilson's concept of a League of Nations was approved in principle without dissent, and he headed home three weeks later with the formal document he wanted in his pocket. But in addition to having alienated Senate Republican leaders by his snub, he had done little to explain to the American people why the League was in their best interest, and he paid dearly for that failure. By the time he returned to Paris in March to push for completion of the entire treaty, word of his waning support at home undercut his efforts to resist the heavy territorial and reparation demands on the Germans, particularly from the French.

The finished document dismayed the defeated Germans, who had been led to believe, or at least hope, that Wilson's Fourteen Points would provide the framework for a peace of reconciliation. At the insistence of the French particularly, the treaty branded Germany "the sole and only author" of the war and demanded the surrender of eight hundred "war criminals," as well as reparations designed to redeem all Allied costs—and keep Germany weak.

To be taken from Germany were Alsace-Lorraine, Upper Silesia, Posen, West Prussia and other territories. Danzig (now Gdansk) was to become a "free city" separated from Germany proper in a corridor to the Baltic for a restored Poland that also sliced off East Prussia. The Rhineland and the Saar, the rich coal regions along the Rhine, were to be occupied for fifteen years under French mandate, and Germany was to be stripped of her colonies.

Also, although the defeated German people were now in the grip of widespread starvation, they were ordered to turn over 140,000 head of cattle, 30,000 horses and whatever was left of their merchant fleet. The German army and navy were to be dismembered, never to be restored, except for a peacekeeping Reichswehr limited to 100,000 men.

The terms of the treaty were a harsh and bitter pill, but the new German government had no alternative but to sign. Failure to do so by a designated deadline would have brought Allied troops of occupation into Germany against a now-defenseless enemy. On June 28, the signing took place at the Versailles Palace and Wilson at last had a full, formal treaty to present to the Senate for ratification. "It's a good job," he said as he set sail for home the next day.

But the Senate Foreign Relations Committee, chaired by Henry Cabot Lodge, was dead-set against the League. Concern in Congress was real that it might lose its constitutional power to declare war and that American sovereignty might be watered down by League membership and obligations. But Wilson refused to compromise. The committee voted thirty-eight amendments and four reservations to the treaty, dooming it.

Wilson thereupon set out on a thirty-speech tour of the country to make his case. But on September 25 in Pueblo, Colorado, exhausted from the strain of the Paris talks and the fight with Lodge, he suffered what first was reported as a "nervous collapse." He returned at once to Washington, where five days later he had a paralytic stroke.

On November 19, the treaty at last came to the Senate floor with Lodge's amendments and reservations. The convalescing Wilson instructed Democratic senators to vote against it and it failed of ratification. Four months later, a revised version again fell eight votes short of the two thirds required, and the treaty died.

Wilson was now a broken man. Voters compounded his repudiation in November, 1920, when in the presidential election billed as a "solemn referendum" on the League, the Democratic candidate, James Cox of Ohio, was trounced by Republican Warren G. Harding. The next month, Wilson was awarded the Nobel Peace Prize, but it was small consolation. He left the White House on March 4, 1921, felled in health and spirit. He held on for nearly three years until his death on February 3, 1924. At that, he outlived Harding, who died in August, 1923, succeeded by his colorless vice president, Calvin Coolidge.

Wilson, however, remained through all his tribulations a compassionate man. One evidence of that fact came on May 20, 1920, two months after the final rejection of the treaty, when he commuted the death sentence of Lothar Witzke to life imprisonment at hard labor. In 1923, Witzke was released on a plea to Coolidge from the Weimar Republic that the United States "set free their last prisoner of war" —not exactly the precise description of Witzke's status as a convicted spy and saboteur. Working in Witzke's favor was a report that in July, 1921, he had "performed an act of heroism in entering a boiler room after an explosion in the prison, preventing possible disaster."

Witzke's release did nothing, however, to clear up the mysteries surrounding the explosions of armaments in America and on the high seas before America's entry into the war. And with the rejection of the Versailles Treaty, the United States was not a party to the reparation terms imposed on Germany. Still, there were many claims by private parties in the United States against Germany for damages sustained, particularly in the period of American neutrality.

Rejection of the Versailles Treaty obliged the United States to enter into bilateral negotiations with the new Weimar Republic on a separate peace pact. In October, 1921, the Treaty of Berlin was signed. Among its provisions was the creation of a commission governing war claims involving the two countries that gave new life to the unsolved cases of Black Tom and Kingsland.

On August 10, 1922, Washington and Berlin by executive agreement established the Mixed Claims Commission to settle all disputes and determine the exact amounts to be paid. Most of the claimants were private American and German citizens and companies seeking restitution for actions by either country since the 1914 outbreak of the war. Each country was to appoint one commissioner and together they were to choose an umpire. In the event the two commissioners could not agree on a claim, the umpire would decide, and his decision would be final. Each country pledged to cooperate fully in arriving at the truth and justice of all claims, which eventually totaled 20,434.

Most were resolved quickly, except those relating to Black Tom and Kingsland, in which the allegation of sabotage and German complicity had to be proved. In these cases, the German pledge of full cooperation would in practice fall far short, and indeed the cases themselves would be subject to sabotage of sorts in a relentless German effort to disavow and avoid responsibility.

Although the Weimar Republic was in power now, many officials, bureaucrats and diplomats of the old Imperial Germany still held significant posts in their country's service. Instability threatened the new regime from the start. There were Communist uprisings, assassinations of leading political figures, a failed 1920 conservative putsch and, in January, 1923, occupation of the industrial Ruhr by France, on grounds of unpaid reparations.

Resentment mounted toward the Versailles "Diktat," as it was now called in Germany, and toward the political "traitors" who had lost the war and then the peace. Free Corps troops roamed the streets and other rabble-rousers emerged, among them an Austrian fanatic, a twice-wounded enlisted soldier of the Great War named Adolf Hitler. He seized upon the trampled spirit of the nation and aroused the impoverished middle class with strident attacks on the Weimar Republic and all those who had "betrayed" Germany by signing the Versailles Treaty. Scapegoating of German Jews became a trademark of his tirades. His "Beer Hall Putsch" in Munich in 1923 was crushed but became the cauldron from which Hitler's National Socialist German Workers Party was forged. Convicted of treason and jailed for nine months, Hitler used the time to write his rambling diatribe, *Mein Kampf*, and upon his release resumed his quest for power.

Amid this internal turmoil, many of those who had run the civil government for the inept and insulated Kaiser Wilhelm during the war were called on to keep its machinery going. For many of them, as well as for the unshakably proud German nation, the two sabotage cases represented a challenge to national honor and reputation as much as they did claims for reparation. In defense of Germany's good name and that of her officialdom, every effort had to be undertaken to secure acquittal.

Germany, presumably in the belief that an American as umpire of the Mixed Claims Commission would be obliged to bend over backward to be fair, urged just such an appointment, and the United States not altogether wisely agreed. Supreme Court Associate Justice William R. Day was selected, but Day died in 1923 and a Houston lawyer, Judge Edwin B. Parker, replaced him.

In the first six months of the Mixed Claims Commission, 12,425 claims totalling $1.5 billion were filed, and the remaining 8,009 over the next five and one-half years. In 1925, the commission assessed Germany $2.5 million to be paid to American claimants in the *Lusitania* sinking. By 1933, all but a relatively few of the claims were settled. The outstanding cases included 153 by American citizens claiming they had suffered losses of about $23 million at Black Tom and Kingsland. These, known as "the sabotage claims," constituted the prime focus of the commission from its inception until 1939, when after much more intrigue a resolution finally was rendered.

Black Tom and Kingsland were only two of nearly two hundred suspected incidents of German sabotage in America or on the high seas. In a few others, arrests were made and criminal convictions obtained, as already noted. But the task of proving conclusively that the German government was to blame in these civil proceedings seemed so monumental that few victimized firms were willing to undertake the cost and effort.

Each country assigned an agent to prepare and present the case before the commission. In addition, the various Black Tom and Kingsland claimants in time hired international lawyers to assist him.

The most important of these claimants were the Lehigh Valley Railroad, the proprietor of the Black Tom facilities, and the Canadian Car and Foundry Company Limited, which owned the Kingsland plant. At first, eminent lawyers consulted by the two firms discouraged them from even filing claims before the commission because the task of proving the German government's guilt in the specificity required by the agreement creating the commission was so exacting. At the same time, however, the size of the claims offered temptingly huge commissions to any law firm that could win the cases.

In the spring of 1924, the Lehigh Valley approached Amos J. Peaslee of the New York firm of Peaslee and Brigham to handle the Black Tom case. Peaslee, a tenacious man of strong Quaker convictions, knew it was a long shot but agreed to accept the case on a contingency basis, realizing that if he could win, the financial reward would be immense. In time he was asked to represent Canadian Car and Foundry as well.

There was a certain irony in Peaslee's selection. A major in the American Expeditionary Force at General Pershing's headquarters during the war, he was assigned after the armistice to the American Commission to Negotiate Peace. As such, he participated in the drafting of amendments to the League of Nations covenant, the Senate rejection of which required the separate peace treaty that created the Mixed Claims Commission.

Peaslee thought at first he could win the case on the basis of police and Justice Department records in hand. In August, 1924, he filed a brief with the commission that confidently proclaimed that "the evidence is so overwhelming and convincing. . . . that it was not deemed necessary to burden the record unduly with a multiplicity of documents." Instead, he noted three key items. The first was the November, 1914, circular telling all German naval attachés and agents that it was "indispensible" to recruit non-German "deck hands, among whom are to be found a great many anarchists and escaped criminals," to cause explosions on munitions-bearing ships and to create chaos in loading and unloading them. The second was the critical cable from Zimmermann to von Bernstorff listing Irishmen in America who, on Sir Roger Casement's word, could be recruited for similar purposes. The third was a note from sabotage paymaster Albert to Berlin saying he was "supporting the authorized military agent, Herr von Papen, in his work on the questions of munitions."

Regarding Kingsland, Peaslee cited a general order from von Falkenhayn on November 2, 1914, to all military attachés to be provided unlimited funds for "setting incendiary fires to stocks of raw materials and finished products," and a notice that special agents would be dispatched with "explosives and incendiary devices" and a list of available saboteurs. This digest also listed von Papen's note to von Falkenhayn of April 9, 1915, thanking him for sending von Rintelen to direct the effort "to curtail the supplies of war materials for our enemies in every way possible."

But this evidence was not nearly specific enough to build a case of German intent, complicity and direct responsibility that would stand up in an international court of law. To do that, Peaslee came to realize he would have to prove a clear link between the German government and the actual perpetrators of the sabotage.

Peaslee's first big break came in January, 1925. Nash Rockwood, a trial counsel for the Lehigh Valley, was working on the Black Tom case and had been mentioned in newspaper stories about it. One night he was having dinner with two friends, Harry Reiss and his young wife, at the Hotel Chatham in New York. Mrs. Reiss observed that she had seen Rockwood's name in the stories and informed him, as he reported later, "I could tell the court a thing or two about the Black Tom affair. I know exactly what happened." And she proceeded to tell Rockwood all about Martha Held's house at 123 West Fifteenth Street.

Mrs. Reiss, it turned out, was the former Mena Edwards, "The Eastman Girl," now settled down in married bliss. As she spoke, however, her husband interrupted and insisted that "if you are going to tell all that you know about that matter you ought to be paid for it, and well paid." Rockwood informed Peaslee, who after hearing her story agreed to pay her $2,500 and a like amount if she was called on to testify, plus another $5,000 if the Lehigh Valley claim eventually was allowed.

Meanwhile, the German government stonewalled on all requests for official documents and access to individuals Peaslee wanted to interview. Although the kaiser was gone, the militarist influence in the German psyche remained strong, as did the determination to protect the integrity of the diplomatic service against allegations that its members had engaged in improper activities.

In 1925, Field Marshal von Hindenburg was elected president to maintain stability. Adoption of the Locarno Pact, admitting Germany to the League of Nations, also required her to accept the existing western frontiers and the demilitarization of the Rhineland. But French troops remained in the Ruhr and the resentment toward Versailles, fanned by Hitler and other radicals, continued to provide a poisonous undercurrent. On top of all the rest, to be convicted before an international tribunal as a nation that had acted dishonorably would be the final insult; the sabotage cases against Germany had to be discredited and beaten, at all costs.

To that end, in April, 1925, the German government produced signed statements from Jahnke and Witzke, both now back in Berlin, disavowing any involvement in either Black Tom or Kingsland. Jahnke attested that "the explosions of war material in the United States happened either by chance or were due to the activity of anarchistic, radical groups of laborers, especially the IWW." Witzke charged that his jail confession was forced from him by police who "beat me on the head with rubber sticks until I broke down."

The Germans also produced an affidavit from Captain Boy-Ed observing that American munitions plants "sprang from the ground like mushrooms and had to be run with unskilled laborers and insufficiently trained supervisors," and hence "accidents" happened. Another affidavit from von Papen said the 1915 cable regarding the recruiting of Irish saboteurs was the work of a minion in Section 3B that he ignored. None of the four witnesses was made available to Peaslee for cross-examination.

When the German agent Karl von Lewinski, a former German consul in New York, filed his first basic defense before the Mixed Claims Commission, he acknowledged that some minor violations of American neutrality had occurred that "the German Government deeply regrets." But he insisted none were aimed at American property or citizens, and that even these "ceased altogether in the course of 1915, due to the energetic attitude of Germany's representatives in the United States" to stop them. Evidence to the contrary, he said, was based on "hearsay, rumors, gossip, statements made by stool pigeons" all in the hope of profiting from the claims provisions of the Treaty of Berlin.

Black Tom, he said, was caused by "spontaneous combustion," negligence or a disconnected act of incendiary, and the Kingsland fire was nothing more than "an industrial accident" in which "the fire was spread by the act of the workman who threw a bucket of water in the burning pan of gasoline and alcohol, causing the fire to spread in a thousand directions."

Von Lewinski also sought to discredit the testimony and reputation of Mena Edwards Reiss. He noted that she

> pictures herself in a most compromising manner, as a frequent visitor to a house of entertainment of a most dubious type, to which she was introduced by a Frenchwoman [who] was in the habit of making trips back and forth on German boats across the Atlantic as the guest of the captains or other officers of the boats.

Stymied by the lack of German cooperation, Peaslee through Secretary of State Lansing went to see Admiral Hall, the old boss of British naval intelligence. With customary British aplomb, Hall listened to Peaslee's tale of frustration and then led him to his basement, where he showed his visitor a cache of more than 10,000 cables, radiograms and letters intercepted and decoded by the occupants of Room 40, Old Building, who had plucked the Zimmermann telegram from the air with great effect in 1917. It was a bonanza for Peaslee, mentioning four men in the German operation who warranted checking out: Paul Hilken, Fred Herrmann, Willie Woehst and Raoul Gerdts. In time, all would figure in the proving of the case.

Discovery of the Hall cables, copies of which under commission rules went to the German side, appeared at first to break German resolve. Agent von Lewinski proposed a deal: Germany would pay $18 million, or about half of what the claimants were seeking, on the condition a settlement would not constitute an admission by Germany that she had been guilty of wrongdoing. Again, the preservation of honor was the foremost consideration. It turned out, however, that Berlin merely was stalling, hoping Congress would pass pending war-claims settlement legislation that would take Germany off the hook.

Peaslee anticipated that the Germans would challenge the authenticity of Hall's cables, 264 of which were filed with the commission. But Berlin decided that because they were so readily verifiable, to challenge them and lose would weaken the German case. Instead, the German side took note, correctly, that the cables intercepted by Hall did not provide any direct link between the German government and specific saboteurs of either Black Tom or Kingsland, as required to establish proof of culpability. It meant that Peaslee and other American lawyers were in for a relentless manhunt—one that before the case was over would take Peaslee on the then-arduous Atlantic crossing no fewer than thirty-six times.

Among those located was von Rintelen, who had sent Canadian Car and Foundry a letter in 1926 offering to tell all about the Kingsland fire in return for immunity and $10,000. Hall found him in Paris and learned that von Rintelen apparently had been rebuked in his efforts to get money from his own government. Hall told him Peaslee wouldn't pay for testimony. Hall encountered von Rintelen in Paris again in 1928, when "The Dark Invader" informed him that Berlin finally had paid him off in devalued marks, worth the equivalent of five American dollars! (Later, when Hitler came to power, von Rintelen moved to England. Although he was vehemently opposed to the Nazi regime, in 1940 he was arrested and sent to a British detention camp for German nationals on the Isle of Man, where he stayed until his release at the end of World War II. He returned to England and died there in 1949 at the age of seventy-two.)

As Peaslee pursued the leads found in Hall's cables, he was joined by another sleuth of bulldog tenacity, Leonard Peto, vice president and general manager of Canadian Car and Foundry. Together they pored over the cables, focusing eventually on the one from von Eckhardt in Mexico City to Section 3B in Berlin on April 12, 1917. This was the cable that referred to Paul Hilken as von Eckhardt's source of operating funds and to the inquiry from "Herrmann, a smart, fair-haired German with an Anglo-Saxon accent," as to whether to proceed with the firing of the Tampico oil fields as commissioned by the General Staff and Hilken. Hilken clearly was a central figure, and he became their next target.

Peaslee located the Baltimore steamship executive, now working in New York. At first in their interview, Hilken flatly denied having had anything whatever to do with Black Tom or Kingsland. But as Peaslee and Peto proceeded to quote from intercepted cables mentioning him, he finally confessed in a cross-examination taken down by a stenographer.

Hilken recounted his recruitment by von Rintelen to serve as paymaster for Captain Hinsch and Anton Dilger. He told of the meeting at Section 3B in Berlin in February, 1916, at which he met Fred Herrmann and was told by Marguerre and Nadolny that the sabotage was to begin at once—not, as Berlin later insisted, only in the event the United States entered the war.

The term the Germans used to describe Section 3B—"Political Section"—was an obvious cover for its role as the headquarters for intelligence and sabotage, Hilken confirmed. He laid out the story of Dilger's "germ factory" in Chevy Chase and Eddie Felton's crew of black stevedores injecting horses slated for shipment to Europe. Felton soon afterward was tracked down living in Baltimore and he confirmed the whole affair.

In making his sweeping confession, Hilken sought to paint himself as a well-meaning man whose family background led him to help the German cause during the neutrality period. He was a classic example of the German youth indoctrinated to loyalty to the fatherland. Although he was born in the United States as was his mother, both his parents were of German heritage and bound to German traditions.

"Our home was German," Hilken testified later in a Baltimore courtroom. "We were not allowed to speak English at home; it was always German. We were sent to school in Germany for two years and when I was eight years old and returned to the United States, I could not speak English and had to learn English again." When he went to Lehigh University, he said, "I still spoke with a German accent and was made fun of. I was called 'Prince,' 'Dutch,' 'Duke,' 'Bismarck' —always some connection with German. And as my initials were Paul G. L. Hilken, I was called Paul 'German Lloyd' Hilken."

Hilken told Peaslee and Peto that Hinsch had called him from the New York office of North German Lloyd the morning after the Black Tom explosion, complaining that the official there, Carl von Helmholt, had refused to give him two thousand dollars and that he needed the money at once. "I sent him the two thousand dollars in cash," Hilken said. "I asked him later, 'Why did you need that two thousand dollars in such a hurry?'"

Peaslee: "What did he say?"

Hilken: "Well, he seemed much elated over the Black Tom explosion. I asked him whether he had anything to do with it and he said, 'You had better not ask any questions.'"

In another exchange, Hilken told of making the payment "early in August, 1916," and that "Hinsch told me at that time that he had hired the men that set fire to Black Tom."

Hilken also told Peaslee and Peto that he supplied nearly $70,000 to Hinsch and Herrmann for payment to the perpetrators of various other acts of sabotage, and that he knew that Herrmann was living in Chile. Peaslee and Peto prevailed on Hilken, now intent on proving his loyalty to postwar America, to go there at their expense to try to persuade Herrmann to testify. Armed with the major briefs in the case he sailed for Valparaiso, arriving there early in January, 1929.

But Herrmann, now married to a Chilean woman and skeptical of Peaslee's offer of immunity from prosecution, refused even to give Hilken a statement to take back. He did, however, read the briefs and afterward, Hilken reported on his return, "He said, 'Well, they have got the right man, Mike Kristoff. Why don't they go after him? Why do they bother me?'" Herrmann denied too that he really was the "Rodriguez" who was at the bench next to Theodore Wozniak at the time of the Kingsland fire, or that he had ever used that name. Hilken returned empty-handed to New York in early February.

In the meantime, Peaslee and Peto also went to South America. Learning that Raoul Gerdts was in Colombia, they met him at Barranquilla on the day after Hilken's arrival in Chile. Gerdts demanded $100,000 for his testimony, a preposterous amount, especially because the investigators knew little about him other than that he had been associated with Herrmann. They agreed finally to pay him $10,000, duly reporting the payment to Robert W. Bonynge, the American agent representing U.S. claims before the Mixed Claims Commission, a former Colorado congressman and New York lawyer.

The price turned out to be well worth it. Gerdts told them in detail how he and Herrmann had fled the United States to Cuba and then Mexico after the American entry into the war. He told them how, because Herrmann could not get money from the suspicious von Eckhardt, Herrmann wrote a message in lemon juice in the *Blue Book* magazine asking for $25,000 and how he, Gerdts, then took the magazine to Hilken. Peaslee and Peto were tantalized by the story, but they did not appreciate at the time the role this particular piece of information would ultimately play in the case.

Gerdts also told the two investigators that when he was first employed by the Germans in New York in July, 1916, Hoppenberg —apparently to test him—pinned an envelope to the inside of his coat and had him deliver it to "Fred March"—a Herrmann alias—at the McAlpin Hotel.

"During the time I was there," Gerdts reported, "a man came there who I think was Mike Kristoff. . . . I remember this man resembled the photograph in the police bulletin . . . which offered a liberal reward for information regarding his whereabouts. Herrmann gave him, whom I am pretty certain was Kristoff, the same envelope that

Herrmann received from Hoppenberg." After the man had left the room, Gerdts said, Herrmann "told me that the envelope contained a large sum of money and that a few days hence I would observe accounts in the newspapers of a 'sensational accident.' Just as he stated, a few days later the Black Tom terminal explosion occurred."

On another occasion in mid-January, 1917, Gerdts said, "while we were riding in a Buick roadster that he [Herrmann] used himself, he showed me the ruins of the Kingsland assembly plant and told me, 'Behold our work of a few days ago.'" Neither of these observations, however, was the kind of solid documentation Peaslee and Peto needed to tie the late Kristoff and Herrmann, and through them the German government, to responsibility for the Black Tom and Kingsland disasters.

In January, 1929, the Germans sprung what would have been an amusing divertissement had it not been received so seriously. They produced a sworn statement from one John Grundman, a Lehigh Valley barge captain at Black Tom the night of the disaster. He contended that the explosions could be blamed not on some nefarious scheme of German sabotage, but on—the New Jersey swamplands' notorious mosquitoes!

On that night, Grundman swore, he saw "there on the end of Pier Seven, right beside the watchman's shanty . . . a fire . . . kind of burning rubbish, more gleaming than burning high, to produce smoke . . . to drive away the mosquitoes. . . . It was about the worst place in Jersey, on account of the swamps there." And that was the only fire he saw on Black Tom that night, he said.

The American side produced testimony that none of the guards on duty that night had seen the fire of which Grundman spoke, and that there was no watchman's shanty where he said he had seen one. Nevertheless, New York's newspapers shouted reports that those damned Jersey mosquitoes were the real culprits in the explosion that had rocked Manhattan as never before.

Two months later, in March, 1929, the German side produced another deposition much less sensational but much more damaging to the American case. Carl Ahrendt, the clerk Hilken said had delivered the money to Hinsch in New York the morning after the Black Tom explosions, swore that the delivery actually was made in the previous January, and hence could not have had anything to do with Black Tom. He offered a story full of persuasive detail. He knew it was wintertime when he went from Baltimore with the money, he said, because he had loaned a friend his overcoat to attend a fancy automobile show in Baltimore. "I therefore had to go to New York wearing a rather shabby overcoat, the sleeves of which were too short for me," Ahrendt recalled with seemingly irrefutable and convincing detail.

The Germans at the same time produced another witness swearing in persuasive detail—also, interestingly, involving an overcoat—that the payment occurred in January, 1916. Charles Muhlenbrock of the New York office of North German Lloyd told of how a drunken Hinsch was waiting when he arrived at work:

> I can positively fix this day as having been in the wintertime because Captain Hinsch was wearing an overcoat and I distinctly remember him taking it off . . . I further remember the incident because Captain Hinsch was visibly under the influence of liquor. In fact, to put it plainly, he was drunk, and so much so that he required assistance in the removal of his overcoat, and in retaining his balance while doing so. . . . The disgust which I felt with Captain Hinsch for such a breach of conduct that was expected of the company's officers made a deep and lasting impression on my memory.

Hinsch's condition was so obvious, Muhlenbrock said, that his boss, von Hemholt, dictated a memorandum for the file in case Hinsch decided to make an issue of his refusal to give him the two thousand dollars he asked for.

Here were two witnesses with stories of such indelible detail that challenging them would be a monumental task, as the time for oral arguments before the Mixed Claims Commission at last arrived. And so it proved to be.

19. Justice Cheated

For ten days in April, 1929, the commission hearings proceeded, based on more than seven hundred exhibits from the American side, only one of which included Hall's more than four hundred cables, and the German side's flat denials, based on affidavits not subject to cross-examination.

German agent Von Lewinski, in his oral argument, offered an incredible defense against the allegation that Germany had withheld evidence unjustifiably. It was all the fault, he said, of the war, the brief Red revolution and the terms of the Versailles Treaty. Documents were destroyed wholesale at the end of the war to keep them from the enemy and then from the Bolsheviks, he said, and then in meeting "an obligation imposed by the treaty." In accordance with its terms, he said, "the General Staff [of the Imperial German Army] was abolished and everything that the General Staff had, had to be eliminated also."

Because an Inter-Allied Commission of Control established by the treaty was mandated "to see that in the future no military organization in Germany could rise again," von Lewinski blandly explained, it was incumbent on the German government after the war to destroy everything that had anything whatever to do with the General Staff or any other future source of militarism. It was not enough to wipe out the military structure and munitions plants, he said. All support facilities had to go, including all papers dealing with the war and even the buildings that housed them!

Here again was that famed Teutonic thoroughness and total compliance with official orders — but this time with a profoundly self-serving purpose. This interpretation of the requirements of the Inter-Allied Commission would have been comical had it not been for the importance to the American side of the documents thus lost. The chairman of the Inter-Allied Commission, a Briton named Sir Francis Bingham, in due course informed the Mixed Claims Commission that the notion that complete destruction of all war-related documents and property had been required was pure hokum.

Von Lewinski rested his defense on a challenge to American agent

Bonynge's contention that the claimants had only to prove German intent to commit sabotage and that such acts took place. Germany could be held responsible, the German agent argued, only if "acts can be traced back, link by link, long as the chain may be, to the German Government or to a German authority." Instead of achieving that, he said, the claimants were relying simply on "the American theory of German animus—that any act done was meant to do harm in behalf of the German government or its interests" out of a natural hostility toward America.

On the contrary, he suggested, Germany bent over backwards to stay in her good graces and keep her neutral. But Bonynge, citing von Bernstorff's admitted role in ordering the destruction of property in China and Canada and encouraging incitement of riots in the United States, asked: "If he was willing to do these things, was he not more willing to do that which would be more effective for Germany, namely destroy the munitions here in the United States, destroy them in our munitions factories?"

Some forty-five hours of oral argument were offered, and plans were made for the commission to reconvene in September, at the Peace Palace in The Hague. The date was postponed, however, when Judge Parker died unexpectedly. He was replaced by another American, Roland W. Boyden, a Boston lawyer whose firm was involved with a number of large banks doing business with the German government.

Facing the prospect of having to review the whole case before a new and possibly tougher umpire, Peaslee and Peto sought to strengthen their case. They got a lead in August, 1929, when the German side suddenly filed affidavits signed by Theodore Wozniak denying again that he had started the Kingsland fire or that he was the "Karowski" who had turned up in Mexico in 1917. He had appeared one day at the German consulate in New York, made the statement, and disappeared again, the Germans said. In the affidavits, Wozniak claimed that in August and September, 1917, when "Karowski" was in Mexico, he was working for the Santa Clara Lumber company in Tupper Lake, New York, in the Adirondack Mountains near Saranac. It was clear from the affidavits that Wozniak and his German lawyers had been at Tupper Lake gathering material for the affidavits, so Peaslee and Peto hired detectives to stake out the town, in case he returned to further build his alibi.

For months nothing happened and the search for Wozniak continued well into the fall of 1929 and the dark days of late October when the stock market crashed, sending reverberations from Wall Steet to Unter den Linden and around the globe. Soon the Great Depression was enveloping the German economy. Unemployment mushroomed; with it came more discontent and, with Hitler and his Nazi henchmen stirring the pot, rampant street violence. The old diatribes of the failed Beer Hall Putsch of 1923 were heard again, and this time they fell on more responsive ears. With Nazi membership now approaching 200,000 Hitler courted the army leadership, and infiltrated its ranks with his S.A. men.

These developments, however, were far from the minds of the American investigators as they sought to track down Wozniak and connect him to the Kingsland fire. Two new allies surfaced, Edwin and Carl Herrmann, brothers of Fred, both American citizens concerned about his safety and legal standing. Peaslee and Peto persuaded them to go down to Chile and urge their brother to come home and face the music; they agreed. Although Herrmann was not ready to return to the United States, he did agree to meet Peaslee and Peto in Havana in late March, 1930. Fred Herrmann had lost his bank job in Valparaiso and was desperate. Assured he would not be prosecuted, he consented at last to return. It was in Havana, however, that the American investigators hit paydirt with him.

In the course of a long conversation, Peaslee at one point asked Herrmann casually: "Did you ever know a man who used the alias 'Francis Graentnor'?" Without hesitation, Herrmann replied: "Oh, yes. That was Captain Hinsch." Peaslee did not allow himself any visible reaction, but as soon as Herrmann left the room he phoned Bonynge. He had the missing link in Kristoff's tie to the German saboteurs— the man who had hired him, the Baltimore-based overseer for the merchant submarine *Deutschland* on its missions to neutral America.

Herrmann also admitted that he was called "Rodriguez" by Hinsch. The testimony fed the suspicion that Herrmann himself had bribed the real Rodriguez, Wozniak's workbench neighbor at Kingsland, to stay home on the day of the fire and had taken his place, helped Wozniak spread the fire, and then escaped with him. Herrmann denied it, but even so his testimony substantially strengthened the American case, particularly with his fingering of Hinsch as "Graentnor." Other witnesses subsequently substantiated that Hinsch had used that alias.

Herrmann told how Hinsch had introduced him to Wozniak, a man with "a heavy, thick black moustache and dark eyes, looking sort of cuckoo, [with] staring eyes"; how Wozniak got Rodriguez a job at Kingsland with him and how he, Herrmann, met them periodically, paying them thirty-five or forty dollars a week each and giving them several of the incendiary "pencils" or glass tubes, also referred to by the saboteurs simply as "glasses."

He also told in detail about the meeting in Berlin in February, 1916, at which the heads of Section 3B, Marguerre and Nadolny, gave him the first such "glasses," instructing him on their use—as soon as he got back to the United States, not just in the event America entered the war. In fact, he said, he told his German bosses "that if the United States ever got into the war I was going to quit insofar as work in the United States was concerned, and I did. All of us beat it in various directions when the breach of diplomatic relations came."

Herrmann also confirmed Eddie Fulton's germ-inoculating mission. The Germans regarded this operation against horses, he said, as a much greater "moral" offense against American neutrality and the laws of warfare than any other act of sabotage, and hence they feared its disclosure above all. Blowing up munitions plants would save the lives of Germans in the war; but injecting anthrax and glanders germs into horses "was a dirty trick," Herrmann said. "We never knew it would be allowed in any sort of open or closed warfare."

It was because the handling of germs was considered "dirty" work, both physically and ethically, that black stevedores were chosen to perform the inoculations. In the blatant racism that reigned at the time, Herrmann described the operation this way: "On the germ question, they had about eight or ten coons in these different places putting these germs around." He and others used the word "coon" repeatedly, with never an objection recorded by any of the lawyer-interrogators on the American side.

What was needed now to tighten up the Kingsland case was corroboration from Wozniak. The search for him continued. On July 4, 1930, the stakeout at Tupper Lake finally paid off. He was spotted by the manager of a local hotel, who phoned one of the detectives. In the best tradition of a Keystone Kops movie reel, American investigators including Peaslee and Peto rushed to the Adirondacks town and played hide-and-seek with Wozniak. A car chase ensued, in which he was forced to the side and served with a letter from the American agent demanding that he testify. That night, suitcase in hand, Wozniak tried to give his pursuers the slip, boarding a train for New York. One of the detectives climbed aboard unnoticed and tailed him all the way. In the meantime, both sides collected affidavits from lumbermen at Tupper Lake to establish that Wozniak did or didn't work there when "Karowski" was in Mexico. It came down to which side the commission would believe.

Another issue in that same category was whether Hinsch had collected two thousand dollars from Hilken in July, 1916, the day after Black Tom, or the previous January. Now the Germans filed memoranda and correspondence from the files of North German Lloyd professing to prove that the payment was made seven months before the Black Tom explosions. Bonynge reexamined Hilken, who said he recalled two payments, one in January and one the following July, and that he had "undoubtedly" gotten the details confused.

This admission was certain to compromise his testimony before the commission that the two thousand dollars was a direct payoff for Black Tom. Peaslee pleaded with Hilken to go back to his home and office and search for some record that would help to restore his credibility on the payment after Black Tom.

As the commission prepared to reconvene at The Hague, the German side suddenly produced a host of new affidavits from key figures, again with no opportunity for the Americans to cross-examine or even check them independently. They came from Hinsch, Marguerre, Woehst and Ahrendt—dubbed by the Americans "the Four Horsemen" of Germany's fraudulent defense; from three Italian workmen at Kingsland all testifying about the poor condition of the shell-making machinery there; and from the head of the Kingsland security guards reporting the sighting of sparks from the machines.

Hinsch admitted he had been involved in the making of "dumpling" incendiary devices to be placed on ships and in the inoculation of horses, but that these deeds had been done before he became overseer of the activities of the *Deutschland,* and that at the time of Black Tom and Kingsland he had no time for anything else. The fact was, however, that the *Deutschland* made only two trips during that period and was in American ports only forty days out of ten months from its first call at Baltimore in July, 1916, to the American entry into the war.

Hinsch's affidavit did mention one thing, though, that later would help dispel the haze blanketing the sabotage cases. He specifically acknowledged that during this period "Herrmann showed me about seventy-five to one hundred small glass tubes for causing fires, and he demonstrated how these tubes could be concealed in a pencil." His use of the words "glass tubes" would ultimately take on critical significance in the case. Marguerre in his affidavit also used the words in telling how, after Herrmann took the first batch of incendiary devices to America, "we had a trunk made with a double bottom in order to pack glass tubes therein in a secret partition." But he insisted they had nothing to do with either Black Tom or Kingsland.

Also critical in time was the testimony of Carl Ahrendt, the lowly clerk in the Baltimore office of North German Lloyd at the time of the two-thousand-dollar payment to Hinsch, that he had never heard from Hinsch or anybody else about sabotage activities. These flat denials eventually helped break the back of the German defense, when irrefutable evidence to the contrary was discovered.

The hearings at The Hague proved to be essentially a contest over the credibility of Bonynge's star witnesses, Paul Hilken and Fred Herrmann, and an argument as to whether it was enough for the American side to prove German complicity in sabotage, without proving specific details and tying them to specific people. "What the American agent treats as mere details," von Lewinski argued, "namely how it was done, who did it, and whether the person who did it was really a German agent—these so-called 'details' form the actual, and I claim the only, issue in the present procedings." Herrmann's confession, von Lewinski argued, was squeezed from him with financial inducements and hence was not credible.

Von Lewinski's associate, Dr. Wilhelm Tannenberg, went after Hilken, accusing him of perjury in first saying Hinsch had told him nothing about Black Tom and later saying Hinsch had told him suggestively, "It is better not to ask any questions." Similarly, he said, Hilken first said he knew nothing about the Kingsland fire but then, after falling in league with the American investigators and reading Herrmann's version, corroborated it.

The German defense strategy was transparent: to harp on the inconsistencies and conflicts in the versions testified to by Herrmann and Hilken before and after each had decided to throw in with the American side. In a case that clearly was going to ride on the commission's weighing of circumstantial evidence and the credibility of witnesses—

a case without a "smoking gun"—the German strategy was as deft as it was simple.

Bonynge summed up by bringing the case back to its origins—the German embassy under Count von Bernstorff in his dual role as neutrality-preserver and sabotage-overseer:

> The late President Wilson, with a tolerance that seemed almost impossible, would not believe it until the evidence accumulated so rapidly that no longer could he believe, as he thought at first, that it was incredible that any nation in this age would commit such acts as those the testimony shows conclusively were committed by . . . a supposedly friendly power, which had its duly accredited representative at the Capital at Washington dealing with the President of the United States.

While all the subversive acts were going on, Bonynge said, there was von Bernstorff "assuring him that Germany was not doing these things; trying to cover up his tracks while he himself was engaged in fomenting strikes among workmen, in issuing false passports, in organizing an invasion into territory of another friendly power of the United States. . . . Finally the evidence became so convincing that Germany was in fact waging a secret warfare against the United States that even President Wilson could no longer withstand the convincing evidence that was brought to him." The Mixed Claims Commission, Bonynge concluded, could now do no less.

But Bonynge was very wrong. On October 16, 1930, the commission ruled unanimously that the American side had established that the German government had authorized sabotage in neutral America, but the Americans had not proved to the commission's satisfaction that German agents had perpetrated either Black Tom or Kingsland. And so the case was dismissed.

Regarding Black Tom, the commission said, it was unable to conclude that Michael Kristoff did indeed cause the disaster, and it did not believe that Lothar Witzke or Kurt Jahnke, with their alibis of having been elsewhere, were involved at all. And while Captain Hinsch may have been the "Francis Graentnor" said to have hired Kristoff, the commission observed, the American side did not prove sufficiently that Kristoff was a German agent. The commissioners accepted Hinsch's story that he gave up sabotage when he took over the *Deutschland* assignment, and they accepted the testimony of the

Italian workmen contending that while Wozniak was at the site of the fire, it was an accident caused by faulty machinery. And finally, "the discrepancies and improbabilities of Herrmann's story," the decision said, convinced the commission "that Wozniak was not guilty." The evidence was clear, the commission judged, that Herrmann was "a liar, not presumptive but proven."

Hall wrote a consoling letter to Peaslee. "I am so sorry for you, my dear Amos, and my sorrow is mixed with fury when I think how the Germans are now chuckling. I think that hurts more than anything, as it is the first time they have got away with a bluff since the war."

At least one onlooker in the United States, the German-language *New Yorker Staatszeitung*, greeted the decision with satisfaction. "Germany has won a great victory through the decision," it said editorially, "not on account of the sum involved, but because of the fact that the commission is bearing a brilliant testimonial to the honesty of Germany."

The *Washington Star* also hailed the decision. "War passions and war psychology were responsible for disordered thinking all over the world," it decided. "Innocents suffered everywhere along with the guilty. All the resultant damage cannot be repaired, but the outcome of the Black Tom and Kingsland cases is a heartening indication of a readiness to make, though tardy, such amends as are possible."

Also expressing a sense of vindication was Ervin J. Smith, head of one of the detective agencies that had investigated Black Tom in 1916. "The real story of the explosion," he told the *New York Times*, "is this: The watchmen employed to guard the millions of dollars' worth of war materials, sugar, salt, flour and explosives were bothered by the mosquitoes that infested the swampy land about Black Tom. They built themselves a smudge fire to drive them off. A spark from this fire ignited some excelsior which had been left carelessly under a box car on a siding less than a hundred feet from the watchmen's shanty."

Fourteen years after the Black Tom disaster, after exhaustive investigations by more than forty insurance companies and a small army of high-powered, high-priced lawyers, here was the old mosquito theory, still alive and well! That is, at least for the readers of the prestigious *New York Times* and several other newspapers. The Danville, Virginia, *Bee* practically rejoiced over learning that Black Tom "was primarily due to native-born New Jersey mosquitoes." Editorially, the paper reminisced:

What extravagant stories were told of the affair! German agents abroad in New York, enemy spies making their first decisive coup in America to stun its people by an example of German efficiency and terrorism, special emissaries from the emperor of Germany reporting directly to him, and his imperial majesty the brains of the plot! . . . But it was a simple accident after all.

And *The Nation* magazine noted:

Mosquitoes as the indirect cause of the Black Tom explosion and fire in July, 1916, will seem altogether possible to residents of New Jersey who know their mosquitoes. . . . As it stands, [the decision] will serve to increase the friendly feeling of Germany toward an erstwhile enemy nation.

There was no friendly feeling in return, though, from the indefatigable American investigators who remained convinced of Germany's guilt. They refused to accept the idea that the case was closed, and before many weeks had passed, an unexpected discovery suddenly revived their hopes. On Christmas Day, 1930, Paul Hilken, now estranged from his wife, was back at their old house in Baltimore rummaging through a box of old papers, at the urging of the American sleuths. He came upon something he had forgotten all about: a tattered issue of *Blue Book* magazine, dated January, 1917.

What Hilken found was the magazine Raoul Gerdts brought from Mexico in 1917, in which Herrmann wrote the secret message in lemon juice asking for $25,000—the secret message that demonstrated for the sake of identification that he knew all about the German sabotage operations in the United States, and who was involved in them. The front cover was torn off but otherwise the magazine was intact. All through the prosecution of the case against Germany, the magazine and the coded message it bore had remained a secret, all but forgotten even by those who were involved in its writing and transmission. It did not remain so for much longer.

Hilken at first hesitated giving it to the American investigators. He felt he had been badly treated in the manner in which the German side had been able to brand him a liar in the commission's decision. But in mid-April, he received a surprise visitor—Fred Herrmann—and told him how he had found the old *Blue Book*. Herrmann, likewise chagrined at how the commission decision had painted him, immediately recognized that the magazine was the key to their vindication. He persuaded Hilken to bury his pride and take it to Peto. He did so.. Fourteen years earlier, by passing a hot iron over the pages, Hilken had made Herrmann's lemon-juice message visible. Now, as he lay the *Blue Book* before Peto, the message could still be clearly read.

Noting the numerals written for names and places, discarding the first number and turning to the indicated page in the *Blue Book*, Hilken demonstrated how the tiny pin pricks on the page spelled out the coded words. The critical names in the sabotage operation were thus quickly sorted out. Peto was amazed and ecstatic. The Germans had used this coding procedure often during the war and the Allies were familiar with it; he had no doubt about its authenticity. Ironically, had von Eckhardt not been suspicious in 1917 when Herrmann sought money to blow up the Tampico oil fields, Herrmann never would have written the lemon-juice message. Peto immediately urged Bonynge and the other leading American investigators to push for reopening the case.

At the same time, another significant development was unfolding that might persuade the commission to reconsider its dismissal. The Germans categorically denied that Wozniak was in Mexico in the summer of 1917 as part of the German sabotage apparatus that fled there after the American entry into the war. But through the perseverance of a new investigator in the case, a young New York lawyer named John J. McCloy, new evidence was discovered.

McCloy was a member of the firm of Cravath, deGersdorff, Swaine and Wood, which had as a client one of the American claimants, the Bethlehem Steel Company. McCloy knew his way around Europe, having served as a field artillery captain in France and Germany during the war. After the commission threw the case out, Peaslee's star went into eclipse and McCloy's firm asked him to move in as a principal associate.

McCloy located two boyhood friends of Wozniak who had emigrated from Poland to Scranton, Pennsylvania, and then to Cleveland. McCloy took affidavits from them in which they said Wozniak had sent them letters from Mexico in 1917, then called on them in Scranton, urgently asked for the letters and ripped them up in their presence.

In April, 1931, three more letters purported to have come from Wozniak turned up. Ivan Baran, a minister and chairman of the

Ukrainian Relief Committee in Chicago, gave them to Peto in exchange for immunity for Wozniak and $2,500 to cover his time and expenses. The three were written in Ukrainian, one from St. Louis dated August 10, 1917, and the others from Mexico City, one on August 28 and the other on September 16.

The critical one from Mexico City complained about Mexico and hinted that he was under the thumb of "these damn Germans." The writer offered that "I did quite wrong by going with the Germans" but "there is no place to go and if there was, why it is dangerous and I must listen to the Germans." He warned Baran not to tell anybody what he had written, and he said he could be written care of "F. W. Karowski." The other letter from Mexico City complained of the heat and observed: "Not writing much because next month will be in New York not far from King"—which the American investigators took to mean Kingsland.

Armed with the Herrmann message in the 1917 *Blue Book*, the purported Wozniak letters, and an actual "glass tube" Carl Herrmann long before had buried in his garden and had just dug up, the Americans petitioned the Mixed Claims Commission to reopen the case. While declining to set aside its earlier acquittal of the German government, the commission did agree to hear additional oral arguments in Boston in the summer of 1931.

The Germans argued first that the case was closed and could not be reopened, and then that both the Herrmann message and the Wozniak letters were fraudulent. They accused the Americans of buying an old *Blue Book* and writing the message in it, a charge that triggered both sides to hire experts in handwriting and the aging of paper. Albert S. Osborn, regarded as the preeminent American in the field, was sought by the commission, but he said he had already been hired by the Germans. The Americans then hired as their expert Elbridge W. Stein, a man recommended to them by—Osborn! It was a circumstance that had important ramifications later on.

An intense battle of the paper experts ensued, the American experts reporting that their tests proved without a question that both the magazine and the lemon-juice message dated back to 1917, the German experts insisting that their tests proved conclusively that they did not. Questions were raised as to the watermarks on the paper and the fading of it; the nature and timing of the pin pricks made; the marks left by the hot iron and the blurring of the handwriting.

The paper experts on each side went to war over the Wozniak letters, too. The Germans did not challenge that they were in Wozniak's handwriting, but they contended, based on the watermark, that the paper could not have been available in 1917.

While all this jockeying was going on, Wozniak himself suddenly reappeared. On May 31, 1931, without warning, he paid an unsolicited call on Peto in his room at the Roosevelt Hotel in New York, demanding to be interviewed so he could clear his name. The astounded Peto, unprepared for so important an opportunity, stalled, telling Wozniak he could not interview him right then and suggesting he return the next day. Wozniak agreed.

Peto rented the room next to his own and the next morning installed two stenographers. Notepads at the ready, they sat in chairs placed against the connecting door to Peto's room and listened attentively. Sure enough, at the appointed hour Wozniak appeared and Peto ushered him to a chair next to the connecting door. As the two men talked, the stenographers scribbled away.

At once, it became clear Wozniak wanted to sell his confession. Each time he began to broach the subject of money, Peto asked him specific questions about the Kingsland fire, as if to determine whether the testimony was worth the price Wozniak might put on it. Unaware of the presence of the stenographers and hence thinking he was not surrendering his payoff, Wozniak spilled the whole story.

Peto: "Supposing Commissioner Anderson* asked you, would you tell him that you did set the fire on behalf of Germany?"

Wozniak: "I would tell him."

Peto: "You admit it?"

Wozniak: "Yes, I admit it. That was set so easily."

Peto: "No witnesses."

Wozniak: "No witnesses. I was scared. . . . I was scared for myself. I had no agents helping me at that time; just a bunch of rags. . . ."

Peto: "Listen, this man Lascola, he said that your machine was throwing all kinds of sparks. That is not true?"

Wozniak: "This machine perfect. Listen, how could the sparks come out? . . . He doesn't know. He is not a machinist."

Peto: "Lascola lied then?"

Wozniak: "Sure."

---

*Chandler P. Anderson, the initial American commissioner on the Mixed Claims Commission.

The interview was going swimmingly. Then, suddenly, one of the stenographers on the other side of the connecting door—coughed! Wozniak, realizing he had been set up, erupted in a fury. He seized the doorknob and tried to force the locked door open. He stooped over and looked through the keyhole, professing to see the eavesdroppers on the other side, although the stenographers by this time had jumped out of sight. Wozniak rushed out of the room into the hall and pounded on the door to the adjoining room. Peto called a hotel assistant manager, who rushed up and led the enraged man out of the hotel.

Peto promptly filed an affidavit with the commission based on the stenographers' notes. He asked the commission to waive its rules for the presenting of testimony only through the agents so that Wozniak could be brought in to testify directly. But the German side refused and Tannenberg charged that Peto had bribed Wozniak to confess.

The Boston hearings again were a contest of credibility, this time mainly over the Herrmann message and the Wozniak letters. But Bonynge, with the stenographers' account of Wozniak's hotel-room confession in hand, also challenged the veracity of the Italian workman Lascola at Kingsland. In three separate statements at the time of the fire, Bonynge pointed out, Lascola never once mentioned "a spark from a defective machine" or "a squeaking machine." The American agent offered an affidavit from a manufacturer who had installed the shell-cleaning machines at Kingsland who avowed "there never was any spark from the machine" and that it was "absolutely impossible that there could have been a spark" because the machine revolved too slowly to produce one.

Another Italian workman, Eugene Urciuoli, acknowledged in his affidavit, Bonynge noted, that he was not in Building 30, the site of the fire, at the time it happened. Inasmuch as the commission in its decision had relied on these witnesses in concluding that an industrial accident had caused the fire, he argued, here alone were sufficient grounds to reopen the case. Together with the Herrmann message, which alluded to Hinsch paying off Wozniak for the Kingsland job, and the Wozniak letters, which placed Wozniak in Mexico as part of the German apparatus, the German complicity was established, Bonynge argued.

The American agent also relied on the Herrmann message as grounds to reopen the Black Tom matter. He pointed to the sentence in the decoded message warning that the "Hoboken bunch," specifically including Kristoff, "if cornered . . . might get us in Dutch with authorities." Bonynge asked: "In Dutch for what? If it was merely observation [of munitions plants], of course they would not get in Dutch." The very fact that Herrmann mentioned the Jersey City Terminal (Black Tom) and Kingsland, he said, established sufficient connection of both crimes with the German sabotage community.

In its earlier decision, Bonynge noted, the commission had held that it had not been sufficiently established that Kristoff was in the employ of Germany at Black Tom. Now, he concluded, "there cannot be the slightest kind of doubt that Kristoff was a German agent, and that he started this fire . . . and that Germany therefore is responsible for it."

The Germans realized that the Herrmann message was the stronger of the two new pieces of evidence offered by the Americans, and that the Wozniak letters were the weaker. Tannenberg, who now had taken over as the German agent, understood that if he could cast serious doubt on the veracity of any of the new American evidence—or, better, suggest outright fraud in any single piece of it—he could very likely harpoon the entire American effort to have the case reopened. So he focused on the Wozniak letters.

He marveled at the carelessness of a supposedly accomplished saboteur telling Baran in one letter to address mail to him as "F. W. Karowski," his alias, and then signing the letter, as he did, with his real name, T. I. Wozniak. One of the letters had so much information in it, he noted, that if seized it would have surely incriminated a man said to have the craftiness of a spy. It was all too preposterous, he said. Furthermore, he charged, stains on one of the letters had been, according to his paper experts, placed on it after the letter was written to indicate age, and a hole cut in one of the letters might have excised "the watermark which would have identified the paper as being manufactured sometime after 1917."

As for the Herrmann message, Tannenberg told the commission:

> I readily concede that if this document had been found in the archives of the State Department as a document or message intercepted in 1917, there would perhaps be hardly any defense as to its authenticity. But this document is now produced by Paul Hilken, and is identified only by Paul Hilken and Fred Herrmann. The commission found that these two gentlemen . . . had perjured themselves, by giving one affidavit after

another repudiating their previous statements. . . . In order to accept this message as authentic, and as meaning what the American Agent says, the commission must rely on the testimony of two witnesses who have been proven to be liars and perjurers.

Once again, Bonynge was being stymied by his own witnesses' tarnished credibility. He asked the commission to look beyond Herrmann's and Hilken's previous inconsistent record for telling the truth and to consider how the message itself dovetailed with the rest of the evidence. That argument, however, ran against the commission members' already demonstrated inclination to cast both Herrmann and Hilken aside as "proven liars."

The next important development once again came from Paul Hilken's attic. In December, 1931, his estranged wife, while going through old belongings, came upon a diary her husband had kept during the war. Entries referred to his visit to Berlin in 1916 and his meetings with von Papen and Marguerre and Nadolny of Section 3B, at which he met Herrmann and the orders to use the incendiary devices were given.

Another entry told of Hilken's having dinner at the "Astor Roof with Sir John [Hamer] and crowd" on August 4, 1916. It reinforced earlier testimony about a dinner there at which Hinsch was present, confirming that he was in New York a few days after the Black Tom explosions. Most important, however, was still another entry indicating that six days later, on August 10, Hilken paid two thousand dollars to Hinsch, as he had testified earlier.

About six weeks after the diary was found, Hilken also located some old checkbooks. The stub in one of them, for check Number 115 dated August 10, 1916, noted payment of two thousand dollars for "Capt. H., Lewis, etc." The reference obviously was to Hinsch and to Herrmann, known to have often used the aliases "Lewis" and "March." Shortly afterward, Hilken delivered the new evidence to Peaslee.

The check stub, the American side confidently hoped, would offset the detailed, colorful testimony by Ahrendt that he had gone to New York from Baltimore in dead winter in a tattered overcoat, thus placing the payment to Hinsch six months before Black Tom. Hilken always contended that there must have been two such payments to Hinsch. The diary entry and check stub now stood as tangible confirmations of that view.

As the American investigators thus shored up their case in the hope of persuading the commission to take another look, one of the earliest important figures in the German sabotage effort in America during the neutrality period came to light again in a significant way. Franz von Papen suddenly surfaced as chancellor of Germany in a lightning series of events that ultimately put Adolf Hitler in power.

Von Papen was now a member of the Centrist party of Heinrich Brüning, the man Hindenburg had appointed as chancellor. But he saw Hitler's National Socialists as the vehicle for inflaming and enlisting mass support for a resurrection of the military-leader class and, ultimately, the downfall of the Weimar Republic. Hitler, by now a force to be reckoned with, challenged von Hindenburg for the presidency in March, 1932, and, while he lost, he received some thirteen million votes.

In the streets of Germany's major cities, the Nazi party's strongarm force, the S.A., now numbered some four hundred thousand, or four times the authorized ceiling for the Reichswehr, the Weimar Republic's standing army. Fearful of the ruthless Brown Shirts, the government banned them from public demonstrations after the election.

The real power in Berlin now was General Kurt von Schleicher, who had been instrumental in Brüning's appointment as chancellor. As the economic depression bred public discontent with Brüning, von Schleicher cast about for a weak replacement who would offer no power threat to the German army. To the astonishment of nearly everyone in Berlin, he settled on von Bernstorff's old military attaché in Washington.

Von Papen, now fifty-three years old and a lowly member of the Prussian state parliament, was appointed as chancellor on June 2 by the pliable von Hindenburg, who wanted anyone but Hitler in the post. To obtain Hitler's acquiescence, von Schleicher obliged von Papen to dissolve the Reichstag and call for new elections, at the same time lifting the prohibition against Hitler's Brown Shirts. Amid widespread street violence by them, the Nazi party captured 230 seats in the Reichstag, a plurality for the first time. Already von Papen's days were numbered, with Hitler's reign of terror soon to begin.

Now came the most audacious effort yet to kill the still-gasping American case by thoroughly discrediting the Herrmann message as a blatant fraud. In a move that at first baffled the American investigators, the Germans introduced as evidence 409 copies of three different magazines—assorted issues of the *Blue Book*, *Red Book* and *Adventure*. Accompanying this pile of old magazines was an affidavit from Herman Meyers, proprietor of Abraham's Book Store in New York, dealing in second-hand books and magazines, in which he testified that Albert Osborn, the Germans' handwriting and paper expert, the previous October (1931) had come in asking for a copy of the January, 1917, *Blue Book*—the same issue containing the Herrmann message. When Meyers told him he had sold his only two copies a few months earlier, Osborn bought copies of the month before and after that date.

A week later, Meyers said, Osborn came in again with Tannenberg, then the German counsel, who proceeded to buy all of Meyers' remaining 1917 copies of the *Blue Book* and all the *Red Book* and *Adventure* magazines subsequently offered in evidence. Meyers, in an affidavit for Tannenberg, said he had sold one of his two copies of the January, 1917, *Blue Book* to a man he "vaguely" remembered as "tall and possibly between thirty and forty years old"—a description that comfortably fit Herrmann.

What the Germans were up to soon became clear. On two facing pages at the beginning of Hilken's *Blue Book*, there were "plus" and "minus" pencil markings next to the titles of most of the articles in that issue. These marks had not drawn particular notice until the German side introduced all the other magazines. In total, they bore 154 similar markings on their contents pages, 137 minuses and 17 pluses.

The Germans produced affidavits from two brothers, Horace and John Qualters, telling how Horace had collected these magazines and as he read articles would mark them with a horizontal line on the contents page. Then John would read them and mark a vertical line through the horizontal, creating a plus sign. In late 1930, Horace said, he sold all the magazines to Abraham's Book Store. At Tannenberg's request, he identified them as those sold. The Germans were alleging that the January, 1917, *Blue Book* containing the Herrmann message had not been in Hilken's attic since 1917 at all, but really was part of the Qualters collection sold to the book store in 1930, and an unvarnished fake.

The American investigators were astounded. The charge set off another battle of the paper experts. The American experts countercharged that the marks in the other magazines were phony, made by one pencil in the hand of one individual. The Germans countered that their agents in Mexico in 1917 had invisible ink and never would have used lemon juice to write a secret message. The Americans disputed the claim.

To prop up the authenticity of the Herrmann message, the American sleuths tracked down Adam Siegel, the man who dictated the message to Herrmann as he wrote it in lemon juice. Siegel was uncovered in Reval, Estonia, one of the Baltic states later gobbled up by the Soviet Union, and Herrmann was dispatched to urge him to testify.

The Americans were elated when Herrmann came back with Siegel's signed statement that he had met Herrmann and Gerdts in April, 1917, on a steamer from Havana to Vera Cruz and had gone on with them to Mexico City, where Herrmann sought money from von Eckhardt to resume his sabotage work. Siegel confirmed that when von Eckhardt balked, Herrmann wrote the secret message, first in longhand and then in lemon juice in the *Blue Book* as Siegel dictated it to him from the longhand text. Gerdts then took it to Hilken in Baltimore, he said.

"Herrmann showed me today a magazine similar to that used at that time to send to Baltimore," he stated, "likewise the photographs of the printed pages on which the report to Baltimore was written in lemon juice at that time. These above-mentioned photographs were signed by me today." There was one hitch, however. Siegel refused to have the statement notarized because, he told Herrmann, he did not want the people in Reval to know of his wartime activities for the Germans.

When the Americans filed their statement with the commission, the Germans immediately dispatched their own agents to Estonia and came back with another Siegel affidavit, signed before the German chargé d'affaires in Reval, charging that Herrmann had misrepresented himself as an agent of Germany dictating how he should respond. He revised his story to say that "I can no longer swear whether it was a magazine or a bound book." He also insisted "positively that during that time single sheets of the printed volume were not pricked with a needle under certain letters." Nor did he know, he said, most of the names in the message until Herrmann read them to him in Reval. Just as quickly as the first Siegel affidavit seemed to assure the credibility of the Herrmann message, the second cast a shadow over it.

Finally, there was one other piece of hanky-panky by the Germans to undercut the claimants' chances. Unsuspected by the Americans who had hired Elbridge Stein as their paper expert on the recommendation of the Germans' expert, Albert Osborn, the two were in collusion. Osborn, on the sly, conveyed to members of the commission a suggestion that Stein had written a report for his American employers questioning the authenticity of the Herrmann message. Stein himself then charged the American lawyers with having suppressed it, when in fact they had never received any such report from him. When Bonynge confronted Stein, the paper expert retracted his charge of suppression while still insisting he had written such a report. The suspicion thus planted, the commission umpire acknowledged later, contributed importantly to his doubts about the authenticity of the Herrmann message as the commission reconvened in November, 1932.

As the American side knew, credibility of documents again would be the deciding issue. There was now a strong sense that the case against the Germans could have been made much better by relying on the Herrmann message alone, referring as it did to both Black Tom and Kingsland. It was an unfortunate complication now to have to depend also on the Wozniak letters, the authenticity of which was much shakier and which sought to establish only that Wozniak was in Mexico in 1917 and thus by inference part of the German operation that fired Kingsland.

Bonynge in his presentation accordingly focused on the Herrmann message, attacking what the Americans called "the Qualters Hoax" and particularly the strange role played by Osborn, who was supposedly an impartial expert but who actually had functioned as an investigator for the Germans. Osborn, he charged, "not only was acting as an expert in examining these documents, but also was endeavoring to secure nonexpert evidence . . . and became an advocate for Germany."

Bonynge argued that the discovery of Hilken's diary and checkbook provided solid corroborating evidence that Hinsch was "Graentnor" and that Kristoff was a hired German saboteur. He pointed out that the date on Hilken's check stub, August 10, 1916, noting the two-thousand-dollar payment to "Capt. H., Lewis, etc.," was the day before Kristoff said he went to the McAlpin Hotel to be paid by "Graentnor."

Bonynge also produced entries in Hilken's diary that indicated regular Sunday meetings between Hilken and Hinsch in Baltimore. But

Paul Koenig, detective for Hamburg-Amerika Line, who recruited and directed spies and saboteurs

View of destruction on Black Tom Island, New York Habor, after explosions of the night of July 29–30, 1916

Remnants of Canadian Car and Foundry plant, Kingsland, New Jersey, after fire of January 11, 1917

Forged passport, wig, and moustache disguises of Robert Fay, German soldier sent to America to fasten bombs to rudders of ships

Field Marshal Paul von Hindenburg, Major General Erich Ludendorff, and Kaiser Wilhelm II

Major General Erich Ludendorff, who favored resumption of unrestricted submarine warfare, in conversation with the famed "Red Baron," Manfred von Richtofen

Above left: William Jennings Bryan, U.S. secretary of state 1913–15, who resigned in protest against what he considered Woodrow Wilson's insufficiently neutral posture toward Germany

Above right: Robert Lansing, secretary of state from 1915 through 1920, who favored a more interventionist foreign policy

Left: Colonel Edward House, Wilson's adviser and personal negotiator

Right: Robert W. Bonynge, lawyer and former Colorado congressman who served as the chief American agent in arguing the sabotage case against Germany after the war

German Chancellor Theobold von Bethmann-Hollweg, second from right, who sought to prevent resumption of unrestricted submarine warfare

President Wilson announcing to Congress that diplomatic relations with Germany have been broken off, February 3, 1917

Ambassador von Bernstorff, center, with wife and daughter, left, arriving at Hoboken, New Jersey, en route to Germany after the United States broke off diplomatic relations with Germany

President Wilson riding to Buckingham Palace with King George V of England while en route to peace conference at Versailles, December, 1918

S.S. *George Washington* arriving in New York Harbor bringing President Wilson back from peace conference, 1919

there were none between late April and early June, 1916, when Kristoff claimed to have been in the Midwest with "Graentnor"—and when Kristoff was absent from his regular job at the Tidewater Oil Company.

To substantiate the American contention that the fire at Kingsland was caused by an incendiary "pencil" placed in the shell Wozniak was cleaning, the American agent produced one such "pencil," manufactured for the claimants by an American chemist according to Hermann's specification. Bonynge showed it to the commission—the glass tube placed in a crayon pencil. While it would ignite itself within forty minutes if left upright, he said, it could be ignited at once by striking it, which, he contended, was what Wozniak did.

Tannenberg intentionally gave priority to the weaker link in the American case, the Wozniak letters, and only then attacked the Herrmann message. He concentrated on making the case that Wozniak was not in Mexico in 1917 and could not have written the letters from there. He blandly ignored a long list of witnesses the American side had corraled at Tupper Lake saying none had ever seen Wozniak there, and he brushed aside his own failure to produce corroboration that Wozniak was there in 1917, and hence not in Mexico. Instead, he argued that since Wozniak in an affidavit had described Tupper Lake landmarks before having gone there to seek witnesses in 1929, and since records showed he had been elsewhere in 1916, 1918 and 1919, then he must have been there in 1917!

Wozniak, Tannenberg suggested in the strongest way, probably wrote the letters for the American side for money, when he was down on his luck after having failed to get financial support from the German side. Then, he said, the Americans faked the stains on them by photostatic trickery. And if the Wozniak letters, said by the American side to be authentic, really were fakes, he argued, then very likely so was the Herrmann message similarly attested to by the same experts. What probably happened, he suggested, was that Hilken, knowing the commission had specified that it could not accept anything either he or Hermann said without corroboration, simply manufactured it.

As for the use of lemon juice, Tannenberg said, Ahrendt had testified that in July, 1917, Anton Dilger brought from Germany a large supply of powder for making invisible ink. So why, he asked, was lemon juice used in the Herrmann message? "The simple answer," he said, "is that in the latter part of 1930 and in the beginning of

1931, no invisible ink of the kind used during the war was available."

The members of the commission, and the umpire, could not be blamed if by now they were thoroughly confused by the Qualters testimony, by the experts and nonexperts alike. And confusion was the German side's ally. Once again, the commissioners split and the umpire, now Supreme Court Associate Justice Owen J. Roberts, ruled against the Americans. His decision suggested strongly that the German strategy of attacking the Wozniak letters as fraudulent, and in so doing casting doubts on the more important Herrmann message as well, had worked.

Roberts declared categorically that the Wozniak letters, for which Peto had paid Baran $2,500 and promised immunity to Wozniak, "are not authentic." Most telling to him, he said, was the reference that Wozniak would "soon be back in New York near to 'King.' This is the sort of admission that Wozniak above all men in my judgment would not naturally or normally have made," Roberts wrote. "The references to Karowski and the Germans and to 'King' too well piece out the claimants' theory of the case." And he questioned why Baran would cut a piece out to have the paper analyzed for age if he had had the letters since 1917. "He needed no confirmation of their age," Roberts wrote.

As for the Herrmann message, the umpire said he couldn't decide whether it was authentic or not. If it could be believed, he said in an opinion tantalizingly bitter to the American side, it would prove the charges. But he was not convinced. The fact that Herrmann did not identify the message until April of 1931, he said, was also suspicious. "We need only note in passing," he said, "the Commission's former finding that Herrmann is a liar, not presumptive but proven."

The Herrmann message itself, Roberts wrote, was entirely too perfect in meeting the specific requirements of the American proof to be genuine. "The document comprises 254 words," he noted. "Those that have to do with the request for money amount to only twenty. All the remainder are wholly irrelevant to the purpose at hand. . . . But enough has been said to show in how extraordinary [a] manner this document dovetails with all the important and disputed points of the claimants' case, and how pat all these references are, not to the request for funds but to the claimants' points of proof. . . ."

As for the Qualters magazines, Roberts acknowledged that he was thoroughly confused—which after all was the Germans' purpose in submitting them. "While the evidence arouses suspicions," he wrote, "I cannot find in it alone enough to reach a certain conclusion." And after examining about one thousand pages of expert testimony, the umpire could only observe that "many of the opinions of the experts on the one side are countered by diametrically opposite results stated by those on the other." So much for expert opinions.

The American investigators were at a loss to understand how the umpire could be so blind as not to recognize the Germans' fraud. But Roberts was an American and he was bending over backward to demonstrate fairness. The Americans concluded that their only hope now was to prove beyond the shadow of a doubt that the Germans, in their desperation to defend their national honor in the case, had indeed resorted to fraud on a grand scale against the commission itself.

20. Justice Served

The Germans' determination to maintain the integrity of their diplomatic service in the Black Tom–Kingsland case was bolstered by events at home, where the fervor of nationalism was surging with the political fortunes of Adolf Hitler. Von Papen, inept as chancellor, secretly threw in with Hitler, proposing a coalition. He assumed that once it was struck, his own continuing influence with von Hindenburg, who had vowed never to make "that Bohemian corporal" chancellor, would enable him to command the upper hand.

But Hitler had other ideas. He insisted on being chancellor, with von Papen as vice chancellor, and von Hindenburg reluctantly acquiesced. On January 30, 1933, Hitler at last took power in Germany. If the leaders of the Weimar Republic had considered a guilty verdict in the American sabotage cases an unbearable humiliation, so much more did Hitler and his fanatical flock.

The American investigators, bent on proving German fraud, focused first on the accounts of the three Italian workmen at Kingsland. They ferreted out the fact that they had been located by one of the German lawyers and that parts of their affidavits were dictated by him. The stenographer who took the affidavits swore in one of his own that the German lawyer "used his language entirely and without but one or two interruptions" by the Italian witnesses.

The Americans also established through records that two of the Italians were not working at Kingsland at the time of the fire, and that all had been promised money by the German side. Safety records at Kingsland and testimony of the plant manager indicated there had never been even the smallest fire in Building 30, site of the 1917 fire. An actual cleaning machine of the sort used at Kingsland was located at an army ordnance depot, tested and found not to produce a single spark, as the Italian workmen had sworn it had.

To prove fraud, the American side pleaded with the commission to grant subpoena power. But the German commissioner refused. The Americans thereupon turned to Congress and a month later, on June 7, 1933, Congress finally acceded. Immediately, subpoenas were sought and issued for Wozniak, Baran, Herrmann, Hilken, the Qualters brothers and Ahrendt. The German side sought to quash the subpoenas, but without success. The German defense at last began to show signs of erosion.

The Qualters brothers were the first to crack. Horace, testifying under oath, said the Germans had never told him about expert opinion challenging the sequence of markings, and had he known he never would have insisted on what he had first testified. The disputed *Blue Book*, he said, was "entirely different than the magazines I sold to Abraham's" but the Germans told him it probably had been artificially aged. John Qualters also testified that the marks in the disputed book "are too small. . . . They were not made by me."

One subpoenaed witness who did not change his story, however, was Ahrendt, located in Detroit, where he was now North German Lloyd's representative. He insisted he didn't know Hinsch in 1916 or that Hinsch had anything to do with distributing germs or incendiary "glass tubes." This bit of unshaken testimony seemed to add nothing to the case at the time, but ultimately it was to prove pivotal.

Most important was the subpoenaing of papers of North German Lloyd and its former Baltimore director, Henry Hilken, father of Paul, and those of the Eastern Forwarding Company, created to handle the wartime arrangements for the merchant U-boat *Deutschland*. The Germans fought the subpoenas bitterly, for obvious reasons. The papers produced a bonanza of evidence supporting Paul Hilken's testimony that he was the paymaster for extensive activities of Hinsch and other German operatives, through the Eastern Forwarding Company front.

Hilken testified that he "used various accounts because it [the sabotage money] had to be jumbled up so it could not be traced." He put some in an account with a broker, he said, who "was simply making wash sales so as to hide the real purpose of that account, which was the payments to Dilger and Hinsch in Mexico. . . . I could not hang that on a bell so that everyone would know."

The subpoena power also uncovered sources of Eastern Forwarding Company disbursements, witnessed by checks and receipts. The senior Hilken, eighty years old and then the respected German consul in Baltimore, was obliged to review them, and he grudgingly testified that none of them was for any business activities of his shipping company. The obvious conclusion was that a separate "sabotage account" was maintained by Paul Hilken from which the controversial August, 1916, payment to Hinsch was made. Records of the company also showed that Hinsch, despite his denials, was in New York at the time of Black Tom.

In mid-July, Gerdts gave an affidavit in Colombia acknowledging that he had bought the lemon used by Herrmann "and I saw him writing the message myself." And a month later, Wozniak, responding to a subpoena, repeated basically the story he had given earlier to Peto in the episode of the hidden stenographers. He said he had met German agents in a cemetery near Kingsland, and, shown a photograph of Hinsch to identify, he blurted: "I cannot tell for sure the truth. . . . But I can seventy-five percent bet on this man. . . . I think this man was in Mexico. . . ." Then, quickly, he added: "Maybe I see him before the border—in the United States." The Americans at once seized on the remark about Mexico as a telltale slip—an admission by Wozniak that he had indeed been there in 1917.

All this finally persuaded commission umpire Roberts to reopen the case. To German howls of protest that the commission's work was done, he replied: "Every tribunal has inherent power to reopen and revise a decision induced by fraud."

The Americans continued to seek more evidence. McCloy scored another breakthrough in January, 1934, in Dublin. He obtained a lengthy affidavit from James Larkin, the organizer and agitator for Irish independence, on how key German embassy officials in Washington, including von Papen, tried in 1914 and later to buy his services to recruit other Irish radicals to foment strikes and commit acts of munitions sabotage. Larkin's testimony did not confirm definitively either Black Tom or Kingsland but did provide prime corroboration that, rather than ignoring the Irish recruitment cable of 1915 to von Bernstorff central to the American accusation, the Germans had acted vigorously on it. Larkin said that Wolf von Igel, von Papen's deputy military attaché and eventual successor, told him that if American munitions shipments could be slowed, Germany would break through the Western Front, call for an armistice and recognize a revolutionary government in Ireland.

Larkin told of being given demonstrations of German incendiary devices in Hoboken, New Jersey, and how he heard of specific plans . . . for destroying the munitions at the Jersey City terminus by means of a loaded barge exploding alongside the pier or jetty. The barge, it was stated, already arranged for was a Lackawanna Railroad barge, it being explained that the detonation from these explosives would result in the explosion of the explosives stored in or about the vicinity.

Here was corroboration of what the American side suggested all along had happened at Black Tom, when the barge *Johnson 17* exploded. What excited McCloy even more, however, was Larkin's use of the term "Jersey City terminus" and, shortly afterward, "New Jersey terminal." Up to this point in the interrogation, McCloy had never mentioned Black Tom. Later, Larkin told him, when the Germans again tried to recruit him in Mexico in 1917, they claimed "their chief success . . . was what they termed the New Jersey terminal explosion. They stated that of the five men who were involved in that explosion, two were then located in Mexico City." The German lawyers promptly charged that McCloy had bribed Larkin to make these statements.

One other avenue also was explored by the Americans, with some success. Peaslee, hearing through British intelligence that many German wartime documents were in the Austrian Archives, went to London and interested a publishing house there in putting out a book on relations between the Central Powers and the United States during the Great War. Then he proposed the book to an eminent Hungarian historian, Dr. Otto Ernst, who Peaslee knew had done considerable research in the Austrian Archives in Vienna. Ernst accepted and plunged into the research with the assistance of two Austrian archivists, none of the three knowing the real intent of Peaslee in organizing the project.

In April, 1935, Ernst uncovered a considerable volume of German material sent by Austrian liaison officers stationed at the German General Headquarters during the war. Included were summaries of German activities in the United States that specifically mentioned the Kingsland fire and other munitions plant explosions and fires in the New York area.

At this juncture, a new German tactic surfaced. Hitler, his expansionist appetite whetted by his march into the Rhineland, was beginning to cover his flanks. On May 5, 1936, the American chargé d'affaires in Berlin received a call out of the blue from the minister-president of the Reichstag, Hermann Goering. The German government, Goering proclaimed, hoping to launch a "broad program of better relations with America," wanted to settle the sabotage cases, once and for all.

This feeler, carrying as it did the weight of a gesture from Hitler himself only a week before the commission was to hear the allegations of fraud, suggested that Berlin knew the jig was up. Hitler appointed a prominent Nazi party official, Hauptmann von Pfeffer, as his special representative. He was an early organizer and leader of the feared S.A.; in the words of McCloy years later, "a Nazi from Naziville, and a great friend of Hitler." In a meeting with Joseph Flack, the American first secretary in Berlin, von Pfeffer confided that the Foreign Office, interested in vindication, not a deal, was "hostile" to a settlement and was trying to convince Goering and Hitler that the State Department didn't want one, either. Flack assured him that his department wanted the sabotage cases settled, but that any settlement "must be unconditional," not tied to any larger package of agreements.

As this hopeful development unfolded, the commission met again in Washington on May 12, 1936. Bonynge personally reviewed the "Qualters Hoax," including the new evidence of the collusive role of Osborn and Stein in it. The Germans again replied by trying to switch the subject to the Wozniak letters, arguing that since the Americans were coming before the commission with soiled hands, their allegations of fraud had no credibility.

But this time Justice Roberts emphatically disagreed, in a way that astonished the American side and jolted the Germans. He took the unusual step of submitting an affidavit of his own, reporting that Stein in 1932 attempted to talk to him directly and privately in violation of commission rules, but was rebuffed by the umpire. Shortly afterward, Roberts said, the German commissioner informed him that the American side had suppressed a Stein report challenging the authenticity of the Herrmann message. Then, he wrote, when Osborn in one of his affidavits called it remarkable that Stein had not submitted an opinion on the message's age, "the impression remained [with Roberts] that there had been a withholding of a report which might have shed light" on the issue. And that impression, Roberts said, had prejudiced his own judgment against the American side.

On that note, Roberts closed the hearings, with the Americans now supremely confident. And at the same time, the prospects for a settlement with the Hitler regime—perhaps for this very reason —appeared to be brightening. Although Goering announced that Germany was asking for an "immediate postponement" of the commission's deliberations, it went ahead, and on June 3 ruled to permit a full hearing on the fraud charges. A new German commissioner, Dr. Victor L. F. H. Huecking, went along, doubtless recognizing that Roberts would so rule if the issue came to him on a split vote.

On the next day, Goering invited the United States to send a delegation to Germany to discuss details of a settlement with von Pfeffer. The Mixed Claims Commission thereupon granted a three-month postponement in its deliberations, and an elated Bonynge set sail for Europe. He expected to go to the Foreign Office in Berlin but was rerouted to Munich, apparently to circumvent Foreign Office hostility to the settlement. Negotiations proceeded apace, with von Pfeffer frequently conferring directly with Hitler on the terms.

The Summer Olympics were going on at the time in Berlin, and the American negotiators, who now included McCloy, were invited to sit in Hitler's box. These were the Olympic Games at which the Fuehrer and his dictums of Aryan superiority were mightily shaken by the superlative feats of black American athletes, particularly the magnificent track and field star, Jesse Owens, who won an unprecedented four gold medals. McCloy later recalled sitting next to Goering and enjoying "a window on the center of the Nazi regime."

On July 6, both sides signed an agreement, to be carried out by the Mixed Claims Commission. Called the Munich Agreement, it provided for 153 Black Tom and Kingsland claims to be paid on the basis of fifty percent from a special deposit account of German funds created by the War Settlement Act, and proceeds from German bonds deposited by the German government with the United States Treasury. The fifty percent was calculated at just over $25 million, but only about $20 million was available for parceling out.

Further complicating the matter, however, was the fact that of nearly seven thousand awards made by the commission in response to other claims, all those amounting to $100,000 or more were held in abeyance until all litigation was completed. The Black Tom and Kingsland claims were, obviously, in this category. If they were granted in full, it was clear that none of the other unsatisfied awardholders would be

302 *Germany on Trial, 1919–1939*

paid. These other awardholders, therefore, hoped that the Black Tom and Kingsland claims would be rejected by the commission, finally and irrevocably, so that their smaller claims could be settled. The other awardholders sent a lawyer to Berlin and petitioned the commission to be heard.

The Hitler regime, however, seemed to be cooperating, and by November all appeared to be on track. Then, suddenly, the Germans filed a new motion before the commission asking that all the Kingsland claims be thrown out. The reason: the Canadian Car and Foundry Company, owner of the Kingsland plant, was a wholly owned subsidiary of a foreign corporation, and hence did not fall under the jurisdiction of the joint German-American tribunal!

For the next four months, the matter was up in the air, until on April 5, 1937, the German ambassador in Washington, Hans Luther, handed a formal letter to Secretary of State Cordell Hull: Berlin was reneging on the entire deal, and blaming the Americans.

Although it had been explicitly agreed that the settlement was not to be contingent on any other matter of German-American relations, Luther's letter argued that "it was to be the prerequisite for such a settlement that it was to be the first step in a thorough-going improvement in the relations between the two countries, and that it was by no means to be made to appear as if the German Government were willing to accept any responsibility whatever for the claims made in the complaint." Furthermore, he said, all claims still pending were to be resolved, not just those regarding Black Tom and Kingsland.

For sheer audacity, the letter was a match for anything the Germans had tried previously in the long bizarre history of the case. If the Americans had any doubts up to now about the capacity of the Hitler regime for raw deceit, they were dispelled. The question remained, however, whether Berlin ever had an intention of settling or was simply stalling for time, or whether the monkey wrench tossed in by the protesting awardholders had really queered the deal.

Bonynge tried to get the commission to go ahead on the basis of the signed Munich Agreement, but the Hitler regime formally advised the commission that it considered the agreement null and void, and in July the umpire ruled that the commission was powerless to enforce it. So the American side went back to proving German fraud.

The case was going around in circles now, dragging on into the summer of 1938, when participants on both sides had increasing difficulty keeping their minds on it, rather than on the ominous developments across the Atlantic. Hitler, having long since consolidated power in Germany, had annexed Austria on April 10, 1938, behind the facade of an engineered Anschluss, while the old Allied powers fretted but refrained from taking a stand against him.

As the new Germany thus moved relentlessly forward, a single piece of paper from the past unexpectedly surfaced that at last proved its undoing in the sabotage cases. On June 7, as Nazi jackboots thundered through the streets of Vienna in a roundup of terrified Jews and open looting of their most prized possessions, United States Attorney Simon Sobeloff was rummaging through the subpoenaed files of the Eastern Forwarding Company in Baltimore. He came upon a seemingly innocuous letter dated January 19, 1917—eight days after the Kingsland fire—from Carl Ahrendt, the company's clerk then working in the New London office, to Paul Hilken in Baltimore.

The letter itself was a typed covering note accompanying four business letters that Ahrendt was forwarding to his boss. At the bottom, however, unmistakably in Ahrendt's handwriting as later matched with other samples, was the following postscript:

> Yours of the 18th just received and am delighted to learn that the von Hindenburg of Roland Park won another victory. Had a note from March who is still at McAlpin. Asks me to advise his brother that he is in urgent need of another set of glasses ["glasses" underlined]. He would like to see his brother as soon as possible on this account. [Signed] A.

Two days later, Hilken sent a reply, returning the business letters and instructing Ahrendt on what to do with them. His last paragraph said: "You might write our friend March that his brother will be in New York Tuesday and Wednesday, and for him to phone the Astor 9 a.m. Tuesday regarding an appointment."

At first the American investigators did not realize what they had. But as they reread Ahrendt's postscript and pondered its meaning, the underlined word "glasses" jumped out at them. Of course! It had to refer to the "glass tubes," the "pencils," the small incendiary devices first brought from Germany to the United States by Herrmann in 1916.

In an earlier examination, when Bonynge asked Herrmann about the South American activities of German agent J. A. Arnold, he said: "I am quite sure they sent him those glasses from—."

Bonynge interrupted him at that point and asked what he meant by "glasses," and Herrmann replied: "Why, these tubes."

The response dovetailed with Marguerre's admission in his affidavit of August, 1930, that after sending Herrmann to America in early 1916 with a supply of the new incendiary pencils, "we had a trunk made with a double bottom in order to pack glass tubes therein in a secret partition."

The Americans went on with their deciphering of the postscript. "March," they already knew, was an alias used by Herrmann, and his "brother" was probably Hinsch, although they allowed that the word also could have referred to Hilken.

Next, the American sleuths considered the phrase "von Hindenburg of Roland Park." That obviously could be no one but Hilken, whose home was in the Roland Park section of Baltimore. And the "victory," clearly, was the success of the sabotage of the Kingsland plant, for which Hilken was the paymaster, the overseer—the "von Hindenburg."

Beyond this deciphering of the Ahrendt postscript was Ahrendt's unwitting admission in it that he knew all about what Hinsch was up to. In other words, his flat denials, repeated only months earlier in a subpoenaed cross-examination by Peaslee, were bald-faced lies. Hence his sworn testimony that Hinsch never was paid for acts of sabotage, and specifically that he never received two thousand dollars in August, 1916, right after the Black Tom disaster, was also stripped of credibility.

What Sobeloff had struck upon was nothing less than "the smoking gun." The Germans had been scrupulously careful about not committing their sabotage exploits to paper. But here was a business letter preserved in the files that the Germans obviously felt could safely stand scrutiny. It was a colossal blunder.

Also found in the same batch of papers were several letters written by Edward Salzer, another clerk in the Baltimore office during the same period. The principal one, dated December 16, 1916, less than four weeks before the Kingsland fire, also was a business communication to Hilken, then in New London. The important part said: "Yours of yesterday duly received, and will try to keep L. warm until Captain Hinsch comes to Baltimore about New Year."

The American investigators concluded that "L." was "Lewis," another of Herrmann's aliases and the one used by Hilken on the August 10, 1916, check stub recording the two-thousand-dollar payment to Hinsch after Black Tom. "L." needed to be kept "warm," the Americans figured, because he was asking for or demanding something that only Hinsch could supply or satisfy.

This lode of damaging documentation from Baltimore jolted the Germans. They thrashed about desperately to discredit it with typically audacious "explanations." They conceded the obvious that "the von Hindenburg of Roland Park" could only be Hilken. But they argued that the "victory" for which Ahrendt congratulated him must have been nothing more than some business success, such as the news that a second German merchant submarine was headed toward America, as reported in the *New York Times*.

Second, the Germans said the word "brother" could not have referred to Hinsch because other correspondence indicated he would not have been in New York on the days Hilken's reply said March's "brother" would be there. If the reference was, as it seemed, to Hilken himself, then the suggestion that "glasses" really meant the incendiary glass tubes had to be wrong, they argued; Hilken testified earlier that he had nothing to do with them! Here the Germans were selectively invoking the credibility of a man they had, when the purpose served them, branded a liar.

Finally, they insisted "glasses" didn't refer to the glass tubes at all; what Ahrendt really was talking about in the postscript was—money! Herrmann needed money, the German defenders said, because he and Woehst had just rented an apartment. They produced a letter from Woehst to Herrmann written around the time of the Ahrendt postscript that said: "The place is rented, but I have to pay April ahead as well as September month's security, which is together $300. I promised to pay this on Tuesday. . . . Enclosed is a contract. Do not lose it. . . ."

Herrmann, the Germans said, quite naturally had dropped a note to Ahrendt asking him to let Hilken know he needed the money —using the code words "set of glasses." The Germans in America had corresponded repeatedly over the previous several years and never hesitated using the word "money." This explanation was ridiculous, but they stuck to it. They also produced other letters to contend that "L." was not "Lewis" but a man named Lenoir who had offered his services as a counterspy. This one didn't wash either.

The breakthrough scored by the Americans was little-noticed. The case had dragged on for so many years that it had vanished from public attention and remembrance. Besides, the world had much graver things to consider now. British Prime Minister Neville Chamberlain, his black umbrella in hand, flew to Munich and naively delivered the Sudetenland from Czechoslovakia to Hitler on the empty promise that this would be Der Fuehrer's last territorial claim.

The climactic sessions of the Mixed Claims Commission occurred in January, 1939, at the Supreme Court in Washington. Bonynge, armed with the Ahrendt postscript, presented a devastating case of fraud and duplicity against the German side, casting Ahrendt as its convincing tool. Every time the American investigators came up with new evidence, he noted, Ahrendt was put forward to rebut it, in seven different affidavits, most notably in the matter of the payment to Hinsch after Black Tom.

Referring to the Ahrendt postscript's reference to "glasses," the American side pointed out this exchange in the cross-examination of Ahrendt under subpoena by the American lawyers:

Q. "Did Captain Hinsch show you at any time during the years 1915, 1916 or 1917 any explosive devices or little glass tubes?"

A. "No."

Q. "Did he show you at any time pencils that contained little glass tubes?"

A. "No. . . . To this day I have never seen anything like that."

But the most colossal fraud against the commission, Bonynge said, was the convoluted German effort to discredit the Herrmann message, and to mislead the commission intentionally that the Americans had suppressed vital evidence—the supposed Stein report on the authenticity of that message.

In conclusion, Bonynge observed: "I am rather inclined to think that there are some miracles in this case. One of the miracles is that at such a late date the Ahrendt postscript finally turned up." But a greater miracle, he said, was the American claimants' ability to overcome all the obstacles thrown in their path by the German government's blatant use of fraud.

There was no doubt now how the commission would vote. A new

American commissioner, Colonel Christopher B. Garnett, and the new German commissioner, Huecking, would split, and umpire Roberts would rule in favor of the Americans. But before that could happen, the Germans threw in one more monkey wrench. Roberts received a terse letter from Huecking. "I beg to apprise you of the fact," it said, "that I retire from the post of German Member of the Mixed Claims Commission." Beaten, the Germans were simply picking up their marbles and going home!

Roberts, Huecking charged, no longer had an "open mind" on the case. He was right about that. The Germans gambled on having an American as umpire; but the assumption that he would bend over backward to be fair had been stretched too far by the overwhelming case against them. The Nazi regime now obviously hoped that this boycotting of the commission could yet frustrate the American claimants and somehow avoid public condemnation.

Undeterred, Garnett proceeded to write a 480-page opinion. The Nazi government meanwhile notified Secretary of State Hull that with Huecking gone, no further commission action would be considered valid. Garnett concluded his opinion by quoting from the umpire's 1932 decision observing that if he had found the Herrmann message to be genuine, which at that time he did not, he would "hold Germany responsible" for both the Black Tom and Kingsland disasters. Inasmuch as the message's authenticity had now been conclusively established, he wrote, so had Germany's liability, "and the cases are in position for awards."

Roberts immediately agreed, accepting Garnett's massive opinion as his own. Seventeen years after the Mixed Claims Commission was established, its work was over. All that remained to be done now was the allocation of the German funds in escrow at the United States Treasury Department—about $20 million, plus German bonds with a face value of about $500 million. But the German government had long since defaulted on the bonds and they were thought to be virtually worthless.

Admiral Hall wired Peaslee: "Heartiest congratulations to you, Greatheart. Triumphal vindication and justification of your many years' work." Peaslee wrote back that if it hadn't been for Hall's intercepted cables "we would never have even started on the pilgrimage."

One of the great ironies of the case, however, was the fact that in the overall arbitration of claims, Germany received about three times as much repayment as did the United States clients. "Germany received about $500,000 of seized property," Peaslee informed Hall. "It induced the United States to consent to the creation of a War Claims Arbiter who gave awards of about $85 million in favor of Germans against the United States for ships that were seized and used for war purposes. The Germans have already received in cash an additional $45 million respecting this. They were even paid for some ships which the German submarines sank!" Now that the Germans were on the short end, he marvelled, they seemed to believe they "could defeat justice by trying to render the Commission impotent to act!"

A thoroughly humiliated Nazi regime was not a gracious loser. The official German news agency in Berlin denounced the decision of a "rump commission" as "devoid of all legality" and "the opening gun of a new anti-German campaign in America."

The atmosphere was, indeed, getting more poisonous. Three days after the commission's decision, a *Washington Post* editorial noted "much discussion of the very disturbing coincidence" in which three submarines—one American vessel, the *Squalus*, one British and one French—all had sunk under mysterious circumstances, one of them on the very day of the Black Tom–Kingsland decision. "These explosions occurred so long ago that their memory, and also their moral, seem rather dim and distant today," the *Post* said. "Yet history repeats, and its lessons are often highly instructive. This reminder of German government techniques . . . is not to be overlooked."

A *Washington Evening Star* editorial observed that the decision "climaxes, but does not end, a true story of international intrigue as weird as any tale ever conceived by writers of popular fiction. . . . The whole sordid Black Tom–Kingsland episode has served one good purpose, however. It has shown the need in this country of an efficient counter-espionage system in time of peace as well as war."

That such a system was imperative was emphatically underscored by an exploding Europe. On August 23, the Nazis signed their infamous nonaggression pact with the Soviet Union and on September 1, Hitler sent his hordes hurtling into Poland. World War II was on, as the British and French honored their pledges to come to Poland's aid.

War, however, did not deter the Mixed Claims Commission from finally concluding its business. On October 30, it made these awards: the Lehigh Valley Railroad, $9,900,322; the Canadian Car and Foundry Company, $5,871,105; the Black Tom underwriters, $2,095,607; the

Kingsland underwriters, $1,311,023; the Bethlehem Steel Company, $1,886,491; the Delaware and Lackawanna Railway Company, $32,676. Still outstanding was a $600,000 claim from other awardholders, who continued in the courts to try to block these payments.

(At this final meeting, note was taken of the death of Robert Bonynge at the age of seventy-seven, of a heart attack. Two weeks after Bonynge's death, Count von Bernstorff, in retirement in Geneva and an outspoken anti-Nazi, died at the age of seventy-six).

Some critics of Franklin D. Roosevelt's neutrality policy seized on the news of the awards to lecture the president. The *Washington Daily News* wrote:

> If we repeal the arms embargo and start selling munitions to the Allies, even though they pay cash and come and get it, we may as well take for granted that there will be more explosions similar to those which occurred at Black Tom Island and Kingsland 23 and 22 years ago. The German Government probably has as many secret agents in this country as it did then.

But FDR persevered in building up the nation's armaments-making capacity, moving the country ever closer to the status of a de facto belligerent, even as the country had been under Wilson in 1916 and 1917, but now with a much clearer sense of national purpose. If Roosevelt was no Wilson, neither was Hitler the kaiser. To Roosevelt, the present danger was clear.

In the first week of September, 1940, the New York newspaper *PM* warned specifically of a meeting of Nazi agents "in which plans to dynamite the Hercules Powder Company were discussed." The plant, in Kenvil, New Jersey, about thirty miles northwest of the old Black Tom site, was making smokeless gunpowder to fill $40 million in federal contracts. Sure enough, on September 12, a series of huge explosions ripped through the Hercules plant, killing 29 workers, injuring 125 others and sending shock waves felt 125 miles away.

It was, it seemed, Black Tom all over again, but worse because of the terrible loss of life. Yet the head of the company's explosives department, William C. Hunt, told reporters:

> The company is at a loss to explain the cause of the fire and the explosions. The buildings in which the powder was located were separated by substantial brick walls and there was a sprink-

ler system in all of them. We thought all safeguards possible to prevent such an occurrence had been taken.

He added: "We have no suspicions of any sabotage." Nevertheless, the FBI immediately sent agents to the site, and a thorough investigation ensued. It was inconclusive.

Meanwhile, the court fight over the awards money dragged on, as World War II raged in Europe. The money remained frozen in escrow until twelve years later, when a postwar conference in London between the United States and yet another German government, concluding in 1953, brought about a settlement, providing payment of $95 million including interest for all claimants, not just those involving Black Tom and Kingsland.

Germany had defaulted on her debts after World War I and during the Hitler years. But the new Federal Republic after World War II, wanting to restore its credit, decided to make good on all its obligations in the world community. It issued new long-term bonds to the United States, the money to be paid out to creditors in the sabotage cases in installments over twenty-six years. Thus, final payments were not completed until 1979—sixty-three years after the major acts of sabotage that required them. By that time many of the principals in the case were dead, and the money due them went to their estates. For Peaslee, the outcome meant personal wealth as a result of the contingent-fee arrangement he had with the claimants. He also served as the American ambassador to Australia for a time after the war.

For McCloy, the successful conclusion of the case launched an illustrious public career. In October, 1940, as war clouds moved toward America again, Secretary of War Henry Stimson, impressed by McCloy's handling of a case that dealt so extensively with German sabotage operations, asked him to review the War Department's skeletal intelligence and counterintelligence capabilities and gear it up for the task ahead. Six months later, he became assistant secretary of war, a post he held throughout World War II.

In that position, McCloy was called upon to implement one of the most controversial decisions of Roosevelt's wartime tenure—the rounding up and interning of Japanese-Americans on the Pacific Coast for the duration of the war. It was an assignment that came to plague McCloy for the rest of his life. In the 1980s, victims of the decision pressed a class-action suit against the government, and Congress in 1988 voted restitution.

In an interview in his Manhattan office, McCloy said the decision to intern the Japanese-Americans had its genesis in the experience of the Black Tom disaster. "The Japanese had sunk our fleet at Pearl Harbor," he said. "We knew they had planned subversion to be sure the United States wouldn't recover. The highest concentration of Japanese-Americans was on the West Coast. Roosevelt said, 'Move them.' We moved them to relocation camps to get them out of sensitive areas." As assistant secretary of the navy under Wilson, McCloy said, Roosevelt "knew all about Black Tom. He said to me, 'We don't want any more Black Toms.'"

After World War II, McCloy became president of the World Bank and, in one of those ironies of history, United States military governor and high commissioner of Germany from 1949 to 1952. Thirty-six years later, at the age of ninety-three, he was still going strong, working out of his downtown Manhattan law office high in one of the towers of the World Trade Center, with a clear view of the Statue of Liberty, Ellis Island and what was once the Black Tom munitions terminal.

The America of 1914–17 victimized by the German diplomats and the saboteurs under their direction was a far more innocent and insulated America than the one of World War II and today. Its people believed that the two great oceans on either coast were a certain protection against foreign intrusion, and that representatives of foreign governments were guests who did not abuse the hospitality they received. Acts of violence were dealt with for the most part by local police and there was no domestic intelligence agency to speak of.

But the Black Tom case and all its machinations helped to change that. Hard experience eroded naiveté, and by the time World War II came, the United States was developing a well-trained corps of agents to combat internal subversion. The Bureau of Investigation within the Department of Justice became the Federal Bureau of Investigation in 1935 and soon won glory as a glamorous fighter of domestic crime—and a mixed reputation as an intelligence-gatherer against a host of targets, including political dissenters. The Secret Service, too, developed into a major intelligence arm, with functions ranging from protection of the president to watchdog of the Treasury Department. And in most of the nation's industrial plants today, security is very tight, even in peacetime.

Nevertheless, the new dimension of violence injected by international terrorism now taxes every resource. Skyjackers have changed the face of every airport in the country and foreign embassies continue to be bases for espionage and other subversive deeds. The sabotage schemes of the Black Tom era and the simple devices used to carry them out seem primitive in the age of nuclear weapons and fear of nuclear blackmail. The daring of the saboteurs of that earlier, almost romantic era is more than matched by the fanaticism of their contemporary counterparts.

Still, for sheer, sustained audacity, few episodes in the chronicles of international skullduggery have matched the mischief the German diplomats and their bold minions perpetrated against American neutrality from 1914 to 1917—and the fraud their legal defenders concocted afterward to escape culpability for it. Only the dedication and doggedness of the Americans who labored for two decades or longer to bring them to account were their equal, in a case that remains unique in the annals of war and international justice.

EASTERN FORWARDING COMPANY
INCORPORATED

BALTIMORE   NEW YORK   NEW LONDON,

STATE PIER No. 1.

NEW LONDON, CONN.   Jan. 19, 1917,

Mr. Paul G. L. Hilken,
P. O. Box #1130,
Baltimore, Md.

Dear Mr. Hilken:--

I am enclosing the following letters:-

Letter of J. W. von Lüncl-Brandenburg Hohenzollern,
the letters and packages mentioned in this
are being held at the office awaiting your
instructions as to their disposal.

"   "   L. von Keviczky. Several letters have been
received by Capt. Hinsch from this firm and
have been ignored. Mr. Hoppenberg has also
received a letter and one of the descriptive
folders. I am now sending one which was
addressed to you.

"   "   Burns Bros. Perhaps this letter will
interest you.

"   "   Frank A. Woodmansee. I am enclosing a copy of
their letter of the 11th and your reply of the
14th, mentioned in enclosed letter.

With sincere regards,

Yours very truly,

Ahrendt

Yours of the 18th just received and are
delighted to learn that the "Hindenburg" of
Roland Park won another victory.
Had a note from March who is still at the Affin
asks me to advise his brother that he is in urgent
need of another set of glasses. He would like to see
his brother as soon as possible on this account

NATIONAL ARCHIVES

The Ahrendt Postscript: The postscript handwritten by Carl Ahrendt
on a business letter to Paul Hilken, referring to a request by Fred
Herrmann (alias "March") for "another set of glasses," or glass
incendiary tubes. The discovery of this letter and postscript became
"the smoking gun" in the Black Tom case.

Appendix I: The Cast of Principal Characters
In General Order of Appearance

THE AMERICAN OFFICIALS

Woodrow Wilson, president of the United States, preserver at almost all costs of American neutrality.

Colonel Edward House, confidant and personal foreign-policy negotiator for Wilson.

William Jennings Bryan, secretary of state, 1913–15, and leader of the pacifist cause.

Robert Lansing, State Department counselor under Bryan and his successor as secretary of state; a strong supporter of interventionism.

James W. Gerard, American ambassador in Berlin, distrustful of the Germans and also an interventionist.

THE GERMAN OFFICIALS

Wilhelm II, kaiser of Imperial Germany, possessor of an illusion of military genius and dominated by the warlords around him.

Count Johann von Bernstorff, German ambassador in Washington with the dual mission of nursing Wilson's desire to keep America neutral while overseeing Germany's sabotage plots against her.

Captain Franz von Papen, military attaché in the German embassy and director of the sabotage operation in its early phase; later chancellor of the postwar Weimar Republic and a predecessor of Adolf Hitler, whose rise he assisted and whose stooge he became.

Captain Karl Boy-Ed, naval attaché in the German embassy and von Papen's partner in the early sabotage plots.

Doctor Heinrich Albert, commercial attaché in the German embassy and paymaster for the sabotage operations.

Wolf von Igel, deputy to von Papen and eventually his successor as military attaché.

Franz von Bopp, German consul general in San Francisco and director of sabotage operations on the West Coast.

Rudolf Nadolny, head of Section 3B of the Foreign Office in Berlin, ostensibly the political bureau but actually headquarters for directing sabotage in the Western Hemisphere.

Hans Marguerre, chief deputy to Nadolny in Section 3B and partner in the direction of sabotage against the United States.

Field Marshal Paul von Hindenburg, World War I German military chief and later president of the Weimar Republic who appointed Hitler as chancellor of Germany.

Gottlieb von Jagow, German foreign secretary and ally of von Bernstorff in debate with the German General Staff over relative values of keeping America neutral and resorting to unconditional submarine warfare, certain to bring America into the war on the side of the Allies.

Theobold von Bethmann-Hollweg, chancellor of Germany during the period of American neutrality who also sought to hold off unrestricted submarine warfare.

Arthur Zimmermann, undersecretary to von Jagow in Berlin and eventually his successor as foreign secretary; advocate of enlisting Mexico and Japan as allies against the United States and author of the famous "Zimmermann telegram" designed to accomplish that alliance.

Heinrich von Eckhardt, German minister to Mexico, Berlin's ranking diplomat in the Western Hemisphere after von Bernstorff's departure and chief contact for German saboteurs who fled to South America to carry on their work after America's entry into the war.

Adolf Hitler, chancellor of Germany, 1933–39, during the decisive stages of the sabotage investigation and trials.

Hermann Goering, ministerpresident of the German Reichstag and initiator of negotiations in 1936 between the Nazi regime and the United States for the settlement of sabotage claims.

Hauptmann von Pfeffer, Nazi party official and former head of the Sturmabteilung, or Brown Shirts, appointed as Hitler's special representative to negotiate with the American side.

THE PERPETRATORS

Horst von der Goltz (alias Bridgeman Taylor), German professional agent who attempted to blow up the Welland Canal linking Lakes Ontario and Erie in the Canadian province of Ontario to slow the flow of troops and supplies to American ports.

Hans von Wedell, German reserve officer in New York who produced false passports that permitted German reservists in the United States to get back to Germany upon the outbreak of war, and German agents to slip into the country.

Werner Horn, German reservist who sought to destroy the Vanceboro Bridge linking the Canadian Pacific Railroad in the Canadian province of New Brunswick and the state of Maine.

Martha Held (alias Gordon), German former opera singer who ran a house on Manhattan's lower West Side used as a rest and recreation center and hideaway for the plotting of sabotage by German diplomats and sea captains, and reputed to be a brothel.

Captain Franz von Rintelen (alias Emil Gache), German naval reservist with banking and social connections in New York, sent to America by Berlin to impede shipment of munitions by whatever means necessary; self-styled "The Dark Invader."

Doctor Walter Scheele, German chemist sent to America in 1893 to provide intelligence on American manufacture of explosives; employed by von Rintelen to manufacture the first incendiary devices for use against munitions-carrying ships in American ports and at sea.

Robert Fay, German soldier transferred from the front to America to manufacture his own invention—a bomb fastened to a ship's rudder and activated by its rotary motion.

Anton Dilger (alias Delmar), German chemist who established a laboratory in a house in Chevy Chase, a Washington, D.C., suburb, to breed anthrax and glanders germs for the mass inoculation of horses and mules scheduled to be shipped to the Allied powers.

Edward Felton, Baltimore stevedore recruited to direct a team of black dock workers in the inoculation of horses and mules in and near East Coast ports.

Fred Herrmann (alias Lewis and March), American-born youth of German parentage recruited as a spy on British shipping in Scotland, transferred to America by Section 3B as a courier with new incendiary devices and as a saboteur in the United States and later in Mexico.

Paul Hilken, Baltimore official of the North German Lloyd steamship line and son of a former German consul in Baltimore, recruited as sabotage paymaster after the return of Albert to Germany.

Carl Ahrendt, clerk for Hilken who steadfastly denied knowledge of sabotage activities until his writing of a telltale postscript on a business letter betrayed him, and the whole German defense.

Raoul Gerdts (alias Pochet), Herrmann's driver and companion in New York and courier who brought pivotal message from Herrmann in Mexico to Hilken after American entry into the war.

Captain Frederick Hinsch (alias Francis Graentnor), German merchant ship skipper assigned to direct docking and loading of the German merchant submarine *Deutschland* as a cover for assignment as von Rintelen's successor as field director of sabotage.

Paul Koenig, detective for the Hamburg-Amerika Line recruited to head a team of bodyguards and intelligence-gatherers for von Papen and other German diplomats and to be liaison with saboteurs.

Kurt Jahnke, German-born naturalized American citizen and former Marine who directed sabotage activities on the West Coast under von Bopp and was sent east; a prime suspect in the Black Tom explosions.

Lothar Witzke (alias Pablo Waberski), German seaman on a cruiser to Chile; interned there, he escaped to San Francisco where he was teamed up with Jahnke by von Bopp and also sent east; another Black Tom suspect.

Michael Kristoff, an immigrant drifter and waterfront worker recruited by the Germans and suspected of teaming with Jahnke and Witzke in the destruction of Black Tom.

Theodore Wozniak (alias Karowski), Polish immigrant recruited by German agents and placed in the Kingsland plant; prime suspect in the fire that destroyed it.

"Rodriguez," mysterious worker assigned to the bench next to Wozniak's at Kingsland and suspected of being a German plant functioning as Wozniak's accomplice.

Willie Woehst, German army lieutenant sent to America to assist Hinsch, Herrmann and Koenig in sabotage operations.

Charles Wunnenberg, German engineer and explosives expert used as a recruiter of other saboteurs and known as "The Dynamiter."

Adam Siegel, German agent in South America who teamed up with Herrmann and Gerdts in Mexico City and played a pivotal role in the writing of Herrmann's invisible message to Hilken crucial in the Black Tom case.

OTHER IMPORTANT PARTICIPANTS

Mena Edwards Reiss, known as "The Eastman Girl," a New York model who frequented Martha Held's house in New York and provided testimony about the activities of German diplomats, seamen and saboteurs there during the period of American neutrality.

Admiral Sir Reginald Hall, retired British naval officer and World War I chief of British naval intelligence whose staff broke the German code and provided key German cables and telegrams in the Black Tom case.

Horace and John Qualters, brothers whose collection of 1917 magazines and whose reading habits therein provided the material on which a major hoax in the case was based.

Albert S. Osborn, prominent American handwriting and documents expert hired by the German defense to provide expert evidence on papers submitted by the American claimants, and who provided more than that.

Elbridge W. Stein, another American documents expert and close friend of Osborn hired by the claimants to provide expert evidence for them, and who provided more—for his friend Osborn.

James Larkin, leading Irish agitator for independence from Great Britain, fomenter of strikes in the United States and a recruiting target of the German saboteurs.

THE AMERICAN PROSECUTORS

Amos J. Peaslee, New York lawyer and lead investigator for the chief American claimants, the Lehigh Valley Railroad, owners of the Black Tom terminal, and the Canadian Car and Foundry Company, owners of the Kingsland plant, for the early phases of the case.

Leonard Peto, vice president of Canadian Car and Foundry and an active associate of Peaslee in the investigation.

John J. McCloy, New York lawyer who assumed the lead in the investigation after two American defeats and brought important new evidence to light.

Robert W. Bonynge, Denver and New York lawyer and former Colorado congressman appointed to argue the case as the official American agent before the Mixed Claims Commission established to hear the allegations against Germany and render a decision.

THE GERMAN DEFENDERS

Doctor Karl von Lewinski, appointed first German agent to defend the German position before the commission.

Doctor Wilhelm Tannenberg, first German counsel before the commission, later succeeding von Lewinski as German agent.

THE JUDGES

Chandler P. Anderson, initial American commissioner on the Mixed Claims Commission.

Colonel Christopher B. Garnett, successor to Anderson as American commissioner.

Doctor Wilhelm Kiesselbach, initial German commissioner.

Doctor Victor Huecking, successor to Kiesselbach as German commissioner.

William R. Day, former associate justice of the U.S. Supreme Court, initial umpire on the Mixed Claims Commission.

Edwin B. Parker, successor to Day as umpire.

Roland Boyden, successor to Parker.

Owen J. Roberts, associate justice of the U.S. Supreme Court, successor to Boyden.

Appendix II: Chronology of Major Events

1914

July 7: Von Bernstorff summoned to Berlin before outbreak of war.

Aug. 2: Von Bernstorff sails for America with sabotage instructions and bankroll.

August: Russian navy recovers German naval code book, delivers it to British Naval Intelligence.

Aug. 22: Von Papen instructs Koenig to establish intelligence and sabotage ring in New York.

September: Von der Goltz fails in attempt to blow up Welland Canal.

Nov. 2: German General Staff issues directive to military attachés in neutral countries to recruit anarchists for sabotage.

Dec. 15: Foreign Office cables von Bernstorff to attempt to blow up Canadian railways.

1915

Jan. 1: Roebling wire and cable plant in Trenton, N.J., blown up; suspected start of German sabotage involving nearly 200 destructions before American entry into the war.

Jan. 26: Foreign Office cables von Bernstorff, von Papen urging recruitment of specific Irish agitators for sabotage.

Feb. 2: Horn captured attempting to blow up Vanceboro bridge.

April 2: Scheele sets up front in Hoboken, N.J., to manufacture incendiary devices.

April: Von Rintelen, Fay arrive in U.S. with sabotage assignments; Germans covertly start setting up own munitions plant in Bridgeport, Conn., to divert war materials and drive up labor costs.

May 7: *Lusitania* torpedoed off Irish coast.

May 15: Unexploded bombs found in hold of ship docking at Marseilles; devices traced back to von Rintelen operation.

July 2–3: U.S. Capitol bombed, financier J. P. Morgan shot by protester against munitions shipments.

July 24: Dr. Albert falls asleep on New York elevated train, awakes, rushes off leaving portfolio with plans for Bridgeport plant, other German schemes.

Aug. 13: Von Rintelen captured by British at Dover as he attempts to return to Germany.

Aug. 30: Documents of Austro-Hungarian Ambassador Constanin Dumba, revealing Vienna instructions for subversion and implicating von Papen, Boy-Ed, seized by British; Wilson demands recall of Dumba.

Oct. 24: Fay arrested, further implicates von Papen, Boy-Ed.

Dec. 1: Wilson demands recall of von Papen, Boy-Ed.

Dec. 28: Von Rintelen indicted for fomenting strikes in American munitions plants.

1916

Feb. 16: Key meeting at Section 3B, Berlin, of Hilken, Herrmann, Dilger with Nadolny, Marguerre to plan sabotage and use of new incendiary devices on their return to America.

July 9: German merchant submarine *Deutschland* arrives in Baltimore; provides front for Hinsch's sabotage activities.

July 30: Explosions destroy Black Tom terminal.

Aug. 10: Hilken makes $2,000 payment to Hinsch for Black Tom.

1917

Jan. 11: Fire destroys Kingsland plant.

Feb. 1: Germany launches unrestricted submarine warfare; marks end of von Bernstorff's effort to keep America neutral.

Feb. 4: Wilson breaks off diplomatic relations with Germany; sends von Bernstorff home.

Feb. 24: London informs Wilson of the Zimmermann telegram.

April 2: Wilson asks Congress for declaration of war.

April: Herrmann in Mexico writes Hilken invisible message for funds to blow up Tampico oil fields, sends Gerdts to deliver it.

1918

Jan. 16: Witzke arrested as spy crossing from Mexico to U.S., later confesses role in Black Tom but recants.

August: Witzke convicted in Texas military court and sentenced to hang; only man thus sentenced in U.S. in World War I.

Nov. 11: Armistice ends World War I.

1919

Jan. 18: Peace conference convenes in Paris; Wilson attends.

June 28: Germany signs Versailles Treaty, including League of Nations.

Nov. 19: Senate rejects League and treaty.

1920

May 20: Wilson changes Witzke's sentence to life imprisonment.

1921

October: Senate ratifies Treaty of Berlin with Germany.

1922

Aug. 10: U.S., Germany establish Mixed Claims Commission to adjudicate all private claims arising from war, including sabotage.

1923

September: President Calvin Coolidge, after appeal from Berlin, releases Witzke as last held prisoner of war.

1924

Spring: American claimants hire Peaslee on contingency basis to pursue sabotage claims.

1925

January: "Eastman Girl" comes forward with detailed testimony on planning of sabotage at German safe house in Manhattan in neutrality period.

1926

May: Von Rintelen promises to tell all to Kingsland owners—for $10,000 and $300,000 life insurance policy: he is turned down.

1927

Summer: Kristoff located in New York jail, is released, disappears again.

1928

April 3: Kristoff dies of tuberculosis in Staten Island hospital.
July 28: Germany files brief with commission claiming Kingsland fire accidental.
Dec. 28: Hilken, confronted with intercepted cables, confesses sabotage role including $2,000 payment to Hinsch for Black Tom.

1929

Jan. 10: Hilken goes to Chile in failed effort to get Herrmann to confess.
January: Peaslee, Peto locate Gerdts in Colombia, where he tells them of delivering Herrmann secret message in 1917.
March: Ahrendt testifies Hilken payment to Hinsch made before Black Tom, not after.
April 3–12: First oral arguments before Mixed Claims Commission in Washington.

1930

March: Peaslee, Peto meet Herrmann in Havana, persuade him to return to testify.
July 4–7: Wozniak located in Tupper Lake, N.Y., trying to build alibi against American charge he was in Mexico with German agents in 1917; after car chase is served with American demand that he testify.
Sept. 18–30: Oral arguments before Commission at The Hague.
Oct. 16: Commission rules against claimants, dismisses case against Germany.

Dec. 25: Hilken finds 1917 Herrmann message in his attic.

1931

April: Hilken turns Herrmann message over to Peto.

May 27: Letters Wozniak purportedly wrote from Mexico turned over to American investigators.

May 31: Wozniak confesses to Peto in New York hotel room as hidden stenographers take notes, then storms out, denying guilt.

July 31–Aug. 1: Oral arguments in Boston.

December: Hilken's estranged wife finds his wartime diary, checkbook supporting claim he paid Hinsch $2,000 for Black Tom.

1932

May 18: Rumor of suppressed American report adverse to authenticity of Herrmann message passed to umpire Roberts; he falls for it.

Oct. 28: Germans launch "Qualters hoax" defense against Herrmann message.

Nov. 22: Oral arguments in Washington over authenticity of Herrmann message, Wozniak letters.

Dec. 12: Umpire Roberts decides against Americans again; rules Wozniak letters fake, disbelieves Herrmann message.

1933

April 14: American investigators find evidence of German fraud in eyewitness testimony that Kingsland fire started by accident.

May 4: Americans petition commission for rehearing on grounds fraud committed.

June 7: Congress authorizes use of subpoena power in sabotage cases.

Dec. 15: Umpire agrees to rehearing on fraud charges.

1934

Jan. 2: Larkin gives McCloy detailed affidavit of German sabotage activities, attempts to recruit him.

1935

April: Historian working for American claimants finds evidence of Section 3B sabotage activities in Austrian Archives.

1936

May 5: Goering sends feeler to Washington offering negotiations to settle sabotage claims.

May 12: Oral arguments on fraud charges.

June 7: Commission agrees to postponement pending settlement negotiations.

July 6: Munich Agreement on settlement of sabotage claims reached.

Sept. 24: Other claims awardholders file to block payment.

Nov. 24: Berlin asks commission to throw out Kingsland portion of case, arguing no jurisdiction since Kingsland Canadian-owned.

1937

Jan. 5: Bonynge files 153 claims under Munich Agreement.

April 5: Nazi regime backs out of Munich Agreement.

July 5: Umpire rules commission powerless to enforce Munich Agreement.

1938

June 7: Ahrendt postscript substantiating key elements in American case found in subpoenaed papers of German shipping firm in Baltimore.

1939

Jan. 16–23: Final oral arguments in Washington; claimants offer new evidence, Germans attempt to discredit it, charging fraud.

Feb. 28: American commissioner, umpire informally advise German commissioner they agree Germans committed fraud and case should be reopened.

March 1: German commissioner quits commission in obvious attempt to thwart decision adverse to Germany.

June 15: Commission meets without German member; umpire rules
  fraud committed, German guilt proved; Germany protests "rump
  commission."
Oct. 30: Awards of nearly $50 million made to American claimants;
  other awardholders' lawsuits hold up payment.

1941

Jan. 6: U.S. Supreme Court refuses to review case, lets awards stand.
  Final arrangements for payments not completed until postwar conference with Federal Republic of Germany in London in 1953, and
  final payments made in 1979.

Appendix III: Note on Sources

The basic source materials for this book have been culled from the official records of the Mixed Claims Commission of the United States and Germany maintained from 1922, upon the creation of the commission, through 1941, and stored at the National Archives in Washington. Those used here are among 1,032 cubic feet of documents, describing German sabotage during World War I generally and the investigation into the Black Tom and Kingsland explosions particularly, in Record Group 76, "Records of Boundary and Claims Commissions and Arbitrations," in the custody of the General Branch of the Civil Archives Division.

Included are eyewitness accounts of both of the explosions as well as affidavits from witnesses; originals and copies of reports of local and federal investigative agencies and private detective agencies into the causes of the explosions and the activities of the principal suspects; memoranda, briefs and drafts of briefs, correspondence, and other working papers of the American and German agents in the case and lawyers for the claimants; official motions and petitions before the commission, and its replies; and expert opinion on evidence submitted.

The records also include complete transcripts of all oral arguments before the commission, complete with affidavits and other documents filed, on the following dates: April 3–12, 1929 in Washington; September 18–30, 1930 at The Hague; July 21–August 1, 1931 in Boston; November 22–24, 1932, May 12–15, 1936, September 15, October 26, and December 1, 1937, January 16–27 and October 30, 1939, all in Washington. All decisions of the commission umpire, culminating in the 480-page finding of the last American commissioner, adopted in toto by the umpire, also are included.

The archives files contain as well copies of German messages intercepted by the British, dealing with activities of German agents in the United States and Mexico during World War I that document Ambassador Johann von Bernstorff's role as the responsible authority for the overall German sabotage operation; transcripts of the testimony of key witnesses and suspects in interviews by the American and German agents and associated lawyers; biographical sketches of some of the suspected saboteurs; and hundreds of newspaper clippings providing accounts of the investigations and the commission's deliberations.

This basic material has been supplemented with descriptions of the actual explosions appearing in the days immediately afterward in the *New York Times* and in later investigative accounts of the case in the *New York Sunday News, New York Sunday Mirror, New York American, Washington Sunday Star, Washington Post, Baltimore Sun* and *Baltimore Post*.

Also, these books were particularly helpful in retracing the details of German sabotage in World War I and the search for the perpetrators: *Three Wars With Germany*, Sir Reginald Hall and Amos J. Peaslee (Putnam, 1944); *The Enemy Within*, Captain Henry Landau (Putnam, 1937); *My Three Years in America*, Count Johann von Bernstorff (Charles Scribner's, 1920); *The Dark Invader*, Captain Franz von Rintelen (Lovat Dickson, 1933); *Throttled! The Detection of the German and Anarchist Bomb Plotters*, Thomas J. Tunney (Small, Maynard, 1919); *The German Secret Service in America, 1914–1918*, John Price Jones and Paul Merrick Hollister (Small, Maynard, 1918); and *The Zimmermann Telegram*, Barbara Tuchman (Viking, 1965). The memoirs of von Bernstorff and von Rintelen, while obviously self-serving, do provide glimpses of the events from the German point of view and of the men themselves, and have been excerpted with that consideration in mind.

Finally, the one surviving principal in the investigation of the case against Imperial Germany, John J. McCloy, granted two long interviews and his associate in the case, Benjamin Shute, now deceased, also provided his recollections. Henry G. Hilken of Bethesda, Maryland, son of Paul Hilken, the German paymaster for clandestine activities and later key American witness, provided personal reminiscences of his father.

For the historical background, particularly President Woodrow Wilson's efforts to maintain American neutrality in World War I, and the diplomatic and military considerations that drove German policy in the same period, I have drawn principally from these books: *Woodrow Wilson and The World War*, Charles Seymour (Yale University Press, 1921); *Woodrow Wilson and the Progressive Era*, Arthur S. Link (Harper and Row, 1954); *America's Entry into World War I*,

Herbert J. Bass, editor (Dryden Press, 1964); *Woodrow Wilson: The Politics of Peace and War,* Edmund Ions (American Heritage Press, 1972); *Too Proud to Fight,* Patrick Devlin (Oxford University Press, 1974); *Echoes of Distant Thunder,* Edward Robb Ellis (Coward, 1975); and the papers of Robert Lansing, Manuscript Division, Library of Congress.

Index